HISTORY AS TEXT

History as Text

The Writing of Ancient History

edited by

Averil Cameron

The University of North Carolina Press

Chapel Hill and London

First published in the United States 1990
by The University of North Carolina Press

Library of Congress Cataloging-in-Publication Data

History as text : the writing of ancient history / edited by Averil
Cameron.
    p.   cm.
    "First published in Great Britain in 1989 by Gerald
Duckworth & Co., Ltd."—T.p. verso.
    ISBN 0-8078-1889-5
    1. History, Ancient—Historiography.   I. Cameron, Averil.
D56.H57 1990
930'.072—dc20   89–14675
                                                CIP

First published in Great Britain in 1989
by Gerald Duckworth & Co. Ltd.
The Old Piano Factory
43 Gloucester Crescent, London NW1

Photoset in North Wales by
Derek Doyle & Associates, Mold, Clwyd
Printed and bound in Great Britain by
Redwood Burn Ltd, Trowbridge

Contents

For Sue
who gave or lent me so many of the books

And in memory of Arnaldo
who would not have liked it

Preface

This collection contains eight chapters by different authors (one of them myself) on aspects of the problem of textuality as it affects our shared discipline of ancient history. The general introduction explains how each of them addresses the general theme – one that concerns methodological issues much debated in relation to other periods of history but rather less so, if I am not mistaken, in relation to our own. We have many excellent books discussing the source material for ancient history, and the methods that historians may adopt, but the upheaval in interpretative approach which has been going on in history as in other disciplines in recent years is not often discussed with specific reference to antiquity. It is hoped therefore that this book will help to set the discussion going.

The presentation which has been adopted is that in addition to the general introduction each chapter is itself preceded by an editorial foreword in which I try to bring out the specific issues raised in it and link them to those presented in the rest of the book. These chapter introductions set the individual contributions in context and should provide the reader with running comments which help him to see the coherence of the whole. Despite the natural variation between the chapters themselves, I hope that the introductions show how each chapter touches on apsects of the central problem, which is in fact an issue common to all historical writing, ancient history included. Finally a brief postlude draws at least some of the threads together.

Again the Institute of Classical Studies, London, provided the setting for initial consideration of these issues, and thanks are due to its Director for continued encouragement.

A.M.C.

Contributors

Helen King is Lecturer in History at S. Katharine's College, Liverpool Institute of Higher Education.

M.J. Wheeldon is completing his doctorate at King's College London.

John Henderson is a Fellow of King's College, Cambridge.

J.W. Rich teaches in the Department of Classical and Archaeological Studies at the University of Nottingham.

Maria Wyke teaches at Newnham and Corpus Christi Colleges, Cambridge.

Dimitris Kyrtatas holds a teaching appointment at the University of Crete.

Sr. Charles Murray teaches in the Department of Theology, University of Nottingham.

Averil Cameron is Professor of Late Antique and Byzantine Studies, University of London.

Introduction: the writing of history

'Is there anything outside the text?'
'What on earth do you mean?'

One can easily imagine just such an exchange, with the second speaker being an ancient historian. For on the whole, the field of ancient history has remained remarkably impervious to the ferment that has been going on during the past generation in other disciplines, notably philosophy and literary criticism, and which is now increasingly making its mark on the history of later periods. The question of the relation between history and rhetoric – in reaction to the extreme position that there is no difference between the two – is indeed in danger of becoming one of the most hackneyed themes of current writing.[1] But in their approach to literary material, and in their conception of their task as historians, ancient historians still mostly tend to divide into two groups – those who like to think they concern themselves with 'hard data' and those who are overtly interested in the literary side of things. Naturally one can pass from the one to the other, or combine both approaches: but in this context 'literary' generally carries a rather traditional meaning, denoting part of what is in a more general sense meant by 'historiography', that is, the techniques of style, content and treatment employed by a given Greek or Roman historian. 'Historiography' also brings in his methods of work, his conception of his subject and his task, and particularly the effects upon his writing of his own chronological and social context; but the tacit assumption is that one engages in such inquiry mainly as a means to the end of discovering what is reliable in the work of this or that Greek or Roman historian, with a view to being able to use it in one's own reconstruction. The study of the ancient sources is thus seen

---

[1] Besides the basic works by Hayden White, *Metahistory* (Baltimore, 1973); *Tropics of Discourse* (Baltimore, 1978); *The Content of the Form: Narrative Discourse and Historical Representation* (Baltimore, 1987), see for instance *History and Theory*, Beiheft 19 (*Metahistory: Six Critiques*) and 25 (*Knowing and Telling History: the Anglo-Saxon Debate*); Edward Said, *The World, the Text and the Critic* (Boston, Mass., 1983) – which is not to suggest that any of the works mentioned are themselves open to that description.

1

2   *Introduction: the writing of history*

to provide the raw material for the modern historian.[2]

Although written texts are also themselves historical documents in their own right,[3] many ancient historians, it would be fair to say, continue to regard historiography in the more traditional sense as being necessary, perhaps, but not of particular interest to themselves – even sometimes as a sort of sub-genre, less intrinsically important than the discovery of new information or the establishment of new 'facts'. Defined in this way, it must always run the risk of appearing simply a preliminary to the modern historian's real task of adjudicating between the sources. To borrow Geoffrey Elton's terminology, he must behave like a barrister conducting a cross-examination in which the individual source is in the dock – the verdict will decide for fact or fiction.[4] 'Primary' sources, it is assumed, will be given most honour, 'secondary' relegated to the inferior position which the name implies. This is how many of the Anglo-Saxon ancient historians now at their most productive were trained, and it is a mode to which we cling with all the tenacity of those firmly moulded in youth.

Except that the whole basis of such an approach has been undermined. Texts no longer straightforwardly respond to study; neither the concept of a text nor that of an author is what it used to be; authorial intention is neither a safe guide nor even in some quarters a respectable concept. The subversive ideas of deconstruction have made headway even in the conservative field of classical scholarship,[5] although they tend to concentrate for good reason in particular areas – Greek tragedy and mythology for instance, where after all Lévi-Strauss and subsequent French scholars had paved the way. Latin literature, for good reason, tends to fall behind, as Maria Wyke's chapter in this volume makes clear. But in ancient history, the legalistic approach is generally set not against an alternative mode of interpretation based on deconstruction or hermeneutics, but rather, as it is in Fogel and Elton's book, against forms of social or economic history based on statistical information. Thus, in relation to contemporary British ancient historians, we have seen in recent years

[2] Take for instance the assumptions implied in the title *Sources for Ancient History*, ed. Michael Crawford (Cambridge, 1983), in a series entitled *The Sources of History. Studies in the Uses of Historical Evidence*, ed. G.R. Elton.

[3] See E. Gabba, 'Literature', in Crawford, op. cit., 3.

[4] R.W. Fogel and G.R. Elton, *Which Road to the Past? Two Views of History* (New Haven, 1983).

[5] For the conservatism of what is referred to in the United States as 'philology' see John Peradotto, 'Texts and unrefracted facts; philology, hermeneutics and semiotics', *Arethusa* 16 (1983), 15-33. The warmth of some exchanges in e.g. the *Liverpool Classical Monthly* on such methodological issues (cf. *LCM* 11 [1986], 55-64, 163-67) is an indicator of the strength of feeling on both sides. A notable example of post-structuralist criticism of classical texts is Simon Goldhill's *Language, Sexuality, Narrative: the Oresteia* (Cambridge, 1984), there reviewed.

a self-conscious polarisation between the 'collection-of-instances' approach and the sociological approach based on statistical data.[6] It is assumed, at bottom, that there is indeed a preferable course to the accumulation of instances drawn from application of the legalistic approach, and that this preferable course will yield something better – not truth, of course, but 'harder' and more respectable history. Admittedly, in our field there will always be a formidable, indeed all but insuperable, difficulty in that there will never be the quantity of reliable statistical information on which a modern historian can rely, and thus any conclusions must always remain by comparison extremely tentative. Not only that: quite often the data themselves must be drawn from the literary sources whose unreliability as witnesses has been admitted both in principle and in specific instances. Ancient historians are used, then, to admitting that their results may be provisional; indeed, they are quite often proved wrong by the discovery of new material evidence such as a new inscription. Some have so far extended a position of basic cultural relativism and disbelief in the possibility of real historical explanation that they do not even claim preference for their own interpretations.[7] But still, on the whole, the alternative to the legalistic kind of approach is seen in terms of a type of social and economic history based on 'harder', often material, evidence.

It is easy to see why this should be so; after all, Marx and Weber between them guaranteed the centrality of the social and economic approach to the history of the ancient world, while the explosion in the quantity of material evidence with the development of modern archaeology has brought an inevitable change of focus to many traditional topics of enquiry. Another important influence on the practice of ancient history, in recent years at any rate, has come from the direction of anthropology, which has hitherto had its own emphasis on material culture and on the social and economic.[8]

But it was of course from anthropology as well as from linguistics that the structuralist movement and all that followed from it took its beginnings, and it is there that we now see both an emphasis on culture and the ambiguities of its expression and an acute awareness of the extent to which the discipline of anthropology is bound up with the

[6] Cf. the harsh criticisms of F. Millar, *The Emperor in the Roman World* (London, 1977) by Keith Hopkins, 'Rules of evidence', *Journal of Roman Studies* 68 (1978), 178-96, and Hopkins's own statements about desirable method in his *Death and Renewal* (Cambridge, 1983), xiii-xiv: 'hard' history is that based on statistical data, on subjects which lend themselves to such inquiry, while everything else is relegated to the 'soft' category, where description is possible but not demonstration, much less proof.

[7] E.g. Mary Beard and Michael Crawford, *Rome in the Late Republic* (London, 1985), 3-4.

[8] In general, see S.C. Humphreys, *Anthropology and the Greeks* (London, 1978).

question of textuality.[9] So great is the permeation of some current writing on ancient history by anthropological methods and focusses of attention that a given work may be hard to classify – if indeed that matters.[10]

It is fair to say, then, that anthropology offers a fertile source of ideas and comparisons for ancient historians. In view, therefore, of the increased self-consciousness among anthropologists about the procedures of ethnography, we should expect to find among these historians an increasing awareness of textuality in all its aspects – the need to analyse (deconstruct) the actual texts of the society under examination ('the sources'), the need to look for the overt or implicit texts operative in the society itself, the consequences of the fact that the historian himself must produce a text in order to do history at all, and finally, the interplay of all of these. At the same time, it is increasingly recognised that history is after all a kind of literature, and that as such, it must be exposed to the problems of criticism and interpretation which are felt so keenly at the present time by literary critics. When they, like philosophers, are so preoccupied with the relation or non-relation of texts to the world 'out there', history, which is felt in an obvious sense to have a peculiarly close relation to events and facts, must also take its place in the literary debate as one of the kinds of discourse most in need of interpretation and discussion. When literature, or in the language of some critics, rhetoric, is seen by some as essentially related to a real world ('secular' criticism) and by others as irrevocably self-referential and introverted (the 'hermetic' approach), the status of history-writing becomes a major issue, and history a critical subject for analysis.[11]

Whether or not most historians will wish to engage themselves in these literary and philosophical battles, the whole debate does bring to the fore the extent to which the writing of a historical work is itself a 'text upon text'. For history is a matter of interpretation. In order to write history – to generate a text – the historian must interpret existing texts (which will often be, but need not always be limited to, written materials, for ritual and social practice constitute texts too). But he will interpret, or 'read', his texts in accordance with a set of

[9] Culture: cf. the works of Clifford Geertz, especially *The Interpretation of Culture* (London, 1975) and *Local Knowledge* (New York, 1983), which have been very influential on some ancient historians – see King below.

[10] We see this influence prominently in some writing on ancient religion, e.g. S.R.F. Price, *Rituals and Power. The Roman Imperial Cult in Asia Minor* (Cambridge, 1984), with predictable responses from some reviewers.

[11] For an introduction to the issues, see R. Scholes, *Textual Power* (New Haven, 1985), 22ff.; his examples are, for 'secular' criticism, T. Eagleton, *Literary Theory: an Introduction* (Minneapolis, 1983); for 'hermetic' criticism, Paul de Man, *Allegories of Reading: Figural Language in Rousseau, Nietzsche, Rilke and Proust* (New Haven, 1979); further discussion in Said, op. cit. (n.1).

other texts, which derive from the cultural code within which he works himself; and he will go on to write his text, that is, his history, against the background of and within the matrix of this larger cultural text. Thus history-writing is not a simple matter of sorting out 'primary' and 'secondary' sources; it is inextricably embedded in a mesh of text.

The result of this heightened awareness of the interpretative element in history-writing, which has spilled over from the loss of faith in objective truth which can be seen also in other disciplines, especially literary theory, philosophy and anthropology, is in some cases to cause historians to change their choice of subjects. Obviously there are some which lend themselves better than others to this approach. Considerations like these are not going to count for much, for instance, with the 'straight' epigraphist primarily interested in amassing new inscriptions or correcting earlier readings of old ones, or, for that matter, with the historian of the Roman army concerned with collecting more data from which to build up a picture of individual Roman military career patterns. Naturally they will not impress anyone still puzzling over some of the canonical puzzles of Greek or Roman political history, whose very attraction consists in there being just enough evidence available to tantalise, but never quite enough for scholars to come to an agreement. But others seem much better suited to a more self-conscious and interpretative approach: cultural history in particular, and especially religion, offer a particularly good field, and it is no accident that three of the eight papers here are concerned with religious issues. Religion, after all, has often been defined in terms of the creation of an all-embracing view of the world, whether by ritual, belief or the articulation of a theory – or, as commonly, by all three.[12] It is part of culture, if not indeed the defining element of a given culture; it offers rich material which lends itself to an analysis in terms of texts and codes,[13] and it is frequently an area displaying the signs of that change and adjustment which are supposed to be the historian's proper concern.

Although both Greek and Roman religion have attracted this kind of interest, as it happens all three of the papers included here are concerned with early Christianity. Again this is not accidental. First, Christianity is concerned with texts to an exceptional degree – not only with the establishment and interpretation of a canonical set of texts, but also, from its Judaic background, with the practice of teaching and preaching, and finally with the articulation, both oral and written, of a

[12] See e.g. P. Berger and T. Luckman, *The Social Construction of Reality* (Harmondsworth, 1967); C. Geertz, 'Religion as a Cultural System', in M. Banton, ed., *Anthropological Approaches to the Study of Religion*, ASA Monographs 3 (London, 1966), 1-46; M. Mann, *The Sources of Social Power I* (Cambridge, 1986).
[13] See e.g. Mary Beard, 'The sexual status of Vestal Virgins', *JRS* 70 (1980), 12-27.

complex body of doctrine.[14] Individual elements from these three characteristics of early Christianity may be found in Greco-Roman religion, but never together to the degree that they were developed by Christians. Despite its much-vaunted lowly origins, early Christianity, as seen in its texts, soon developed into a highly intellectual and highly self-conscious system, whose practitioners sought both to articulate the faith and to locate it and themselves in relation to prevailing social discourse. It therefore attracts urgent attention from any scholars interested, as M. Foucault was, for instance, in the formation of discourse.[15] At first sight it might seem to present the opposite phenomenon to that which G.E.R. Lloyd, for example, has charted in fifth-century Greece, namely the development in that period of a 'rational' or scientific way of thinking; particularly so when even now so many historians, following Edward Gibbon, still write of the Christian Roman empire in terms of a 'descent' into 'irrationality'.[16] Yet this manifestation of ethnocentrism both grotesquely underestimates the intellectual sophistication of theological discourse and identifies Christianity solely with those aspects which the critic finds most suspect from his own point of view. That there was a strain in Christian theological discourse which emphasised the paradoxical or even the nonsensical in religious language is quite a different matter; it proceeds, indeed, from philosophical considerations about language, and especially religious language, and from the same concerns that theologians have today, as Sr. Charles Murray's chapter demonstrates. If we are concerned about texts and textuality, there is a great deal in the language of early Christian texts to be analysed, as I have tried to show in writing about the theme of virginity. And Dimitris Kyrtatas brings to the fore one important consequence of having a canon of sacred texts – that interpretation, that is, reception, of those texts, will itself vary with the prevailing social and historical circumstances. Literary theory has had a lot to say about shifting interpretations and

[14] The formation and dissemination of Christian discourse is the subject of my Sather Classical Lectures, *Christianity and the Rhetoric of Empire* (Berkeley and Los Angeles, forthcoming). Useful collection of passages from early Christian writers demonstrating this concern in R. Sider, *The Gospel and its Proclamation* (Wilmington, Delaware, 1983).

[15] Cf. *Le Souci de soi* (Paris, 1983); 'The battle for chastity', in P. Ariès and A. Béjin, eds., *Western Sexuality* (Eng. trans., Oxford, 1985), 14-25. The early Christian period was to have formed the subject of a projected volume to be entitled *Les Aveux de la chair*.

[16] G.E.R. Lloyd, *Magic, Reason and Experience* (Cambridge, 1979). 'Irrationality' in late antiquity: Erich Auerbach, *Mimesis, The Representation of Reality in Western Culture* (Eng. trans., Princeton, 1953), 53, cf. 76; R. MacMullen, 'Constantine and the miraculous', *Greek, Roman and Byzantine Studies 9* (1965), 92; E.R. Dodds, *Pagan and Christian in an Age of Anxiety* (Cambridge, 1965). The definition of rationality is all too likely to be supremely ethnocentric: for the problem, see e.g. J. Overing, ed., *Reason and Morality*, ASA Monographs 24 (London, 1985), with R. Horton and R. Finnegan, eds., *Modes of Thought* (London, 1973), M. Hollis and S. Lukes, eds., *Rationality and Relativism* (Oxford, 1982).

audience reception,[17] and here too history can profit very directly.

But there is another reason why early Christianity should form a subject of attention for those interested in the problems of texts and textuality. That is that it raises in acute form the question of objectivity, whether of the subject (can there be an objectively true account of early Christianity?) or of the inquirer (what if the inquirer is himself or herself committed? Indeed, can they *not* be committed?). In other words, the spectre of truth. And if these issues pose themselves more sharply and immediately in the case of Christianity – a part of our own culture on which historians do indeed display their personal histories – they are nevertheless questions now seen as central to history in general.[18] Again in the case of early Christianity, they take a high profile in the specific instance of feminist theology – an activity that is by definition doubly engaged,[19] and which is inevitably a subject of Sr. Charles Murray's chapter and of my own, not to mention the present passionate debate (in some quarters anyway) over the ordination of women. It would be easy for historians not themselves involved in or interested in such issues to dismiss the whole matter as irrelevant to themselves and perhaps also to ancient history. Nevertheless, they pose central issues of interpretation and method which, as some of the feminist theologians see, are basic to the activity of writing history in a much wider sense. Indeed, feminist writers have seized on the present flight from objectivity, with its focus on the text, as support for their own concerns;[20] and while such a claim may not spring from the purest of motives, it does not therefore follow that it is unjustified. Nevertheless, feminist theology is only one branch of theology in general, or rather, of the writing of the history of Christianity by committed insiders. Since however all early Christianity is part of Greco-Roman history, it ought to be of serious interest to all ancient historians from the point of view of the methods to be employed, and cannot any longer be simply ducked by the traditional claim to be writing from a wholly objective or empiricist position.

Apart from the study of ancient religion, a concern for textuality naturally focusses on the reading of the ancient authors themselves. Hence John Henderson's reading of Livy, which while exposing the hidden assumptions made in so many existing studies also necessarily

[17] See for ancient works *Arethusa* 19.2 (1986), 'Audience-oriented criticism and the Classics', with bibliography.
[18] Cf. Paul Ricoeur, *History and Truth* (Eng. trans., Evanston, III., 1965).
[19] See especially E. Schussler Fiorenza, *In Memory of Her* (New York, 1983); ead., 'Remembering the past in creating the future: historical-critical scholarship and feminist Biblical interpretation', in A. Yarbro Collins, ed., *Feminist Perspectives on Biblical Scholarship* (Chico, Ca., 1985), 43-64.
[20] Bernadette J. Brooten, 'Early Christian women and their cultural context: issues of method in historical reconstruction', in Collins, op. cit., 65-92.

raises the question of whether it is possible to dispense with them. John Rich addresses one of the most important 'sources' for a critical period of Roman history – the reign of Augustus – in studying the account given by the late second and early third-century writer Cassius Dio. A situation familiar to ancient historians here becomes acute – what are the consequences for a balanced historical view when we find ourselves largely dependent on one ancient narrative account? For the only other full account of Augustus' reign is that given in the early second-century *Life of Augustus* by Suetonius, a literary work of very different type. This at least is a problem not often encountered by modern historians, and it is one which cannot be solved only by scrutinising the conscious purpose and method of the writer in question – the texture and language of the text he has produced must also be taken into consideration.

M.J. Wheeldon also considers ancient historical works, this time from the point of view of narrativity.[21] What is it that makes a historical work authoritative, that is, why do people believe one historian rather than another? It is becoming increasingly common to answer this question in terms of narrative quality rather than by appealing to outside 'facts' for verification. That is, the arrangement and manner of writing itself cause us to give it authority, that is, to believe it. Perhaps more than we are ourselves today, ancient writers were ready to assent to this view, for they already saw history as far more of a literary enterprise than has been the case until very recently, and were perfectly aware that literary technique could be a valuable tool for gaining credibility. Whereas from the point of view of 'objective', or 'scientific' history it has been common to condemn ancient critics such as Cicero and Quintilian when they made it clear that they saw history-writing in unashamedly literary terms, a text-centred approach will have to look again with more sympathy at these ancient statements; similarly we had better stop condemning as mere plagiarism or 'empty rhetoric' the deep-seated ancient tendencies to embody in their work reminiscences of earlier authors and to follow literary precedents set years, or even centuries before.

In differing ways, both Helen King and Maria Wyke ask questions about interpretation and specifically how – or whether – historical conclusions can be drawn from particular sorts of texts. The strange assortment of Greek medical writings known as the Hippocratic Corpus reveals underlying, or indeed sometimes overt, assumptions about the nature of women which prove to be embedded in the Greek language and therefore likely to be widely influential in forming judgements on a variety of topics; Helen King shows forcibly how language can enshrine sets of attitudes which no one is ever called

---

[21] See e.g. W.J.T. Mitchell, ed., *On Narrative* (Chicago, 1981).

upon to justify or explain and some of which in this case have been seen to be carried over without significant alteration into later views of women, including Christian ones.[22] Women, indeed, provide another obvious topic of attention for this collection, not because feminist writing or 'women's studies' attract more than their share of theory for partisan reasons,[23] but because in the male-centred literary world of antiquity the theme of woman becomes itself a topic attracting an intense concentration of metaphorical discourse. From fifth-century Greek drama[24] to late antique and early medieval Christian literature, woman attracts a particular density of associations, and offers an obvious theme for the attention not just of 'feminists', or women scholars, but of anyone interested in texts and textuality. The example studied here by Maria Wyke is that of Latin love elegy, on which the prevailing consensus at least in Britain seems to be that in some sense these poems must relate to real experience, and the females to whom they are addressed to real women; the debate then centres on what kind of women they might be in the context of the society of Augustan Rome.[25] To maintain on the contrary, as Maria Wyke does, that they are not only literary creations, but in a sense actually represent the process of writing, that their origin is in poetics, not real life, is thus to disturb a whole tradition of sensibility in the appreciation of Latin poetry which wants to be able to find a way of imaginative identification with poet and subject. It is not just a matter of denying that there was a Roman lady easily identifiable with Cynthia, and thus undermining the historical conclusions which have been drawn from this body of poetry, but of casting doubt at a deeper level on what had been thought familiar and comprehensible. For if art does not imitate life, what life is there at all?[26] And how can civilised men continue to appreciate the Greek and Latin classics in the comfortable assumption that their standards are shared and agreed by others? If the notion of objective history is put in doubt, then so is that of a classic,[27] and

---

[22] See also Cameron, below; Ruth Padel, 'Woman: model for possession by Greek daemons', in Averil Cameron and Amélie Kuhrt, eds., *Images of Women in Antiquity* (London, 1983), 3-14. More recent but equally deep-seated and influential attitudes to women in medical writing and practice are brilliantly explored by Elaine Showalter, *The Female Malady. Women, Madness and English Culture, 1830-1980* (New York, 1985).

[23] And more than their share of prejudiced hostility: see the 'review' by T. Fleming, 'Des Dames du temps jadis', *Classical Journal* 82 (1986), 73-80.

[24] See Goldhill (n.5); F.I. Zeitlin, 'The dynamics of misogyny in the Oresteia', *Arethusa* 11 (1978), 149-81; ead., 'Travesties of gender and genre in Aristophanes' *Thesmophoria-zusae*',in H.P. Foley, ed., *Reflections of Women in Antiquity* (New York, 1981).

[25] But see P. Veyne, *L'Élégie érotique romaine* (Paris, 1983) for the opposite view.

[26] C. Prendergast, *The Order of Mimesis* (Cambridge, 1986), an attempt to recapture the shared common stock from which common interpretations can proceed.

[27] F. Kermode, *The Classic*, T.S. Eliot Memorial Lecture (London, 1975).

where more threatening for such a doubt to be sown than in the field of 'classical' literature?

But, lest anyone should be thinking otherwise, literature and history must go together. History is not *just* rhetoric, it is true, even those types of history least amenable to direct falsification by the appearance for instance of new evidence. But rhetoric in the wide sense, that is, all that is implied by textuality, is as much a part of all but the most technical historical writing as it is of literature itself. The ancients knew that history was not the same as poetry, a judgement which modern critics have tended to disdain as self-evident or trivial. Now it does not seem so pointless after all. Poetry and history are distinguished, it may now seem, far less by any appeal for verification to the facts 'out there' than by scope and arrangement of material, by author's intention, if that be still allowed, and by capacity to persuade their audience that that is what they are.

This book does not pretend to cover all the issues. It does not, for example, address the question in any detail of the difference if any between history and fiction. Nor does it consider proof as such, or the status of historical explanation, all of which have received attention in other quarters. It is far from claiming that history can never be objective, that history is nothing but rhetoric, or that there is no distinction between good and bad works of history. But it does show in different ways that what has been going on in other fields, sometimes accompanied by passion, anger and incomprehension on the one side and a degree of patronising superiority on the other cannot simply be ignored among serious historians.

1

The Daughter of Leonides:
reading the Hippocratic corpus

I for one consider it unthinkable to claim that a Piaroa of the Venezuelan rain forest is irrational when he says that rain is the urine of the deity.

Joanna Overing, ed., *Reason and Morality* (London, 1985), 4.

In this chapter Helen King raises two questions which have become central in a good deal of contemporary writing: first, that of the extent to which our notion of our physical selves, and especially in the case of women, is culturally constructed, and second, that of rationality and irrationality – what do we do when confronted with something that is plainly irrational according to the system of classification that we have been taught to use?[1] Both, clearly, involve the problem of texts: in a sense, the self, or in this case, the notion of woman, is constructed by and through a set of texts (see also Chapters 5 and 8), while 'rationality' too is obviously defined by accordance with a set of rules laid down in an agreed set of texts. The texts can be either written or implied, so long as they are nevertheless generally accepted within the culture, but in fact both kinds usually coexist. In the present case, the 'Hippocratic corpus', a body of Greek medical writing loosely ascribed to Hippocrates, the founding figure of modern, i.e. 'rational' medicine, offers an outstandingly good example of textual material at once readily available and open to interpretation and refractory in the unfamiliarity (to us) of the picture it presents. Not surprisingly, the Greek medical writers, and the writers of the Roman empire like Galen, the great doctor and voluminous writer of the second century AD, have already been taken up by historians interested both in the development of ideas about the self and about women, and in the problems of textuality.[2] They should be, it would seem, a prime example of the move towards rationality and scientific thought in

[1] For the latter, see B.R. Wilson, ed., *Rationality* (Oxford, 1979); recent discussions in Joanna Overing, ed., *Reason and Morality* (London, 1985), introduction.
[2] See particularly Aline Rousselle, *Porneia* (Paris, 1983); M. Foucault, *L'Usage des plaisirs* and *Le Souci de soi* (Paris, 1984).

classical Greece,[3] and an important source of information for us about the ideas and practice of medicine, and thus about perceptions of health and 'normality' in antiquity.

Helen King shows that such confident expectations are likely to be disappointed. This material, at first sight so promising, presents many sorts of problems: problems of authorship, coherence, expression, interpretation. How far is it for practical use at all? How do the assumptions it contains square with those prevailing in the general culture of which it is a part? Can we turn with confidence to the Hippocratic corpus when we want to know something about Greek concepts of normality and abnormality? And if not, where can we turn instead?

Aside from questions such as these, which look hopefully outwards from the Hippocratic texts to a 'real' world which they are deemed to represent, the instance chosen for discussion by Helen King poses a different one: that of apparent inconsistency within the context itself.[4] King shows that given the conceptual framework of the corpus, the inconsistency dissolves; it is only our own assumptions which made it problematic. The real problem lies with the too easy identification of these seemingly scientific texts with our own modern preconceptions, when in fact they are as different, as 'irrational', as the beliefs of the Piaroas about rain. It is now recognised, too, that it is perfectly possible to hold inconsistent, or contradictory beliefs at one and the same time – indeed, we do it all the time.

Clearly a body of material such as the Hippocratic corpus must be read with more attention to its own rules of logic, and with less of a tendency to assume that any inconsistencies within it are somehow accretions to be explained away, or excluded from consideration like the materials excluded from the Christian canon (p. 145 below). Now that the certainties of science and the scientific method are themselves being seen as problematic,[5] the notion of rationality as characteristic of modern, scientific thinking is even more vulnerable, however much some philosophers and anthropologists have wanted to hang on to it. It is easy enough for historians to sympathise with the change, and accept, for instance, that one can no longer just write off the apparently strange beliefs of the Piaroas – or even, if it comes to that, of the Greeks and Romans; but they also need to recognise that their own prized historical methods have become vulnerable too.

[3] On which see G.E.R. Lloyd, *Magic, Reason and Experience* (Cambridge, 1979).

[4] Not strictly the same as contradiction: see Sybil Wolfram, 'Facts and theories; saying and believing', in Overing 1985, 72f.

[5] Especially since T. Kuhn, *The Structure of Scientific Revolutions* (Chicago, 1964); cf. P. Feyerabend, *Against Method* (London, 1975); *Science in a Free Society* (London, 1978).

The Daughter of Leonides:
reading the Hippocratic corpus

Helen King

It is perhaps appropriate that a book entitled *History as Text* should begin with a problem from medical history, since this sub-field, for many centuries regarded as less problematic than most in terms of its treatment of its sources, is currently being reassessed and rediscovered. Any study of, for example, classical Athenian society, must contend both with apparent contradictions between the evidence of a range of types of literary production – poetry, drama, speeches, history – and with the knowledge that we cannot privilege one type over the others, as 'what really happened' against 'illusion'. Where the text is medical, such problems of source interpretation may seem to recede a little. The 'reality' which is assumed to lie under the text is something which we can apparently experience directly: the human body, historically constant, naturally given. Anatomy, physiology and therapy can be assessed as either 'right' or 'wrong' in relation to this known body; we are able to compare representation and reality, and to judge the first accordingly. A 'history of medicine', according to those who make such assumptions, simply involves the study of significant 'discoveries' of 'facts'; for example, the circulation of the blood, the existence of the ovaries or the efficacy of quinine.

Such a history of medicine, by assuming the values of the medical present of the historian, misrepresents the ideological nature of these values by presenting them as unquestionable 'facts'. As a result, medical history often fails to appreciate the nature of its sources, and of itself, as 'text'; as culturally specific constructs, the form of which influences the meanings which they present. New approaches to medical history, in contrast, explore discourse about the body as a means both of reflecting and of confirming dominant social values. For example, the way in which differences between male and female bodies are expressed derives from particular social structures and the places of the sexes within these, but also reinforces such structures by locating their origin in unquestionable, 'natural' facts. The power of medicine lies in its ability to make the social appear natural.

In this chapter I want to examine Hippocratic medicine as text, through two descriptions of nosebleeds in women. After introducing these texts, I consider some traditional ways of 'reading' the Hippocratic corpus in general. In the final part I return to nosebleeds to show why they are so important in Greek medicine, and propose a further interpretation which reverses many of the established assumptions about reading ancient medicine – and which, inevitably, has implications for reading all other ancient sources.

1. The daughter of Leonides as a pink raven

Aphorisms 5.33/L 4.544.[1] 'In a woman whose menstrual periods have stopped, blood flowing out of the nostrils is a good thing.'[2] The *Aphorisms* is one of the most copied, most edited and historically most popular texts in the Hippocratic corpus (cf. L 4.445-57). There are therefore textual variants, but for this aphorism there is only one. A number of later manuscripts omit 'In a woman', *gynaiki*; however, in the rest of this section almost all aphorisms start with *gynaiki*, and the aphorism clearly refers to women because *katamênia* can only mean 'monthly periods'. In its format, it is very representative of Hippocratic aphorisms; a short general principle, with nothing to explain why this should be a good thing, and no specific empirical examples to support it. One of the traditions associated with *Aphorisms* claims that 'Hippocrates composed it in his old age as a summary of his vast experience' (Jones 1931, xxxiv). This may tell us nothing about its 'real' authorship, but it is an accurate description of its effect on us as readers, for whom it suggests distillation from years of clinical experience; a large number of particular observed cases from which this general law of nature has been derived by the principle of induction (Chalmers 1978, 1-34). Such a methodology is explicit in the Hippocratic corpus; for example, *Precepts* 1 (L 9.250-2) describes how reason builds up many examples of sense-perception, from which theories can be deduced. To this should be added the point that the perceived format (general principle, scientific law) is, for us, at odds with the content. In our understanding of nature, suppressed menstrual blood cannot come out of the nose. Since the derived law is 'wrong,' what could this tell us about the observed cases on which we assume it was based?

Epidemics 7.123/L 5.468. 'In the daughter of Leonides, the *physis*, having made a start, turned aside; after it had turned aside, she bled at the nose. When she had bled at the nose, a change occurred. The doctor did not understand, and the young girl (*pais*) died.' 'The daughter of Leonides'[3] is a specific, identified individual; in contrast to the *Aphorisms* example, we therefore perceive this as a particular observed case. *Hê physis*, 'nature', here means the menstrual period. It is one of a number of such terms in the Hippocratic corpus, each of

[1] All references to the Hippocratic corpus are to the edition of E. Littré (see Bibliography).

[2] Cf. Ar. *HA* 587b35-588a2; Byl 1980, 60.

[3] Women in the corpus are generally identified as 'daughter of x', 'wife of x' or 'a woman from y'. On the avoidance of using women's names – except those of the shameless and the dead – see Schaps 1977 on the Attic orators. Deichgräber 1982 uses names to support a positivist reading of the *Epidemics*, taking epigraphical evidence from Thasos to date sections using Thasian patients. He concludes that such sections date from the lifetime of Hippocrates or that of his first pupils.

which reveals something of ancient Greek ideas about menstruation; for example, *gynaikeia*, 'women's things' (e.g. *G* 1.20/L 8.58; *Ep.* 2.2.8/L 5.88; *KP* 511/L 5.702), *katamênia*, *epimênia* and *emmênia*, 'monthlies' (e.g. *Aph.* 5.39/L 4.544; *G.* 1.58/L 8.116; *NW* 8/L 7.322; *NW* 16/L 7.334), *ta hôraia*, 'the ripe things' (*SF* 34/L 8.504-6) and *ta kata physin*, 'the natural things' (*G* 3.230/L 8.444; *Ep.* 6.8.32/L 5.356). The contexts for which the rarest of these terms are selected may be instructive. Most texts use 'monthlies'; *gynaikeia* can mean any menstrual period, but is the term chosen to be modified by *prôton* when discussing menarche in *Epidemics* 2.2.8 (L 5.88), 3.17.7 (L 3.122) and 3.17.12 (L 3.136). *Ta hôraia* is used only once, in a context which suggests menarche, perhaps chosen because the first menstrual period is a sign of 'ripeness' (cf. *PP*/L 8.466, *hôrê gamou*). *Ta kata physin* is not specifically menarcheal; the implications of *hê physis* must remain open.

The menstrual period of the daughter of Leonides started, but then turned aside, and came out through her nose. There was a change (*diallagê*), which the doctor didn't understand; the term used is *syneiden*, implying shared knowledge. Since these texts prefer the first person, 'the doctor' is probably not the writer himself, but another practitioner.[4] The writer and his audience thus understand what 'the doctor' did not; the reasons why the patient's condition changed and she died. The death of the patient appears directly to contradict the *Aphorisms* statement that a nosebleed is good when the menses are suppressed. The commonsense reading would suggest that, while the first text is a general principle, the second is a particular observed case. The central problem of the inductive method, moving from the latter to the former, is that the next particular case may be the one which disproves the rule: I have seen 302 black ravens, and therefore propose the rule 'All ravens are black'; but what if the 303rd is pink? How many ravens are necessary to formulate the principle? 302? 30? Are 30 more persuasive than 29? Where do we draw the line (Chalmers 1978, 12-15)? And is the daughter of Leonides the pink raven?

As Geertz (1983, 84) reminds us, however, 'Common sense is not what the mind cleared of cant spontaneously apprehends; it is what the mind filled with presuppositions ... concludes.' There are several types of presupposition present in the explanations traditionally used when two Hippocratic texts apparently contradict each other in this way. These are centred on the idea of authorship. Authors are useful explanatory devices, one of the interpretative models favoured by historians being to identify the ancient writer's personal slant, his political stance, his biases and so on, and then to strip these off in a

---

[4] For criticism of other *iatroi* in general see Lloyd 1979, 90-1; for the gynaecological treatises, Lloyd 1983, 80-1. See also Edelstein 1931, with texts such as *Ep.* 2.1.7 (L 5.78), in which 'the *iatroi*' fail to understand the general curative powers of a nosebleed in a male patient.

triumphant dance of the seven veils to reveal the naked truth gleaming underneath (cf. Gellner 1964, 30). This way of working is so entrenched that an authorless text such as the Hippocratic corpus may be seen as a positive embarrassment; generations of medical historians have therefore endeavoured to produce some authors for it, and to assign contradictions between texts to different authors, or groups of authors.

2. Permitted questions in the Hippocratic research programme

A useful model to apply to traditional Hippocratic studies is that of Lakatos, which regards any scientific discipline as possessing a set of questions, methods and assumptions followed by all those who work in that discipline (1978, esp. 16-17, 48-52; Chalmers 1978, 80-7). This set is called a 'research programme', and it has a 'hard core', an area the assumptions of which are accepted by all scholars working in the field and which are unfalsifiable. This is surrounded by a 'protective belt' of hypotheses to digest anomalies which would otherwise threaten the hard core. A research programme also has a set of questions which can be asked ('positive heuristic') and a set which cannot be asked ('negative heuristic'). The positive heuristic of the Hippocratic research programme included such questions as 'Who was Hippocrates?', 'Which are the "genuine works" written by the great man himself?', 'Who wrote the other works?' The hard core assumed that at least *some* – maybe a dozen – of the works in the corpus really were by Hippocrates, largely based on the later (first century BC onwards) set of letters allegedly from Hippocrates to such notable figures of history as Artaxerxes, in which Hippocrates and his sons travel around classical Greece and intervene at significant points of its history, for example curing a 'plague' affecting the Greeks.[5] The origin of the Hippocratic texts, according to the research programme, lies in the institutions within which early medicine was supposed to have functioned. The temples of Asklepios came to be seen as proto-hospitals or health resorts;[6] their case notes were assumed to be texts such as the *Koan Prognoses* (L 5.588-732) and *Prorrhetics* 1 (L 5.510-72), written up from inscriptions bearing details of case history and treatment. Pliny (*NH*. 29.2) refers to case notes kept at the shrines of Asklepios, which Hippocrates wrote out; similar stories exist in Strabo (8.6.15; 14.2.19). Although Clologe (1905) pointed out that the format of the extant inscriptions at Epidauros bears no relation to the lists of symptoms found in these texts, and Withington published a thorough refutation of the case note theory in 1921, its underlying assumptions remain; in

[5] The 'decree of the Athenians' (*Epist*. 25) honouring Hippocrates for saving Greece from 'the plague from the land of the barbarians' appears in L 9.400-2.
[6] See intro. by Kelly to the 1939 edition of Adams 1849; cf. Kee 1982.

particular, that many of the texts which have survived stand in a close relation to 'the real', that is, to real doctors, patients and diseases.

The development of the imaginary 'author' influences the reading of the text in other ways. Hippocrates developed not just sons, but also a wicked son-in-law who betrays him, and a full genealogy of seventeen generations back to Asklepios, based on Tzetzes (Edelstein and Edelstein 1945, T.213). One of his sons, Thessalos, edits his case notes for publication. This is useful, because it means that differences in style can easily be accommodated: two works can be 'by Hippocrates' even if they are not in the same style, because one is directly from his own hand, the other via his son's editing. Both of his sons were supposed to have called their sons 'Hippocrates' – a common naming convention, but conveniently making four members of the family bear the same name; the father of medicine, his grandfather and his two grandsons. Like the 'edited case notes' idea, this is very useful for the protective belt. How did some works which later readers consider 'irrational', or 'unscientific', find their way into the corpus which bears the name of the great founder of scientific medicine? The answer is clear; an incompetent librarian at Alexandria classified the works of all four men under the same name.

In the words of Wesley Smith, this whole enterprise is 'an etiological myth, an analytical scheme dressed up as a narrative of events' (1979, 30). He traces it back to the 'letters' and to two writers of the first and second centuries AD, Dioscurides and Galen. There is little that one would wish to add to his excellent study of the 'Hippocratic myth'; only perhaps that the progress of the Hippocratic research programme from antiquity shows us that the ancient world was as obsessed as we are with finding an author or authors, with reference to whom differences within the text could be 'explained'.

In Lakatos's research programme model, the function of the protective belt of hypotheses is to absorb anything which would threaten the integrity of the hard core. The classic example of this, used by Smith, is the publication in the 1890s of the first or second century AD *Anonymus Londinensis* papyrus, which includes what are usually assumed to be excerpts from Aristotle's pupil, Menon.[7] The research programme had already decided from one of Galen's commentaries (Kuhn 15.25-6) that Menon's lost work would provide accurate and valuable information on early medical history: yet, of the known works of the Hippocratic corpus, the piece from which Menon gave extracts and which he attributed to Hippocrates seemed most closely to resemble a text called *Breaths* (L 6.90-114), not previously counted as a 'genuine work'. In this potentially threatening situation, historians adjusted the protective belt of the programme; for example,

---

[7] Although Wellmann 1922, followed by Jones 1947, suggests Soranus.

one suggestion was that *Breaths* was by one of the other three
members of the genealogy with the same name (Smith 1979, 36-8).
Menon was right to say that it was by Hippocrates, but it was not by
the great Hippocrates. Strategies such as this maintained the
research programme intact.

The power which the programme exerts even now can be most
effectively demonstrated by the otherwise surprising fact that Wesley
Smith, who in so many ways breaks through its influence by exposing
much of the hard core as myth, also feels obliged to conform to its
assumptions by identifying a 'genuine work'. Using as a basis
pre-Alexandrian evidence – for example, Plato's description of the
method of 'Hippocrates the Asclepiad' in *Phaedrus* 269e ff., used by
Littré (1.294-320) to argue that *Ancient Medicine* is a 'genuine work'
(Edelstein 1939) – he claims that Hippocrates wrote *Regimen* and that
Menon's references are to this and not to *Breaths* (1979, 44-59). Even
more recently, Mansfeld has used precisely the same evidence, but this
time to 'demonstrate' that it is *Airs, waters, places* which is by
Hippocrates (1980; cf. Kucharski 1939; Jouanna 1977). Thus even
where the traditional research programme is being eroded, there
apparently remains a deep need to find a 'genuine work'.

Even where medical historians have abandoned the attempt to
match up texts to Hippocrates, other nameless 'authors' are made to
emerge from the corpus. For example, treatises can be linked on the
basis of perceived similarities of doctrine, language or style, or on the
evidence of self-citation of the form, 'As I say in my treatise on x' (e.g.
Generation, Nature of the Child and *Diseases* 4).[8] Alternatively, groups
which are established in the manuscript tradition may be challenged;
thus Grensemann has tried to distinguish two or more authors,
separated by at least fifty years, within *Gynaikeia* 1 and 2. The
grounds on which he does this are open to criticism; even if some
sections favour *epimênia* for the menses, others *katamênia*, and if we
assume that this is due to a different author and date rather than to
personal preference or total interchangeability of terms, the problem
remains that there is hardly any external evidence on which dating
can be based, since there is little direct discussion of menstruation
outside Hippocratic gynaecology.[9] The possibility of deliberate
archaising – of chronologically later writers consciously imitating the
style of earlier writers – should also be mentioned here, since it makes
dating even more complicated.

The question raised by all such attempts to produce authors for

[8] There is an excellent edition of these by Lonie 1981; on the question see 43ff. Cf. Joly
1977.
[9] Grensemann (1975, esp. p.164) puts author A (*epimênia*) earlier than C (*katamênia*).
See also Grensemann 1982. Joly 1977, 137-8 uses the same criteria to place C earlier
than A.

anonymous texts is why so much effort is invested in them. The only possible response is that this is how the Hippocratic texts have traditionally been read, in order to explain apparent differences in therapy or theory by different dates – as change over time – or by different authors – as variation within one period. Associated with this way of reading the Hippocratic corpus is the assignment of texts to 'schools' of medicine alleged to have existed in the classical period; the incompetent librarian at Alexandria not only confused the four writers called Hippocrates, but even catalogued some medical works from a rival school under Hippocrates' name. Further questions from the traditional research programme's positive heuristic are therefore 'What were the doctrines characteristic of the ancient medical schools of Kos and Knidos?' and 'Which treatises in the corpus belong to each school?' The school of Kos is the rational, scientific one supposedly linked with Hippocrates, and is responsible for all the best treatises of the corpus – however each age wishes to define 'best' – while the 'more primitive' (Kudlien 1968, 321 and n.67) or 'pre-rational' (Kudlien 1968, 325) level of medicine is represented by the Knidian school. Of the texts being considered here, *Aphorisms* is traditionally seen as the work of Hippocrates himself; *Epidemics* 1 and 3 are also usually taken to be 'Koan' and 'genuine works' of Hippocrates, on the basis of their emphasis on observing the course of a disease, while *Epidemics* 7 is thought to be somewhat inferior.[10]

The negative heuristic of the research programme shows its full force when it looks at the major gynaecological treatises, the *Gynaikeia* (L 8.10-462). It classifies them not only as being by someone other than Hippocrates,[11] but also as belonging to the inferior and irrational 'school of Knidos'. As a result of this classification, they are assumed to be of only marginal interest; evidence of the primitive form from which Koan medicine developed, but of little value as objects of study in their own right. It is furthermore considered heretical to read the 'Knidian' *Gynaikeia* beside the 'Koan' *Aphorisms* on 'inferior' *Epidemics* 7.

An alternative model of the Hippocratic corpus, which cuts across such divisions, has however recently been adopted by Smith (1979), Lloyd (1975; 1983), Thivel (1981) and Hanson (1986). This suggests that oppositions between Knidos and Kos and between genuine and secondary works should be abandoned in favour of a new emphasis on the common assumptions of the writers in the corpus; their stock of

[10] On the 'school of Knidos', see e.g. Sarrazin 1921, 9; Joly 1966, 31 (list of 'Knidian' works). Refuted by Thivel 1981; cf. Smith 1979, 142 on Galen's ignorance of such a school. Grmek and Robert 1977, 290 plead for *Epidemics* 7 to be assessed more favourably than is traditional, because 'la qualité des observations est admirable'.

[11] A writer in the epistolographic tradition (*Epist.* 21/L 9.392) however has 'Hippocrates' writing to Democritos, 'As I said in my treatise "On the Diseases of Women", give purges when the womb needs to be purged.' This passage was brought to my attention by Ann Hanson.

shared knowledge and beliefs, and the competition existing not at the institutional level – schools – but at the individual level, where many anonymous practitioners try to innovate within the limits set, in order to gain patients (Lloyd 1979). In the absence of any form of professional licensing, employment depended upon one's ability to persuade; rhetoric became important (Jouanna 1984), as did the presentation of self in a way which would convince patients and their relatives of one's abilities, through dress, manner, language and so on. Lonie, in the first part of an excellent article on 'Cos versus Cnidus and the historians', demonstrates that the 'pre-rational' Knidian school is entirely a construct of the dominant research programme; it 'comes into existence to fill an historical vacuum, the absence of any direct information on the character and development of Greek medicine before Hippocrates' (1978, 50).

If the so-called 'Knidian' texts are compared with the remarks on gynaecology scattered through such 'Koan' works as *Aphorisms* 5 and *Epidemics* 1 and 3, it can be shown that a very similar anatomy of woman exists in both, from which similar conclusions are drawn. Assumptions of female inferiority, of the natural superiority of right over left (e.g. *Ep.* 2.6.15/L 5.136), and of the mechanism of the movement of blood within the body are examples of other features common to both groups of texts (Hanson 1986). It is thus impossible to separate Koan and Knidian ideas fully from each other (Joly 1966, 64-9; Jouanna 1961, 463). Furthermore, it is only by reading across the traditional boundaries between groups of texts that the scope of Hippocratic medicine can be appreciated. The *Epidemics* are written from the point of view of a doctor who sees every type of case, male and female; detailed case histories are given in which the progress of the symptoms to the critical point of the disease is charted, but information on the precise treatment is rare. The *Gynaikeia* gives long lists of remedies for the symptoms which it describes; the descriptions of disorders are not usually tied to particular identified individuals, but are presented in a more general way. The brief comments on women's diseases in *Aphorisms* 5 can similarly only be understood in relation to the fuller accounts of the *Gynaikeia*.

The range of explanations offered by the traditional research programme for the difference between the two texts on nosebleeds in women may now be summarised: they could derive from different authors, different schools, or different dates. In the last case, the *Epidemics* passage would presumably be 'late' because it suggests that the aphorism is 'wrong'; the case history becomes a moment of progress, as the earlier hypothesis is falsified. 'The doctor didn't understand' would thus mean 'The doctor was baffled that his theory didn't seem to be borne out in practice.' On this reading, the daughter of Leonides is the pink raven, the observed case which falsifies the (erroneous) general rule.

3. The daughter of Leonides as a black raven

I would propose, in direct opposition to this, that any reference to a medically correct 'reality' is entirely misplaced: the daughter of Leonides is not a case of observation falsifying a general law, but is another black raven.

Only the traditional research programme prevents us from taking the two texts under consideration here at precisely the same level. Case histories, with their real place names, identified individual patients and descriptions of the course of diseases, intuitively feel closer to reality. However, Lloyd points out that these 'star examples of detailed observations in early Greek science' nevertheless rely on prior theory and on motivations different from those behind modern case histories (1979, 154-5). Furthermore, Lonie has recently drawn attention to the common sense assumption that we 'know' what a case history is. He points out that doctors in our society write up case notes because of particular historical developments in medical institutions, and because of their own positions and responsibilities within such institutions. Such a social context is absent for the authors of the *Epidemics*. Unlike the case histories with which we are familiar, those of the Hippocratic corpus are private notes of points which interest the doctor, and to which he may later return. They provide directions for further enquiry, and they begin the process of putting a structure on that which is observed. They therefore provide evidence, not of what 'really happened', but rather of 'the observer's private and unexpressed sense of what is interesting, relevant, of what may turn out to be useful' (1983, 155).

In Foucault's terms, all sources are equally 'representations'; action, text, speech: observed, read, heard (1966). Each is a veil between the observer and 'reality'; there is no such thing as direct, common sense access to 'reality'. Furthermore, the search for an ultimate, 'correct', true meaning is futile: there is no one 'meaning of', but rather, as the anthropologist Gilbert Lewis has shown in a study of the 'meaning' of a particular ritual practice, there are many 'meanings for' (1980). First-hand reports such as case histories cannot report reality accurately; they do not *present* reality, but they 'represent' – re-present – reality.

Now if both Hippocratic texts are taken as representations in this sense, as equally far from – or near to – reality, they are best referred not to our ideas of the reality of the body, but to their own cultural context. Beneath the apparent difference between their evaluations of nosebleeds lies a shared belief that a menstrual period may be diverted and come out through the nose.[12] Before we can investigate why this

[12] I see little point in 'diagnosing' this as vicarious menstruation, a rare condition in which the mucous membranes of the nose bleed in response to oestrogen, since this

causes a fatal change in the daughter of Leonides, it is necessary to reconstruct the intellectual framework common to the *Aphorisms*, *Epidemics* and *Gynaikeia*; the internal anatomy of Hippocratic woman.

Both Manuli and Hanson have recently drawn attention to the ancient therapeutic procedures which assume that, in a woman, there is a *hodos*, a route extending from the orifices of the head to the vagina. As Manuli vividly describes her, woman is 'an uninterrupted vagina from nostrils to womb' (1980, 399; 1983, 157; cf. Hanson 1981; 1986); a hollow tube with a mouth (*stoma*) at each end. 'Obstruction of passages is a very frequent explanation in Greek medicine' in general (Lonie 1981, 113), and tests for whether a woman is able to conceive often rely on demonstrating that this tube is free of obstructions. Garlic or another strongly-scented substance is placed at the bottom end; if the smell reaches the top end, the woman can conceive (*G* 2.146/L 8.322; *NW* 96/L 7.412-4; *Aph.* 5.59/L 4.554 etc.). A similar belief in a connection between the two ends of the tube can be detected in descriptions of therapy, which include attempts to lure the womb back into place when it is supposed to be wandering about the body; a summary of treatments of the womb in *Gynaikeia* 2.137 (L 8.310) mentions the top end and the bottom end (*anô/katô*) as sites for treatment.[13] If the womb has moved upwards, foul-smelling substances are held to the nose, pleasant-smelling substances to the vulva; the womb is simultaneously repelled from above and attracted down to its correct place (*G* 2.123/L 8.266; 2.154/L 8.330; 2.201/L 8.384). If the womb moves down, the reverse therapy is used (*G* 2.125/L 8.268; 2.137/L 8.310; 2.143/L 8.316 etc.). Another example of the use of the tube in treatment is the section of the *Gynaikeia* in which a woman whose womb must be made to move upwards is encouraged to vomit, presumably to create a space into which the womb will be drawn; at the same time the womb is repulsed from the vulva by foul odours (*G* 2.142/L 8.314; Joly 1966, 44-5). A method of expelling the retained afterbirth is to make the woman sneeze, but to block her nostrils and mouth at the moment of sneezing (*Ep.* 2.5.25/L 5.132).

The nostrils are important in Hippocratic medicine in general as indicators of health. For example, cold *pneuma* coming from the

---

would only obscure the completely different theory underlying the Hippocratics' belief that it is 'a good thing'.

[13] Cf. *G*. 1.66/L 8.136, which says that the fluxes which it describes should be treated both from the top and the bottom, but first of all from the top; in *Ep.* 5.19/L 5.218, a female patient produces bile and blood *kai anô kai katô*; cf. *Nutriment* 45/L 9.116, 'the way up and the way down are one'. A female slave in *Ep.* 5.35/L 5.230 produces after a purge a little 'up' and a lot 'down', yet she dies. The writer adds, 'She was a barbarian.' I suggest below that the end of the case must always be taken as significant in interpreting the rest; does this indicate that *barbaroi* are somehow beyond the pale for Greek medicine?

nostrils when the skin is producing warm vapour is a sign of death (*Ep.* 6.4.22/L 5.312-4); naturally damp nostrils and watery sperm show a weak constitution (*Ep.* 6.6.8/L 5.328) and sexual intercourse dries up the nasal discharge of Timochares (*Ep.* 5.72/L 5.246). These last examples demonstrate that an affinity between the nostrils and the organs of reproduction can exist in the male. Such an affinity is even more pronounced in the female; for example, in *Gynaikeia* 2.133 (L 8.282), the mouth of the womb closes and tilts, and it is striking that the nostrils behave in the same way, being 'dry and blocked, not upright'. Similarly, when the menstrual period is about to start, there is heaviness in the head and pain in the throat (*KP* 537/L 5.706). Ps-Aristotle says that the womb 'breathes in' the seed in much the same way as the mouth and nostrils inhale substances, and that the *hodos* from the vulva to the inside of the womb is like the *poros* from nostrils to larynx (*On sterility* 634b 35; 636b 17-18; 637a 21-35); the anatomical similarities between the top and bottom of the tube, which account for their similar treatment in therapy, are here explicit.

There thus exists a direct route from one end of the female body to the other; Greek theories of the process of menstruation in a mature woman further explain how blood can move from the bottom to the top. The womb itself is seen not as being, in Aretaeus' famous words (2.11/CMG 2.32-3), 'an animal inside an animal', but rather as a jar inside a tube.[14] Like any jar, it has a mouth (*stoma*), which is the focal point for diagnosis and treatment. The patient is often asked to touch it and report on its condition (hard/soft, open/closed) and position (upright/tilted) (e.g. *G* 2.119/L 8.260; 2.133/L 8.280-8; 2.134/L 8.304). If it is aligned with the tube, and with the 'mouth of exit' (*PP*/L 8.466) at the bottom of that tube, then blood can pour out of the jar. Amenorrhoea is not presented as a failure of the body to produce menstrual blood; women naturally produce excess blood, because their flesh is of a qualitatively different texture from that of a man. Women are wet and spongy (*chaunos*), 'like sheepskin' (*G* 1.1/L 8.12).[15] They absorb more fluid from their food because of this spongy texture; blood is always accumulating, and every month the excess must pour out. If it does not appear, the mouth of the womb may have closed, blocking its way outside, or the womb-jar may have tilted, pouring the blood in the wrong direction. Where the mouth of the jar is not aligned with the bottom of the tube, the blood may accumulate or may force a new way

[14] Actually called *to angos*, the jar, in *Ep.* 6.5.11/L 5.318. *Gen.* 9/L 7.482 draws an analogy between womb and cup, and then between womb and jar; the good womb, which bears good fruit, is like a cucumber growing in an *angos*. Cf. also *G* 1.33/L 8.78 in which a difficult delivery is compared to shaking a fruit-stone out of a jar with a narrow mouth. For womb as jar see also the illustrations to the ninth-century AD Mustio papyrus, and ex voto offerings from Kos (Diepgen 1937, 31 fig. 14; 132 fig.40).

[15] In terms of texture and thus of capacity to absorb fluid, sheepskin is to a rug as the female body is to the male. Cf. Heidel 1941, 91; Manuli 1983, 188; Hanson 1981.

out. In *Diseases* 4.41 (L 7.562) it is said that, just as there are four
humours and four bodily sources of the humours, so there are four
routes out of the body which the humours can take: mouth, nostrils,
anus and urethra. *Epidemics* 2.1.7 (L 5.76-8) gives several more
routes, and particularly recommends, if possible, a loss from an
opening below and a long way from the site of the disease. As in women
(above and n.13), so in men it is expected that evacuation of humours
should occur from both 'above' and 'below' (e.g. *Ep.* 5.43/L 5.232). One
area in which the *Gynaikeia* does differ significantly from many other
treatises of the corpus is that the theory of the four humours plays a
very small part (Thivel 1981, 98-9; 1983, 230), since the nature of
woman is dominated by one organ, the womb, and hence by only one
humour, the hot and the wet: blood. There are many routes which
suppressed menstrual blood may take; it may come out through the
groin, the side or the rectum (*G* 1.2/L 8.20-22; *KP* 511/L 5.702).

Because of the affinity between the top and the bottom of the tube,
suppressed menstrual blood may cause headaches (*Ep.* 5.12/L 5.212),
and the other route which blood may take in a woman is that to the
mouth and nostrils. The aphorism under consideration here
encourages menstrual nosebleeds; it is preceded by one saying that
vomiting blood ceases when the menses flow (5.32/L 4.542).[16] These
aphorisms imply that blood can only move in one direction at a time;
however, in the *Epidemics* it is possible to find several cases in which
blood changes direction abruptly, and others in which it uses both
routes simultaneously. In *Epidemics* 1.2.8 (L 2.640-50) a particular
fever affecting both sexes is described. It affects women less than men,
and women are also less likely to die from it unless they suffer after a
difficult labour (L 2.646). In male sufferers, a heavy nosebleed always
leads to recovery (L 2.642; cf. *Prognostic* 7/L 2.126-8): in women, the
fever often brings on the menstrual period, and *parthenoi* suffering
from it have their first menses. In some, nosebleed and menses flow at
the same time, while the daughter of Daitharsis, a *parthenos*, had her
first period and a nosebleed. The writer adds that, to his knowledge,
none of these women died (L 2.648).

The combination of first menses and a nosebleed is also favourable in
the cases of the *parthenos* of Larissa (*Ep.* 3.17.12/L 3.136) and the
parthenos of Abdera (*Ep.* 3.17.7/L 3.122), who have similar symptoms
of fever, thirst and insomnia. The girl from Abdera has menarche at
the beginning of the illness, and a heavy nosebleed on the seventeenth
day: the Larissan girl has the nosebleed first, and menarche shortly
afterwards. Both recover.

---

[16] The two aphorisms are taken together in the commentary of Theophilus (ed. Dietz
vol. 2, p.462). Cf. Ar. *GA* 727a 11-15; *HA* 587b 31ff; Byl 1981, 74. Vomiting blood is not,
however, beneficial for another '*parthenos* of Larissa' in *Ep.* 5.24/L 5.224; her death could
be explained in terms of the fatal nosebleed of the daughter of Leonides (below).

Where these cases differ from both *Aphorisms* 5.32-3 and the daughter of Leonides is that they describe fevers in which natural blood loss is beneficial to both sexes (cf. *Ep.* 4.17/L 5.154), rather than menstruation suppressed for reasons of individual physiology. An intermediate case is the daughter of Philon (*Ep.* 1.2.9/L 2.658), who suffers from another fever in which nosebleeds are thought to be beneficial for both sexes (L 2.650-68). There are four favourable signs in the course of the disease, one of which is the nosebleed (L 2.656); in *gynaikes* and *parthenoi*, the writer adds, there is a fifth sign, a heavy period. However, the daughter of Philon had a copious nosebleed but died on the seventh day. The writer is clearly aware that this requires explanation, and he adds that 'she dined inopportunely' (*akairoterôs*).

The daughter of Leonides apparently has no fever; her surprisingly fatal nosebleed is a diversion of her normal menses. The daughter of Philon has a favourable nosebleed, but dies because she eats at the wrong time. It is possible to reconstruct the reasoning by which both deaths could be explained without falsifying *Aphorisms* 5.32-3, by investigating two variables in the jar and tube anatomy and physiology of woman: the age and the reproductive status of the patient.

The age of the patient, of either sex, is taken into consideration by several Hippocratic writers. *Aphorisms* 3.24-31 (L 4.496-502) and *Koan Prognoses* 502 (L 5.700) list the diseases most likely to affect particular age groups; texts which apply such a division to women include *Gynaikeia* 2.111 (L 8.238-40) and *Nature of woman* 1 (L 7.312). Only one section of the *Gynaikeia*, that which concerns fluxes, consistently gives comments on the age of the patient (*G* 2.115-21/L 8.248-64, except 2.117). A younger woman is given a different regimen (*diaita, G* 2.115, 118; cf. 2.177/L 8.360): a white flux is difficult to cure in older women (2.116, 118, 119), and other fluxes too are more likely to strike and to kill if the patient is older (2.120, 121). Elsewhere in the *Gynaikeia* similar distinctions are drawn. Movements of the womb cause more difficulties in older than in younger women, especially if the woman is near the menopause (2.137/L 8.310). Some conditions are worse in pregnant women (2.174-174²/L 8.354-6), others more common in the childless (2.145/L 8.320). The variables of age and reproductive status would often, but not always, coincide, young women being more likely to have no children.

To discover why fluxes and womb movement are more of a problem in older women, two parallel texts on sudden movement of the womb to the liver in a healthy woman are instructive (*G* 2.127/L 8.272-4 = *NW* 3/L 7.314-6). Those affected are mostly older *parthenoi* and young widows, but it can affect any childless or sterile women who are *ek tôn tokôn*, which Manuli translates as 'outside the logic of generation' (1983, 156). This is the case because such women do not experience the bloodshed of the lochia, the discharge after childbirth, thought to be composed of stored menstrual blood (King 1987); the womb 'does not swell up or become soft or emit [blood]'. The treatment for the widow includes sweet wine poured in the mouth, foul odours applied to the nostrils, sweet smells to the womb, followed by a purgative and cooked asses' milk, an aromatic fumigation of the womb, beetle pessaries (another purgative) and an aromatic injection into the womb. These procedures have in common the drawing down of the womb from the liver; it is significant that they assume the connection between nostrils and vulva. It is best of all, the writer continues, if the widow conceives. As for *parthenoi*, they should take a husband. So far, this is fairly standard Hippocratic advice. The remainder of the section is, however, of a different type, consisting of advice on what *not* to do if the patient is a *parthenos*. Nothing should be applied to the nostrils (*G* 2.127; *NW* 3 reads 'to the womb' here), no purgative should be administered, although strong-smelling substances in sweet wine may be drunk, and she should not put any perfumed oil on her head, nor inhale any.

Variation in disease frequency and treatment in different categories of woman could be explained by the physiological differences believed to exist between them. Women's loose-textured flesh, complete with channels, develops gradually over time. In *Diseases* 4.39 (L 7.558) the network of passages (*phlebes*) throughout the body is described. During the whole of the person's life they are open, allowing the humoral fluids to pass, but at death they close. *Gynaikeia* and some other texts modify this theory. In the young person of either sex, normal growth includes the widening of the channels so that fluids can move around more easily (*Gen.* 2/L 7.472; *NC* 20/L 7.508; cf. Diogenes DK 64B6); but while boys show that they are mature once and for all by producing semen, the channels in girls continue to widen after puberty. Puberty (*hêbê*) is in general a time of sudden changes (*Ep.* 6.1.4/L 5.268)[17] but in girls it does not complete the process of becoming a woman. Normal growth opens the *phlebia* to make 'a way through and a way outside' *Gen.* 2/L 7.472-4), but all three transitional bleedings – menarche, defloration and childbirth (King 1983) – cause changes in the body. For example, a childless woman of any age has denser, more tightly-packed flesh than a woman who has given birth, with less space into which suppressed menstrual blood can travel and consequently more pain if her blood does not leave her body. In a childless woman the *stoma* of the womb will be narrower *G* 1.1/L 8.12; 1.2/L 8.14), although it may be closed by disease in any woman. Childbirth is usually beneficial in easing menstruation not only because the passage of the child opens the 'way out' (*exodos*, *NC* 30/L 7.538), but also because it breaks down the flesh, opening up spaces in

---

[17] Following the reading of Zeuxis, rather than Galen; cf. L 5.268-9; Manetti and Roselli 1982, 5.

the body (*G* 1.1/L 8.10), and widens the *phlebia* carrying blood to the womb (*NC* 30/L 7.538).

A woman who has given birth has loose-textured flesh, open *phlebia* and a complete tube from nostrils to vulva, which can be used in therapy. A young unmarried girl has not given birth and possibly has not even completed the growth process of puberty, so her *phlebia* are narrow and her tube may not be complete: this is why attempts to apply anything to her head or nostrils would have no effect on the womb. These distinctions between women made by age and reproductive status would also suggest that fluxes affect older women more, because their bodies are more open. Women near the menopause are more subject to movements of the womb partly because their bodies are drying out as they age, and the womb will be more likely to travel in search of moisture (cf. *G* 2.137/L 8.308-10), but also partly because there is more open space in their bodies into which the womb can move.

In terms of Hippocratic theory, *parthenoi* are thus physically incomplete women; some are still growing towards menarche, others have bled but their *phlebia* are narrow and their flesh has not yet been broken down (*katarrêgnymi*, *G* 1.1/L 8.10; *NC* 30/L 7.538) by childbirth. Menarche itself is a time of potential danger. In the *Peri parthenión* menstrual blood which is unable to come out of the bottom of the tube instead travels up towards the top, but it becomes lodged in the region of the heart and diaphragm where the channels are 'at an angle' (*PP*/L 8.466-8), and causes illness (King 1983). A nosebleed is 'a good thing when the menses are suppressed' in a *gynê* (*Aph.* 5.33); in *Gynaikeia* 1.41 (L 8.100) it is lochial blood which comes out of the nose, so the patient has obviously given birth and can be considered a complete woman. The complete woman (*gynê*) can be treated by purges and by fumigations at the nose, and can lose blood from the nostrils, because her internal anatomy permits it. In a *parthenos*, a nosebleed is particularly significant – and thus worth noting in a case history[18] – because it shows that the dangerous areas of the body have been successfully traversed, and hence that a certain point of internal physical maturity has been reached.

It is not stated that the daughter of Philon (*Ep.* 1.2.9/L 2.658) is a *parthenos*, or that her nosebleed is seen in menstrual terms. However, the attribution of her death to 'dining inopportunely' recalls a phrase of the *Peri parthenión*, where blood is said to accumulate at menarche because of 'food and the growth of the body' (L 8.466). Since the origin of

---

[18] It may therefore be significant that the writer chooses to note that it is the *first* menstrual period in the cases of the *parthenoi* of Larissa and Abdera; as a critical time, it would be worth noting. Cf. also *Ep.* 2.3.1/L 5.102-4 on the importance of menarche as an indicator.

blood is food, more food means more blood.[19] Having successfully purged the excess, by eating too soon the daughter of Philon foolishly created more blood before her body was ready for it.

What of the anatomical status of the daughter of Leonides, whose nosebleed is due not to a fever but to the diversion of normal menstrual blood? It is not possible to know whether *hê physis* does or does not suggest menarche, while being 'daughter of' rather than 'wife of' is no guarantee of being a *parthenos*.[20] The case histories of *Epidemics* 7, like those of the other *Epidemics* collections, often end with the bald statement of the death of the patient, sometimes also giving the number of days since the illness began, and using either *apethanen* (7.36/L 5.404; 37/406; 81/436; 109/458; 116/462) or *eteleutêsen* (10/382; 14/388; 15-17/390; 19-21/392; 28-9/400; 32/402; 41/408; 49/418; 51/420; 55/422).

In no other case in this volume is the age, sex or any other status of the patient given at this point;[21] yet, for the daughter of Leonides, we read *hê pais apethanen*. If medical history is text, then the selected ending must affect our perception of the whole. The selected end explicitly links her death to the status of *pais*, just as that of the daughter of Philon is linked to 'dining inopportunely'. There is no reason to repeat her identity as 'daughter of', so I would suggest *pais* here should be taken as 'child'. *Weeks* 5 (L 8.636) uses *paidion* from age 0-7, *pais* from 7-14; the next section of *Epidemics* 7 concerns a *pais ephêbos* (7.124/L 5.468), which would suggest the upper limit of the *Weeks* category. These references cannot be pushed too far. In terms of her internal anatomy, being a *pais* would simply suggest that the daughter of Leonides is, as yet, an incomplete woman. In her compact body there are thus no spaces where excess blood can rest: she dies because, although her body is ready to menstruate, it cannot also survive the blood forcing its way up to the nose through channels which are too narrow to cope.[22] 'The doctor didn't understand': he failed to realise that the nosebleed principle only

[19] Cf. *Iliad* 5.341-2 (blood related to consumption of normal human diet); Ar. *PA* 650a 34-5 (blood is the food of the body); *Diseases* 4.38/L 7.554-6. The relationship between food and blood in the Hippocratic corpus is discussed in depth by Duminil 1983, 235ff.

[20] The 'daughter of Telebolos' in *Ep.* 1.2.8/L 2.646 dies on the sixth day after she has given birth (cf. *Ep.* 4.24/L 5.164); the 'sister of Harpalides' in *Ep.* 7.6/L 5.376 has difficulties in pregnancy. 'Daughter of' reinforced by *pais* is, however, a different matter.

[21] *Ep.* 4.15/L 5.152-4 ends with the point that the young man who died of a fever with delirium was 'not very old, only about twenty'. This too forms special pleading since, in the previous sentence, the writer conjectures (*oimai*) that this patient only died because he drank undiluted wine while ill. Drunkenness leads to a sudden increase in the amount of blood in the body (*Breaths* 14/L 6.112); this case thus recalls the daughter of Philon who 'dined inopportunely'. Relevant also is *Ep.* 4.49/L 5.190, the daughter of Histaios, which ends, 'the *paidiskê* died'. Here a purgation, artificially induced, kills; perhaps here too the ending suggests that the patient was too young to take this treatment.

[22] *Breaths* 8/L 6.102-4, discussing pain in the head, describes hot blood being forced through narrow *hodoi*. In the case of the daughter of Leonides, the *hodoi* or *phlebia* are narrow because of youth rather than disease.

safely applied to mature women, to *gynaikes*. This would also explain why suppressed menstrual blood is more likely to come out through the rectum in a *parthenos* than a *gynê* (G 1.2/L 8.22);[23] unable to move up the tube so freely, in a *parthenos* the blood may 'make a *hodos*' through the next nearest orifice.

The 'Koan' and 'Knidian,' 'genuine' and 'spurious' works of the Hippocratic corpus together demonstrate the details of the jar and tube anatomy of woman, such as the affinity between nostrils and vagina, and the process by which a girl grows to become a woman. If we commit the heresy of reading the texts as if the traditional research programme had never separated them, the death of the daughter of Leonides becomes another black raven for the theory of menstrual nosebleeds. This interpretation does not treat the case history as the rationally-observed particular case which causes the general rule to be questioned; instead, it emphasises the point that the particular case can only be observed within the conceptual framework provided by the general rule. I would suggest that the author of *Epidemics* 7.123 is fully aware of the rule that menstrual nosebleeds are salutary and that this is why he chooses to note that this patient was a *pais*. Any description involves selection; as historians, our role is to take into account both the points which the text deliberately brings to our attention, and the points which are so obvious that they are not stated. The medical case history shows that it is precisely those sources which appear to report reality directly which need to be read with the closest attention.

Particular thanks to Ann Hanson for her comments on an earlier draft of this chapter; also to Lesley Ann Jones for access to her unpublished dissertation. The final version was prepared in the perfect conditions provided by the Fondation Hardt, on a visit funded by the British Academy.

Bibliography

Adams, F. 1849. *The Genuine Works of Hippocrates* (London).

———— 1939. *The Genuine Works of Hippocrates* (reissue, with intro. by Kelly) (London).

Byl, S. 1980. *Recherches sur les grands traités biologiques d'Aristote: sources écrites et préjugés* (Brussels).

Chalmers, A.F. 1982. *What is This Thing Called Science?* (2nd. ed.) (Milton Keynes).

[23] L 8.23 does not make sufficiently clearly the point that the text separates blood loss by vomiting from blood loss through the rectum; it is only the latter which is thought to be something particularly affecting *parthenoi*, and this is consistent with the suggestion that the route to the head and nostrils is treacherous in younger women. Damascius comments on *Aph.* 5.33, 'Not only from the nostrils, but also from the rectum' (ed. Dietz vol.2, p.462).

Clologe, C.H.T. 1905. *Essai sur l'histoire de la gynécologie dans l'antiquité grecque jusqu'à la collection hippocratique* (Bordeaux).

Deichgräber, K. 1982. *Die Patienten des Hippokrates. Historische-prosopographische Beiträge zu den Epidemien des Corpus Hippocraticum* (Wiesbaden).

Diels, H. 1893a. *Anonymi Londinensis ex Aristotelis Iatricis Menoniis et aliis medicis Eclogae* (Berlin).

―――― 1893b. 'Über die Excerpte von Menons Iatrika in dem Londoner Papyrus 137', *Hermes* 28, 407-34.

Diepgen, P. 1937. *Die Frauenheilkunde der alten Welt*, Handbuch der Gynäkologie XII.1 (Munich).

Duminil, M.-P. 1983. *Le Sang, les vaisseaux, le coeur dans la collection hippocratique* (Paris).

Edelstein, E.J. and L. 1945. *Asclepius: a collection of the testimonies*, 2 vols. (Baltimore).

Edelstein, L. 1931. 'The Hippocratic physician', repr. in O. and C.L. Temkin, eds., *Ancient Medicine: selected papers of Ludwig Edelstein* (Baltimore, 1967), 87-110.

―――― 1939, 'The genuine works of Hippocrates', *Bull. Hist. Med.* 7, 236-48.

Foucault, M. 1966. *The Order of Things*, section repr. in R.T. and F.M. de George, eds., *The Structuralists: from Marx to Lévi-Strauss* (New York, 1972), 256-85.

Geertz, C. 1983. 'Common sense as a cultural system', in C. Geertz, *Local Knowledge* (New York), 73-93.

Gellner, E. 1964. *Thought and Change* (London).

Grensemann, H. 1975. 'Eine jüngere Schicht in den gynäkologischen Schriften', in *La collection hippocratique et son rôle dans l'histoire de la médecine*, Colloque de Strasbourg 1972 (Leiden), 151-69.

―――― 1982. *Hippokratische Gynäkologie. Die gynäkologischen Texte des Autors C nach den pseudohippokratischen Schriften De mulieribus I, II und De Sterilibus* (Wiesbaden).

Grmek, M. and Robert, F. 1977. 'Dialogue d'un médecin et d'un philologue sur quelques passages des *Epidémies VII*', in R. Joly, ed., *Corpus Hippocraticum*, Actes du Colloque hippocratique de Mons 1975, Univ. de Mons, 275-90.

Hanson, A.E. 1981. 'Anatomical assumptions in Hippocrates, *Diseases of Women I.1*', paper delivered at the *Am. Philol. Ass.*, summary in *SAM Newsletter* 8, 4-5.

―――― 1986. 'The diseases of women in the *Epidemics*', Actes Vᵉ Colloque hippocratique (Berlin, 1984).

Heidel, W.A. 1941. *Hippocratic Medicine: its spirit and method* (New York).

Joly, R. 1966. *Le Niveau de la science hippocratique, contribution à la psychologie de l'histoire des sciences* (Paris).

―――― 1977. 'Indices léxicaux pour la datation de *Génération-Nature de l'enfant – Maladies IV*', in *Corpus Hippocraticum* (see Grmek and Robert 1977), 136-47.

Jones, W.H.S. 1931. *Hippocrates*, vol. 4, Loeb ed. (London).

―――― 1947. *The Medical Writings of Anonymus Londinensis* (Cambridge).

Jouanna, J. 1961. 'Présence d'Empédocle dans la collection hippocratique', *Bull. Ass. G. Budé*, 452-63.

―――― 1977. 'La Collection hippocratique et Platon (*Phèdre* 269c-272a)', *Rev. Et. Grecques* 90, 15-28.

—— 1984. 'Rhétorique et médecine dans la collection hippocratique', *Rev. Et. Grecques* 97, 26-44.

Kee, H.C. 1982. 'Self-definition in the Asclepius cult', in B.F. Meyer and E.P. Sanders, eds., *Jewish and Christian Self-definition*, III: *Self-definition in the Graeco-Roman World* (London), 118-36.

Kenyon, F.G. 1892. 'A medical papyrus in the British Museum', *Class. Rev.* 6, 237-40.

King, H. 1983. 'Bound to bleed: Artemis and Greek women', in Averil Cameron and Amélie Kuhrt, eds., *Images of Women in Antiquity* (London), 109-27.

—— 1987. 'Sacrificial blood: the role of the *amnion* in ancient gynecology', in Marilyn Skinner, ed., *Rescuing Creusa: new methodological approaches to women in antiquity, Helios*, n.s. 13, 117-26.

Kucharski, P. 1939. 'La "méthode d'Hippocrate" dans le "Phèdre"', *Rev. Et. Grecques* 52, 301-57.

Kudlien, F. 1968. 'Early Greek primitive medicine', *Clio Medica* 3, 305-36.

Lakatos, I. 1978. 'Falsification and the methodology of scientific research', in J. Worrall and G. Currie, eds., *The Methodology of Scientific Research Programmes* 1 (Cambridge), 8-101.

Lewis, G. 1980. *Day of Shining Red* (Cambridge).

Littré, E. 1839-61. *Oeuvres complètes d'Hippocrate*, 10 vols. (Paris, repr. Amsterdam, 1961).

Lloyd, G.E.R. 1975. 'The Hippocratic question', *Class. Quart.* 25, 171-92.

—— 1979. *Magic, Reason and Experience* (Cambridge).

—— 1983. *Science, Folklore and Ideology* (Cambridge).

Lonie, I.M. 1978. 'Cos versus Cnidus and the historians', *Hist. Sc.* 16, 42-75, 77-92.

—— 1981. *The Hippocratic Treatises 'On Generation', 'On the Nature of the Child', 'Diseases IV'* (Berlin).

—— 1983. 'Literacy and the development of Hippocratic medicine', in F. Lasserre and P. Mudry, eds., *Formes de pensée dans la collection hippocratique*, Actes du Colloque hippocratique de Lausanne 1981 (Geneva), 145-61.

Manetti, D. and Roselli, A., 1982. *Ippocrate: Epidemie, libro sesto* (Florence).

Mansfeld, J. 1980. 'Plato and the method of Hippocrates', *Greek, Roman and Byzantine Stud.*, 21, 341-62.

Manuli, P. 1980. 'Fisiologia e patologia del femminile negli scritti ippocratici dell'antica ginecologia greca', in M.D. Grmek, ed., *Hippocratica*, Actes de Colloque hippocratique de Paris 1978 (Paris), 393-408.

—— 1983. 'Donne mascoline, femmine sterili, vergini perpetue. La ginecologia greca tra Ippocrate e Sorano', in S. Campese, P. Manuli and G. Sissa, *Madre Materia, Sociologia e biologia della donna greca* (Turin), 147-92.

Sarrazin, P. 1921. *La Gynécologie dans les écrits hippocratiques* (Paris).

Schaps, D. 1977. 'The woman least mentioned: etiquette and women's names', *Class. Quart.* 27, 323-30.

Smith, W.D. 1973. 'Galen on Coans versus Cnidians', *Bull. Hist. Med.* 47, 569-85.

—— 1979. *The Hippocratic Tradition* (Ithaca, New York).

Thivel, A. 1981. *Cnide et Cos? Essai sur les doctrines médicales dans la collection hippocratique* (Paris).

—— 1983. 'Médecine hippocratique et pensée ionienne, réponse aux objections et essai de synthèse', in Lasserre and Mudry 1983, 211-32.

Wellmann, M. 1922. 'Der Verfasser des Anonymus Londinensis', *Hermes* 57, 396-429.

Withington, E.T. 1921. 'The Asclepiadae and the priests of Asclepius', in C. Singer, ed., *Studies in the History and Method of Science* 2 (Oxford), 192-205.

2

'True Stories': the reception of historiography in antiquity

History is a narrative discourse with different rules than those that govern fiction.

> Robert Scholes, 'Language, narrative and anti-narrative',
> in W.J.T. Mitchell, ed., *On Narrative* (Chicago, 1981), 207.

Different because somehow history is held to have a relation to real events, therefore to truth. 'Thus it is quite proper to bring extratextual information to bear on those events when interpreting and evaluating a historical narrative.' By contrast, 'in fiction, the events may be said to be created by and with the text. They have no prior temporal existence, even though they are presented *as if* they did.' At the same time the historian, and especially the Greek or Roman historian, is a writer who must convince, by leading the reader to the conviction that he is telling the truth. How Latin historians achieved that end is the subject of M.J. Wheeldon's chapter.

In one sense history, at least in most of its forms, and as it was commonly written in the ancient world, is certainly a form of narrative. Its plot takes place in time: it is essentially diachronic. It may or may not aim at explanation, but by putting one event before another it usually implies causality even if cannot formally prove it. History may be descriptive, or synchronic, but its subject is still located in time – that is what distinguishes it as history. The ordering of a historical narrative will therefore be a crucial part of its claim to plausibility.[1] On the other hand, historical narrative is distinguished from fictional narrative by its presumed connection with real events, in fact with truth. And in order to be believed, the writer must be able to convince the reader, whether by proofs, assertions, truth-claims or rhetorical devices, that his narrative is actually worthy of belief. Even a post-structuralist historian, who has given up on truth-claims, still has to convince, or he may as well not bother to write at all; indeed, since

---

[1] On time and history see e.g. Peter Munz, *The Shapes of Time* (Middletown, Conn., 1977); Paul Ricoeur, 'Narrative time', in Mitchell, op. cit., 165-86.

he cannot now claim to have *proved* his case, the justification for his activity rests even more strongly on his capacity to persuade the reader of his hypothesis, if only for the time being.[2] The call for a 'return to narrative' in history[3] is itself the product of dissatisfaction with the validity, that is the truth-value, of the results obtainable by other means.

The ancient historians themselves were not worried by modern debates about narrative versus quantitative or other history; on the whole they wrote narrative history because that was what was expected, though it could allow a good deal of room for explanatory essays or 'digressions', or for debate about causes. They also had an armoury of techniques of persuasion – the tropes of the historian, from the authoritative preface to the claim of autopsy, and from authorial intervention to fine writing. The current attention to the techniques of narrative ('narrativity') allows us to return to these well-known *topoi* in ancient historical works with new interest. No longer do they seem the tired repetition of empty rhetorical tricks learnt at school, but rather, legitimate and often highly skilled mechanisms for gaining the reader's belief, in much the same way as the constant imitation of earlier models in ancient, and especially Latin, poetry can now be read as creative memory instead of through the schematic search for model and genre.[4] On this view, history-writing in Greece and Rome was not – as it is often represented – a sterile copying of worn-out *topoi*,[5] but a creative and continuous engagement with the past and with tradition.[6]

Our interpretation of and response to ancient literature is still often impeded by a modern hostility to 'rhetoric' in its narrower sense of technical accomplishment, tropes and the like. After all, beyond a certain stage, Roman education consisted almost entirely of rhetoric, and continued to do so long into the Christian period. The post-Romantic valuation set on originality has therefore led in many of the standard text-books to a devaluing of Latin literature, particularly in its later phases when it is held to have degenerated into the 'merely' or 'purely' rhetorical. It ought now to be possible, when we hear so much about rhetoric in present-day literary criticism, to find new and more satisfactory critical readings of those ancient authors who have

[2] Keith Hopkins, though he denies any claim to truth, and rejects narrative, still calls upon the historian's power to arouse the reader's 'empathetic imagination' (Hopkins 1983, xiv; cf. his characterisation of Peter Brown's technique as 'brilliantly evocative', 232, n.29).

[3] L. Stone, *The Past and the Present* (Boston, Mass., 1981).

[4] See especially Gian Biagio Conte, *The Rhetoric of Imitation. Genre and Poetic Memory in Virgil and other Latin Poets* (Eng. trans., Ithaca, NY, 1986).

[5] Which does not mean that it was not in fact often written in this way, as is obvious from Lucian's satirical treatise *How to write history*, the point of which, of course, is that history should *not* be like that.

[6] Conte, 98.

suffered most from post-Romantic distaste, and especially, to appreciate better the role which rhetorical technique has actually played in helping them to achieve their effects. Some of these issues will recur in Maria Wyke's essay (below, Chapter 5), where it will be seen however that a realist stance is still the most common critical position in relation to Latin poetry; indeed, a recent reviewer described such a stance as 'undoubtedly correct'. That being the case, those critics who, like John Henderson (below, Chapter 3), attempt to subvert the standard expectations, will have even more need of rhetorical devices in order to persuade than the Latin historians studied by him and M.J. Wheeldon, who were at least writing within a set of conventions which on the whole their audience knew and expected to find.

Like Dimitris Kyrtatas (below, Chapter 6), M.J. Wheeldon puts his emphasis on the reception of texts; ancient historiography would command the confidence of its readers (or rather, in the ancient context, its hearers, for literary works were published by public *performance*), if they found what they wanted in the texts. Thus the very rhetorical elements in Latin historical works which are for us most refractory might actually be the most persuasive for an ancient audience. On the whole, we read the ancient historians for purposes quite other, or at least with presuppositions quite other than those in the mind of the ancient reader, and while much effort has been expended on 'source-criticism', it is largely with the intent of separating out and disregarding the rhetorical elements which are thought to have 'distorted' the writer's presentation of reality. Wheeldon shows how dangerous it is in fact to lose sight of the closeness of history and oratory in the ancient world, and how useful it can be for the appreciation of historical works to look at the delivery and reception of oratory. Quintilian's elision of history into oratory, so often quoted as to seem impossibly hackneyed, takes on a new freshness when seen in the context of modern interest in the functioning of narrative. All the same, we still have to make a conscious effort to remember quite how deeply the needs and practices of oratory – speaking – permeated all forms of writing practice in antiquity. It is worth remembering too that it took on a whole new significance and a wider range of possibilities with the development of Christian writing and preaching and with the particular relation to Christianity to the idea of the power of the Word.[7]

The advantage of Wheeldon's approach is that it focusses attention away from the awkward problem of the relation between the text and

[7] Below, p.144f. Since Wheeldon evokes Auerbach's analysis of Tacitean narrative, it is also worth recalling the distinction which Auerbach goes on to make between 'classical' and Christian narrative (*Mimesis*, 40ff.), which deserves a separate treatment.

the 'facts out there', and directs it towards the techniques of the text itself and the relation between text and reader. Whether or not historians nowadays are 'trained to read',[8] it is certain that we do not read the Latin historians in the same way as contemporary readers did. Wheeldon shows us that attention to the way in which ancient readers read them would help us to read them better.

'True Stories':
the reception of historiography in antiquity
M.J. Wheeldon

Much of the current interest in the historiography of the ancient world has been focussed in one way or another on the problem of the 'status' of the ancient historiographical text. Beard and Crawford, for example, address the problem of the authority of *historiae* and other kinds of text as sources for our knowledge of the ancient past.[1] Other studies have been concerned with the relationship between history, rhetoric and poetry in antiquity.[2] Again, in challenging the current preoccupation with the 'rhetoric of history', Momigliano raises the question of the status of propositions in ancient historical writing.[3] This chapter takes as its subject the reception of historical texts in antiquity, and is therefore also intended as a contribution to the assessment of the status of *historiae* in the ancient world, with possible repercussions for their status in our own.

Two questions will be asked: (i) why did readers believe historians' accounts of the past when in many cases we know these accounts to have been fictitious? and (ii) how did this belief affect their evaluation of these texts as worthwhile objects?

I will first consider two approaches to question (i). One is based on cultural presuppositions: the ancients' ethical understanding of reality and corresponding lack of interest in underlying (e.g. social, economic and psychological) influences on events. The other is based on a perception of the rhetorical nature of ancient historical writing: the use of 'oratorical tricks' to convince audiences that what was being presented was the truth. I shall argue that while these approaches are relevant to the task of answering the first question, they fail to take account of certain influential concomitants of the act of reading

---

[8] Dominick LaCapra, *History and Criticism* (Ithaca, NY, 1985), 38, thinks that they are not.

[1] Beard and Crawford 1985, 4.

[2] Wiseman 1979 and 1981; Woodman 1978.

[3] Momigliano 1981; White 1973 and 1978. See also A.J. Woodman, *Rhetoric in Classical Historiography: Four Studies* (London, 1988).

historiae, which must be described in order to understand why the texts were interpreted and evaluated as they were. These are what I shall call the 'contexts' of historiographical reception: the audience's knowledge of the genre, the *auctoritas* of the writer, and what will be termed here the historiographical 'manner of speaking'. Readers in antiquity, that is, did not go to these texts in total innocence of what to expect: in the first place, they would have had some knowledge of *historia* as a genre – the kind of thing that these texts normally provided; secondly, the prefaces to ancient historiographical works influenced the reader's reaction to the narrative of events which followed by presenting an image of the writer as an authoritative source for these events; finally, in the account itself, the narrative manner of speaking (that is, the use of the third person) preserved the impression of authority created in the preface and sustained the reader's expectation of an objective account of events.

Of course, these contexts of reception are not confined to *historiae*; for purposes of comparison I shall try to show briefly how they were also of crucial importance in (for instance) oratory – more important, in fact, than textual strategies of plausibility like *inventio*. The approach adopted here is similar to that of the 'speech-act' theory of literature:

> Speech-act theory provides a way of talking about utterances not only in terms of their surface grammatical properties but also in terms of the context in which they are made, the intentions, attitudes and expectations of the participants, the relationships existing between participants and generally the unspoken rules that are understood to be in play when an utterance is made or received.[4]

In answering the second question, I will argue that by placing *historiae* within these contexts of reception, we will be able to appreciate more readily their status in the ancient world. That is, instead of invoking less helpful comparisons with oratory and poetry, it would be better for us to think of the evaluation of these texts in antiquity as being very similar to the evaluation of a certain class of texts familiar to us today – the non-fictional narrative.

Cultural presuppositions and textual strategies

Auerbach's discussion of Tacitus *Annals* I.16f., in the 'Fortunata' chapter of his book, *Mimesis*, is a famous characterisation of ancient historiographical method.[5] In the Tacitus passage, a common soldier makes a speech of complaint to his fellow-troops about conditions of service, exhorting them to join him in demanding better ones; it is one

[4] Pratt 1977, 88.
[5] Auerbach 1953, 24-49.

of the incidents by which Tacitus represents the beginning of the revolt of the Germanic legions after Augustus' death. His method of dealing with it is, as Auerbach points out, typical of several features of Greco-Roman historiography in general. Although he has the soldier, Percennius, give a list of specific grievances in his speech, Tacitus shows no interest in or understanding of the facts behind his demands, or in arguing against them in objective terms:

> All this, he considers, is not worth treating, and it is evident that he could rely on his readers' not missing anything of the kind either ... a few purely ethical considerations are quite enough to reject them in advance.[6]

Unlike the modern historian who would have sought to get at the facts behind the soldiers' complaints (the levels of pay and prices, past and future government policy on army provision, and so on), or a writer from, say, the Judaeo-Christian cultural tradition (Auerbach's example is from the Gospel of St Mark[7]) whose sympathy with those at the centre of such 'movements in the depths' would on Auerbach's view preclude so high-handed a dismissal, the ancient historical writer was in general unwilling to present evidence or analysis in support of his account, and was profoundly unmoved by any perceived need to understand such grievances from the point of view at which they were voiced.

As Auerbach points out, there is little reason to think that readers in antiquity thought otherwise: both the *historicus* and his audience explained and evaluated historical reality not in terms of social and economic forces but almost entirely in terms of the moral attributes of the characters involved. It was a common justification of history-writing that it provided examples of ethical conduct which the reader should avoid or imitate as appropriate.

Auerbach describes this view of reality as an ethico-rhetorical historical consciousness;[8] one in which there was no difficulty in understanding and evaluating people's actions because, as Aristotle says, 'the line dividing virtue from vice is one dividing the whole of mankind'.[9] Furthermore, the training which a writer received at the rhetorical schools was designed to teach him how to articulate this point of view in respect of the kind of subject-matter he was likely to meet in his historical writing; the relationship between words and the world which ensued from this practice was such that a writer would, in

---

[6] Ibid., 37.

[7] Ibid., 40. But for a quite different view of Mark and the other evangelists, which lays emphasis on the interpretative and rhetorical nature of their writings, see Frank Kermode, *The Genesis of Secrecy* (Cambridge, Mass., 1979).

[8] Ibid., 40

[9] *Poetics* 1448a.

theory, never have had to question the appropriateness of his available means of expression – an assumption which is, of course, alien to a modern language-conscious scepticism about the possibility of historical knowledge at all. D.A. Russell has noted this difference in respect of artistic expression:

> the artist's product ... could not come into existence without a corresponding object outside, on which it depended for its structure and characteristics ... The whole idea of the writer as somehow creating a new world rather than merely a partial image of the world of the senses is in general alien to Greek and Roman thinking.[10]

In a comprehensive scheme of explanation for the reception of historiographical accounts, these two factors, view of the world and view of language in relation to the world, constitute, as it were, 'deep-structural' conditions; that is, relative conditions so uninspected in antiquity that they were generally taken for natural states. Although they are clearly susceptible of more detailed examination, they are not my real interest here; but an analysis of the other contexts of historiographical reception in antiquity may show us how the deep-structural conditions are reinforced by them.

Auerbach describes, for instance, the way in which the historian's conscious art of composition was related to these deep-structural influences on his point of view. This, in turn, raises the question of the influence of rhetorical techniques on historiographical reception: moreover, it has been argued again recently that there was a close relationship between the means of persuasion used by an orator in court and the techniques used by an historian to secure the reader's belief in his version of events. It is argued, for example, that the *historicus*

> had been trained at the rhetorical school to produce persuasive *narratio* for which it was of no significance whether the material used was true or merely plausible (*veri simile*, like the truth) provided that it was convincing. So too with his historical *inventio*: what he had to find was material that would turn the bare annals into a narrative ...[11]

Clearly, the principle of *inventio* applied to both oratory and historiography, allowing writers to devise plausible material for their compositions, in the form of arguments for the orator and 'factual matter' for the historian. However, we should be careful not to overstate the role of *inventio* in oratorical persuasion and in the historiographical 'truth-effect'. It was not a technique which could of itself *convince* an audience. Cicero defines it as *excogitatio rerum*

[10] Russell 1981, 99-100
[11] Wiseman 1981, 389.

verarum aut veri similium quae causam probabilem reddant – that is, the devising of true or merely 'probable' material which may still have to be turned into 'truth' by other means.[12] Moreover, the word *narratio* in oratorical theory referred not to a technique informing the whole speech (which might be suggested by the word 'narrative') but to a part of the speech coming between the *exordium* and the arguments;[13] its function was to offer a plausible statement of the facts of a case, to which jurors could refer during the course of the hearing. It needed, therefore, to be clear and brief, but in certain circumstances – where, say, the facts were particularly repellant and were likely to give offence – the *narratio* could be jettisoned altogether.[14] No orator, then, could hope that this alone could be convincing; it merely provided an underlying narrative which would then be supported by the kind of arguments found in the *De Inventione* and *Rhetorica ad Herennium*.

But we cannot account for oratorical persuasion simply by reference to this combination of narrative and argument. What an orator needed most of all was the art of delivery. This was something universally agreed upon in antiquity, the commonest formulation being of the kind found in *Rhetorica ad Herennium*:

> ... skilful invention, elegant style, the artistic arrangement of the parts comprising the case and the careful memory of all of these will be of no more value without delivery than delivery alone and independent of these.[15]

That is, delivery is more than just the most important aspect of oratory; it is a *sine qua non* of persuasion. We have to remember that in Roman courts, as in some courts today, the audience had not been called to deliberate over the tiny details of a case, to weigh evidence carefully and reserve judgement in cases of uncertainty, but to be persuaded to a single verdict, one way or the other, on the strength of a performance. The invented arguments, however plausible in their written or memorised form, did not count so much as the way in which they were delivered. It is, of course, only possible to make this kind of divorce between 'content' (the written or memorised arguments) and 'form' (delivery) outside the context of performance in the realm of theory or criticism. During the performance itself, if the audience managed to perceive such a separation of form and content, it was likely to lead to the orator's failure, for the arguments would then seem contrived or the orator himself insincere.

In order to account for the persuasive effect of oratory, then, the

---

[12] *De Inv.*, I.9; cf. *Rhet. ad Her.*, I.3.

[13] *De Inv.*, I.27-30; *Rhet. ad Her.*, I.12-16; Cicero, *De Orat.*, II.19.80.

[14] *De Inv.*, I.30; Quintilian, *Inst. Orat.*, IV.2.5-8.

[15] *Rhet. ad Her.*, III.11.19, and see especially H. Caplan's note in the Loeb edition, p.188.

oratorical text must be seen in the context of its performance, and this in turn must be seen in the two further contexts of the audience's expectation of oratory (i.e. to be persuaded) and their expectations of individual speakers (which depended on their knowledge of a given speaker's reputation). Ancient theorists were, in practice, well aware of the importance of the latter. Quintilian, for example, writes of

> the credit which accrues to the statement of facts (*narratio*) from the authority of the speaker; such authority should first and foremost be the reward for our manner of life.[16]

The *narratio*, as we said, comes at the beginning of a speech, after the *exordium*. In terms of the whole process of reception, then, an orator's *auctoritas* is most influential in the transition from the audience's anticipation of a case to the performance itself, helping to narrow what might otherwise be a relatively open-minded approach to the case into a more programmed set of responses. Cicero envisages an ideal version of this in the *Brutus*:

> When it is reported that [the orator] is going to speak, let every place on the benches be taken, the judges' tribunal full, ... a listening crowd thronging about, the presiding judge erect and attentive; when the speaker rises the whole throng will give a sign for silence, then expressions of assent, frequent applause; laughter when he wills it, or if he wills, tears; so that a mere passer-by ... will recognise that he is succeeding and that a Roscius is on the stage.[17]

Although an idealised image, this clearly presupposes the real influence of *auctoritas* to which Quintilian refers. In historiography too, as I hope to demonstrate, much depended on a writer's ability to establish the kind of authority to which readers were accustomed; unless a writer fulfilled this condition of the genre, an audience would be less predisposed to believe his version of events.

The other main aspect of the theory of delivery concerns the orator's voice and gestures – what I shall call here the appropriate 'manner of speaking' the text.[18] There is a further important parallel here between the historiographical 'truth-effect' and oratorical persuasion, for the relationship between *auctoritas* and 'manner of speaking' is the same for both: that is, the 'manner of speaking' should preserve the impression of authority established prior to the work (speech or narrative) itself.[19] However, there is also an important difference, for while the orator has to argue for his case, the historian need only

---

[16] *Inst. Orat.*, IV.2.120; cf. Cicero, *De Orat.*, II.43.182 and *De Part. Orat.* VIII.28.
[17] *Brutus*, 84.290.
[18] Cf. White 1980, 3.
[19] Cf. *De Orat.*, II.211.

42   *M.J. Wheeldon*

narrate 'the facts'.[20] The nature of the argumentative and of the narrative manners of speaking, and the differences between them, can be demonstrated by example. Compare the methods of characterisation in the following two passages, for instance: both pieces refer to the same 'type' (rich, aristocratic ladies with a taste for intrigue, adultery and violence) and the aim – character assassination – is the same in both. The first is from Cicero's *Pro Caelio* and the woman in question is Clodia. The speech contains two *prosopopoeiae* (speeches in character), the first of which requires Cicero to 'call up from the dead' Appius Claudius Caecus, who speaks in the following manner.

> 'Woman, what have you got to do with Caelius, a mere stripling and a stranger? Did you not see ... that it was Quintus Metellus you had married – a brilliant man of the highest courage who had only to step outdoors to surpass his fellows for boldness, glory and prestige?'

Cicero continues the harangue in his own person:

> But as for you, woman ... the accusers are shouting in our ears about debauchery, affairs, adultery ... and that you disapprove of nothing of which they speak. So ... you must now either disprove these things ... or confess that your accusation and your evidence cannot be believed.[21]

Such passages, I would suggest, resist our usual method of reading prose. In particular, it is difficult to make full sense of the *prosopopoeia* which seems somewhat incongruous in the course of what is intended as convincing argument. Clodia herself does not take on life for the reader: we can infer what kind of person she must have been, in a rather general sense, but on the basis of what the passage tells us, we cannot envisage many of her attributes: looks, clothes, speech, the concrete details which place her in a world of objects and other people. The passage feels awkward because the argument and the accusations appear to lack a proper object. What we *are* explicitly told about is her background (via an ancestral procession of personified virtues), which is contrasted with specific offences against the morality which ladies of this background should uphold.

The difficulties of 'reading' the passage in one sense (interpreting, making sense of) are the same as the difficulties of 'reading' in another (enunciation, reading aloud); the full sense of the speech cannot be restored, that is, until one infuses it with something like that which its author did in the course of its delivery, using different volumes, intonations, accents even (in the *prosopopoeia*), and the gestures appropriate to accompany them. As in a dramatic performance, the

[20] *Inst. Orat.*, X.1.31.
[21] *Pro Caelio*, 34-5.

text may be susceptible of various interpretations, but since the orator wishes only to achieve one effect – conviction – any experimentation or 'rehearsal' must be to discover better readings (in both the above senses) of the text.

These requirements of oratorical performance, especially those of gesture, presuppose a further aspect of the oratorical context important in persuasion. For the most powerful impression of reality in oratory was of a non-verbal nature. Cicero had no need to give concrete details of Clodia's appearance, since she was almost certainly present in court for all to see, or was at least known by sight to those in court. In such circumstances, an enumeration of particular attributes would be otiose (for the same reason that the *narratio* or statement of facts was sometimes unnecessary). In oratory, the concrete details of reality are 'given' (i.e. visible) to a greater extent than in historiography. Hence, what the orator should provide are general categories (like the moral and sociological stereotypes of Cicero's speech) which encompass the facts of the case and of which the visible realities become examples.[22]

Let us look next at Sallust's portrait of Sempronia from the *Bellum Catilinae*:

> ... among these women was Sempronia, who had often committed many crimes of masculine daring. In birth and beauty, in her husband and in her children, she was abundantly favoured by fortune; well-read in the literature of Greece and Rome, able to play the lyre and dance more skilfully than an honest woman need, and having many other accomplishments which minister to voluptuousness. But there was nothing which she held so cheaply as modesty and chastity; you could not easily say whether she was less sparing of her money or her honour, her desires were so ardent that she sought men more often than she was sought by them. Even before the time of the conspiracy she had often broken her word, repudiated her debts, been privy to murder; poverty and extravagance combined had driven her headlong. Nevertheless, she was a woman of no mean endowments; she could write verses, bandy jests, and use language which was modest or tender or wanton; in fine, she possessed a high degree of wit and charm.[23]

The first thing one is aware of here is that on the page this is a far more successful job of indictment. It presents no difficulties of reading. Everything we need to know about the character is given explicitly, not left to be inferred or reconstructed. Sempronia's qualities are enumerated in straightforward language and almost the whole passage is coherent in itself outside its original context. She appears in the social settings of class and family, with specific intellectual and

---

[22] Cf. Cicero, *Orator* XIV.45 '... what is proved of the class must necessarily be true of the individual'.

[23] *Bellum Catilinae* (henceforth *BC*) 25 (trans. S.A. Handford).

physical endowments. Her criminal activities are related as fact, not couched in the form of accusations. In short, the portrait seems not to refer to a constructed image, but to an objective historical reality, Sempronia, who, whatever, her real qualities were, existed independently of the writer's characterisation.

We can see by the fact that this passage retains a quality of objectivity outside its ancient contexts of genre, authority and cultural presuppositions, that there is something intrinsic to its 'manner of speaking' which creates this quality, and we shall try to acount for this below. But readers in antiquity would have understood such a passage as representing the facts only when it fulfilled an expectation of truthfulness created by these preceding influences, which we shall now examine in greater detail.

(i) The influence of genre

It will have occurred to the reader by now that throughout this chapter I have treated the notion of genre in a special way. What I mean by this is not only a group of texts which display the same characteristics, but a preconception held by readers about such a group which influences in advance their reading of individual texts in or impinging upon that group; this general idea may then be revised when new texts of this kind are experienced. The approach adopted in this essay presupposes that textual characteristics are only the final influence on reception, conditioned by and moderating in turn the influences which precede them.[24]

In the case of the *historiae* there were, I think, two stages to the generic influence on reception. First, it is reasonable to assume from the available evidence that whatever else was expected of *historiae* in terms of structure and style (which marked them off from *annales*), the single most common expectation of these texts was that they should present a straightforward account of past events. The reader would have learned in school that history recounts *res gestae*, and is to be generally regarded as exclusive of *res fictae* and *res fabulosae*.[25] This helps to explain, as I shall illustrate later, why readers would not have to be *persuaded* that a set of events actually occurred; provided that the other conditions of historical 'truth' were present, and the reader did not himself know of a different version, his attitude to the content would tend to be one of acceptance.

Secondly, before the reader came to the narrative of events itself, the writer's preface would confirm this expectation. These prefaces, as Janson and others have shown, had conventional themes which a

---

[24] Cf. Culler 1975, 145f.
[25] *De Inv.*, I.27; *Rhet. ad Her.*, I.13.

writer was virtually obliged to include.[26] Among these were, first, clear notice of the fact that a writer is engaged in a historical work, and secondly, that what was to follow was a truthful account of the past. The effect that the combined influence of these factors – the reader's knowledge of generic characteristics and the inclusion of these *topoi* in the preface – had on the ancient reception of historiography can be understood as an example of the kind of effect that Marcelin Pleynet describes with reference to literary reception in general:

> It is indeed this word ('novel', 'poem') on the cover of the book which, by convention, genetically produces, programmes or 'originates' our reading. We have here ... a master word which from the outset reduces complexity, reduces the textual encounter, by making it a function of the type of reading already implicit in the law of this word.[27]

(ii) The influence of the narrative 'manner of speaking'

I maintained earlier, in connection with an analogous structure in oratorical persuasion, that the 'manner of speaking' adopted by an ancient historian sustains an impression of authority that should be given in his preface. I shall look at the way in which this impression is given in the next section. But first I want to look more closely at the narrative mode itself, for an understanding of this should help to clarify some of the aims and difficulties that an historiographer had when composing a preface to his work.

It may seem banal to remind the reader that all the Greco-Roman historians relate events predominantly in the past historic and pluperfect tenses and in the third person; that they rarely intrude into their narratives in the first person except to assert the reality of what they relate, or to disclaim responsibility for its truthfulness (usually *en passant*, with an 'ut dicunt' or 'ut fertur'). This feature of ancient historiography is so obvious that it has received little attention as a prerequisite for the 'truth-effect' achieved by these texts. But it can readily be observed that this linguistic mode was neither insignificant nor incidental when we recall that, for instance, Caesar's *Gallic Wars* was written in the third person, though Caesar was himself the protagonist in the events: and that though Xenophon witnessed and took part in the events of the *Anabasis*, he too narrates them in the third person, bringing himself into the story with maximum discretion ('Xenophon, an Athenian ...').[28] Thucydides also refers to himself in the third person in the fourth book of his work.[29] Later, Josephus adopts this mode in the narrative of his *Jewish War*, though he identifies

---

[26] Janson 1964, 66f.
[27] Quoted in Culler 1975, 136.
[28] *Anabasis* I.8.15.
[29] IV.104.4 and *passim*.

himself as a participant in and witness to the events related. In one of the few discussions of this issue, Scholes and Kellogg comment:

> Such men chose this mode not out of pride or humility, but because they associated the third person with formal narrative of the epic and historical kind, with which they associated their own works. To write in the first person is to be less formal and more intimate [30]

The difference between these two forms of representation has recently received valuable attention from structuralist critics.[31] In their writings, two familiar words, 'narrative' and 'discourse', have been used in special senses, to indicate, respectively, the third person and the first person modes. Structuralist theories of fictional realism and of 'truth-claims' in history and philosophy employ this linguistic distinction in accounting for the 'objectivity' of texts whose predominant mode is the third person (and past historic tense, in historiography) and for the 'subjectivity' of those texts using the first person mode or the present tense, or both. Thus, Hayden White, reporting Benveniste, says:

> The subjectivity of the discourse is given by the presence, explicit or implicit of an 'ego' who can be defined 'only as the person who maintains the discourse'. By contrast, 'the objectivity of narrative is defined by the absence of all reference to the narrator'.[32]

Clearly there is a danger in appropriating too comprehensively this linguistic observation; Greco-Roman historiography may use the 'dramatic' present tense, and occasionally the first person, if only briefly. On the other hand, in so far as ancient historiography is characterised overwhelmingly by the third person mode, the structuralist analysis of historiographical truth-effects may prove useful. Two qualifications need to be made first, however, which are important for understanding Greco-Roman criteria of historiographical truth; they concern the context of this linguistic differentiation between objectivity and subjectivity, and the role of the author in the text.

In the first instance, I would suggest that it is more fruitful to take account of the extratextual experience in which the link between the sense of objectivity and the third person originates; the following remarks will of necessity be somewhat schematic, but our analysis would be incomplete without them. The experience I have just mentioned is that of sensory perception, in particular, seeing. In conversation, the objects to which we refer are often present or

[30] Scholes and Kellogg 1976, 72.
[31] White 1980, 3f; Barthes 1977, 109ff.
[32] White, ibid.

remembered as being present to us. As in Cicero's speech about Clodia, no detailed physical description is necessary to prove the existence of an object, since this depends on our sensory and mental registration of it. We may, in speaking, disagree on the accuracy of a subsequent verbal description, but the existence of an object to be described will not thereby be placed in doubt. Moreover, seeing, if it is to occur at all, depends on there being a suitable distance between the perceiver and perceived; objects placed too far away or right in front of our eyes cannot be distinguished, and we need to bring them into focus before the outlines of the objects become distinct. In conversation, furthermore, successful communication depends on the same kind of cultural, generic and linguistic knowledge that is necessary to appropriate reading. That is, once we are in such a position that the object appears in recognisable focus, we have to know what it is correct or appropriate to say in the particular context of communication. Outside specialised contexts which are partly designed to test these conditions (such as fiction, experimental psychology, philosophy of language), it is only when these two conditions of 'seeing and saying' are fulfilled that we feel confident in making 'objective' statements, using the third person ('that was a Charing Cross train'); if the object is out of recognisable focus or we lack the experience of language or situation to describe a focussed object appropriately, we are much more likely to qualify what we say, using the first person ('I think this is a number eleven bus', 'I think this blue is called "indigo" ').[33]

In narrative (the historiographical mode of speaking), it is this distance and certainty which the third person represents, objectifying phenomena in space by setting them apart from the perceivers, 'you' and 'I' (reader and writer). In addition, the past historic and pluperfect tenses augment the sense of objectivity, since they are the only tenses in which phenomena appear to be completely revealed in time, as already seen (or already read) by the reader.[34] In contrast, the use of the first person indicates objects in relation to the peculiar ('subjective') position of the narrator, while the present and perfect tenses always presuppose a relative (because temporary) state of the events or objects described. So, when both or either are used in a text one is unavoidably made aware of the interests of the narrator, and thereby more likely to question the reality of the objects, or version of the objects, narrated.

However, whereas in the first person mode the author or narrator is explicitly invoked, in the third person he is still more or less implied; one cannot, therefore, wholly adapt the linguistic distinction between 'narrative' and 'discourse' into a literary-theoretical statement,

[33] Cf. Stern 1973, 113-28.
[34] Barthes 1977, 112f; White 1980, 3f.

equating 'narrative' with authorial anonymity. Books do, after all, have writers. Readers are always likely to imagine some sort of personality behind what they read, even when they do not use this as a means of interpretation or evaluation.

In the reception of ancient historiographical texts, however, the impression of factual accuracy depended very much on the reader's understanding that a disinterested authority lay behind the text. Whereas structuralist critics emphasise the role played in truth-effects by linguistic forms representing authorial distance, ancient critics and historiographers stressed that authorial distance, both in the literal sense and in the sense of 'disinterestedness', was the best guarantee of truth in historiography. Thus, Lucian remarks that

> some people have been inclined to believe what [Homer] says about Achilles simply on the ground that he was not writing about a living person; they cannot find any reason why he should have lied.[35]

Yet Lucian's own standards seem only to be a more rigorously-expressed version of this; he too thinks that the greatest threat to factual accuracy is the historian's personal involvement in the events which he relates. The historian

> should be independent-minded and neither fear anyone nor hope for anything. If he does he will be like a bad judge who sells decisions out of favour or malice. He must not be upset by Philip's having his eye shot out at Olynthus by the Amphipolitan archer, Aster. Philip must be shown as he is. Nor must he be troubled if Alexander is bound to be angry at a straight description of his brutal murder of Clitus at dinner.[36]

By distancing the writer from the events narrated, the third person manner of speaking presents these events as occurring without the writer's creative involvement, thereby sustaining, first, the impression of disinterested authoritativeness created in the preface, and, in turn, the reader's expectation that *historia* relates *res gestae*.

But there is a difficulty with this argument which we have yet to face: that is the problem of how ancient readers and writers themselves viewed the use of the narrative mode in historiography. That they recognised the obligation on the historian to narrate is clear; Lucian tells us

> After the prooemium, all the rest of the history is a long narrative (*diegesis*).[37]

[35] *Hist. Conscr.*, 40; cf. Cicero, *De Orat.*, II.62.
[36] *Hist. Conscr.* 38.
[37] Ibid., 55.

But does this imply, on the one hand, merely an uninspected requirement of decorum, as Scholes and Kellogg seem to have thought; or does it, on the other hand, imply a recognition that narrative – both the use of the third person and the 'arbitrary' act of selection and arrangement of events – was a necessary and consciously-exploited device of realism? It is difficult to believe that historians who were themselves participants or even protagonists in the events they relate did not become aware, to some degree, of the objectivising effect of the third person, especially when we consider how this would contrast with the first person mode that a spoken, informal report of their own actions would have taken.[38] This is a crucial point in any attempt to discover what the ancients thought about these texts, for if such an insight was available generally, then how could educated readers have regarded *historiae* as texts which offered, in general, true accounts of the past?

Let us look more closely at Lucian's discussion of *diegesis* in historiography. To begin with, we should note that in the quotation above, the terms *prooemium* and *diegesis* refer to the parts of a history; they have been transferred to the present context from oratorical theory, where they name the first two parts of a speech. However, the connection is slightly stronger than this; Lucian adds that the historiographical *diegesis* should

> have narrative excellences to adorn it, advancing smoothly and evenly ...
> A studied clarity should mark both the diction and ... the connections of
> the facts. Everything should be finished and polished. Only when the
> first point has been completed should it lead on to the next, which should
> be, as it were, the next link of the chain ... Rapidity is always useful,
> especially if there is a lot of material. It is secured not so much by words
> and phrases as by the treatment of the subject. That is, you should pass
> quickly over the trivial and unnecessary, and develop the significant
> points at adequate length. Much should be omitted.[39]

Although the position of writers like Caesar encourages caution about making general statements on this issue, I think we can at least say that neither here in Lucian's discussion, nor in Quintilian's brief remark, that history should narrate, not prove,[40] is there any theoretical insight into the truth-effect of third person narration itself. Rather, Lucian associates the requirement to narrate with qualities similar to those found in the oratorical *narratio*: clarity, for example, is a quality of both, which can be achieved, he says, if certain stylistic and structural guidelines are followed (the use of 'plain diction' and a 'smoothness of exposition'). Lucian also includes in *diegesis* the act of

[38] Rambaud 1953, 196f, 208f.
[39] *Hist. Conscr.*, 55-6.
[40] X.1.31.

selecting the events to be narrated, as is the case for the orator. But there is an important difference between the aims and presuppositions of the two kinds of writer. For Lucian includes the act of selection in *diegesis* without any misgivings as to the possibility of prejudicing or falsifying the historical record by this procedure. This is because, as with Tacitus in the *Annals* passage,[41] he sees no problem as to what constitutes the trivial and the significant: the act of selection is not, for Lucian, a literary technique whose purpose is to secure the impression of 'the real'; whereas in oratorical *narratio* clarity, brevity and selectivity serve the end of plausibility, in historiographical *narratio* the precepts as to diction, continuity of exposition and selectivity serve the purpose of clarification. This is all the historian need aim at, since

what [historians] have to say exists and will be said because it has really happened ...[42]

In addition, although plotting, which includes selection, was seen by many critics in antiquity as an essential ingredient of fiction in poetry,[43] selection was not seen in general as an essentially fictionalising act in historiography, for the reasons we have given: the influence of an awareness of textual selectivity on reception was outweighed by the conditions of reception (cultural presuppositions, knowledge of the genre, the writer's *auctoritas*, and the objective manner of speaking) influencing the reader to accept what the historiographer tells him as fact.

However, to resume our account of these conditions of reception, let us now look at the way in which the major Roman historians attempted to establish their credibility with an audience.

(iii) 'Auctoritas' in the historiographical preface

The basic difficulty for the Roman historian in composing his preface was that whereas some claim to disinterestedness was more or less obligatory,[44] the use of the first person mode of itself drew attention to the historian's particular perspective. Therefore, despite the fact that this claim was a conventional *topos*, it was not a subject about which the historian could afford to be artistically indifferent and for which he could rely on conventional phrases. As Syme says, such claims were susceptible of parody.[45] The difficulty was, in fact, not always rhetorical – concerning the means by which to produce an effect on the

---

[41] Above, p.000.
[42] *Hist. Conscr.*, 51.
[43] E.g. Aristotle, *Poetics* 1451b; Plutarch, *Moralia* I.16 (on the deceitfulness of poetry).
[44] Janson 1964, 65f.
[45] Syme 1958, 204.

reader – but sometimes expressive; that is, a problem in the relationship between 'seeing and saying' that we looked at earlier. For the phenomena which a writer was here trying successfully to articulate were not people and events in the external world but more or less elusive abstract concepts, such as the desire to write historiography, the value of the activity to himself, and of the work to the public, and a convincing authorial persona; moreover since a writer could not rely overmuch on rhetorical commonplaces to articulate these concepts into a coherent statement, the success of a preface might depend in the first instance (as I think we can see in the case of Sallust) on the writer's ability to persuade *himself* of the validity of his claims.[46]

Tacitus

The shortest solution to these problems is offered in Tacitus' *Histories*, where a formal preface is omitted altogether, perhaps in a conscious attempt, as it were, to let the facts speak for themselves. At the beginning of the *Annals* the author is less terse. Here, he deflects attention on to the work of previous historians whose objectivity has been impaired by their proximity to the events they relate. The implication, that Tacitus' own work will not suffer from this defect, is not insisted upon: instead, the famous abbreviated claim to impartiality, and the solitary use of a first-person verb, is subordinated to the very end of the preface, in a sentence whose subject appears at first not to be the writer at all, but the period of time covered in the work:

> ... sed veteris populi Romani prospera vel adversa claris scriptoribus memorata sunt; temporibusque Augusti dicendis non defuere decora ingenia, donec gliscente adulatione deterrerentur. Tiberii Gaique et Claudii ac Neronis res florentibus ipsis ob metum falsae, postquam occiderant recentibus odiis compositae sunt. Inde consilium mihi pauca de Augusto et extrema tradere, mox Tiberii principatum et cetera, sine ira et studio, quorum causas procul habeo.[47]

> (But the early history of Rome, prosperous or otherwise, has already been recorded by famous writers. In Augustus' time, there was no shortage of talent, until it was deterred by the spread of flattery. The reigns of Tiberius, Gaius, Claudius and Nero have been falsified, first through fear, when the emperors were still alive, and again when they were dead because of the writers' lingering hatred. So I have decided to say a little about Augustus, especially his latter years, and then move on to the reign of Tiberius and the others – in neither anger nor affection, for I am beyond the usual incentives to these.)

[46] Cf. Cicero, *De Orat.*, II.14.189f.
[47] *Annals*, I.4-6.

Sallust

Most of the scholarship devoted to the prefaces of the *Bellum Catilinae* and the *Bellum Jugurthinum* has concentrated on two problems: the relevance of the prefaces to the narratives which follow them, and the sources of the ideas expressed in them;[48] both of these traditional questions impinge on what we have been examining all along – the writer's necessity to preserve the reader's impression of disinterested authority from the preface to the narrative of his work.

With regard to the first of these problems, both works contain much material not normally found in historical prefaces; this material has to do with the pursuit of glory by virtuous acts, the cultivation of the intellect as the proper aim of mankind, and the relative values of history-writing and politics.[49] Quintilian complained of this that there was nothing in Sallust's prefaces which pertained to history.[50] Whether Quintilian meant that the prefaces had no relevance to history in general or that they were irrelevant to the narratives they preceded, his remark has led some writers to defend Sallust on both charges. Rambaud, for instance, demonstrated that the prefaces express ideas about historiography common in antiquity and that they provide models of interpretation for the events of the narratives.[51] He also pointed out that Quintilian's complaint was, in any case, based not on an examination of the prefaces in the context of the whole works, but on rhetorical prescriptions for what historical prefaces should contain. Janson comments on this subject that the supposed requirements of an historian were that he treat of the topics *de historia, de materia* (i.e. subject-matter) and *de persona (auctoris)*; he says of these prescriptions,

> ... in reality the only conclusion we can draw is that the rules of rhetoric were so general that they could be applied to any material whatsoever ... Consequently, it is frequently difficult or even impossible to decide if a writer has obeyed such a general direction or not. On the other hand it does not matter in such cases if he has.[52]

This tends to suggest that it was a sensible tactic to stick to what was expected of such prefaces anyway; and it is this sentiment which, I think, constitutes the gist of Quintilian's comment. The point is that the topic *de historia* should be made clear at the outset, and should not have to be inferred by the reader, let alone demonstrated in a scholarly article. Yet both prefaces, as we have said, begin with long reflections

[48] See McGushin 1977, 29, 291-5.
[49] *BC* I-II; *BJ* I-II.
[50] *Inst. Orat.* III.8.9.
[51] Rambaud 1946.
[52] Janson 1964, 25.

on ethics, which only after several paragraphs give way to the subject of history; the initial effect on the reader is thereby one of puzzlement, rather than of orientation.

In the *Bellum Catilinae* especially, Sallust does not really spell out the relationship between these moral reflections and the events and characters of his narrative; this is strange, because the idea of history-as-exempla was to hand in his chief stylistic model, Thucydides.[53] To be sure, the implication that his narrative will provide useful examples of ethical conduct becomes clearer after the formal preface, but this idea is never clearly expressed in the preface itself. Indeed, in one passage he offers quite a different reason for recording these particular events: he considers the conspiracy of Catiline

> especially memorable as being unprecedented in itself and fraught with unprecedented dangers to Rome.[54]

But Sallust's hesitancy in stating the public value of *historiae* seems to be more closely related to an unseemly willingness to make known his private ambitions. One is aware of an underlying argument to the effect that history-writing is itself a virtuous act which should make an author worthy of *gloria*; but whatever the respective attractions of *fama* and *virtus* actually were for Sallust, he failed to expunge from the text the impression that his primary interest really lay in personal glory. We read, for example, at 3.1-2:

> pulchrum est bene facere rei publicae, etiam bene dicere haud absurdum est.

> (It is a fine thing to benefit the state by action; even to speak well of it is not to be despised.)

But this does not introduce an explicit statement about the value of *historiae* to the state. Instead, Sallust tells us,

> ac mihi quidem tametsi haud quaquam par gloria sequitur scriptorem et auctorem rerum, tamen in primis arduum videtur res gestas scribere.

> (In my opinion even though the historian does not earn equal glory with the agent of events, nevertheless history-writing is exceptionally difficult.)

In the *Bellum Jugurthinum* this wavering between public and private stances is less evident, but there is still perhaps a trace of it. For example, when Sallust first raises the subject of historiographical

[53] Thucydides, I.22.4.
[54] *BC* V.9-XIII.

value, he says it is unnecessary to explain it to the reader: many have spoken of its value, so it is best to remain silent on the subject. But immediately he introduces an image to explain just this topic:

> Illustrious citizens of our state used to say that the sight of their ancestors' portrait-masks fired their hearts with an ardent desire to merit honour. Obviously, they did not mean that the actual mould of wax had such power over them, but that the memory of what others have accomplished kindles in the breast of noble men a flame that is not quenched until their own prowess has won similar glory and renown.

If the passage ended there, the reader could interpret it as an invitation to provide the 'tenor' of the image for himself – that history, Sallust must mean, has the same effect as these masks. But the passage does not end there, nor does Sallust provide the comparison himself. Instead, the passage continues on a slightly unexpected tack, contrasting the pursuit of virtue in these ancestors with the lust for wealth and extravagance of his contemporaries. When he does offer a concluding comment, he says:

> However, I have allowed myself to be carried too far in expressing the loathing and distaste which I feel for our standard of public morality.[55]

– as if this had been the subject all along. In fact, this was precisely the kind of comment which attracted hostile criticism of his work in antiquity. Readers were not slow to point up the contradiction between the moralising tone of the prefaces and Sallust's own allegedly scandalous private life in the luxury and splendour of his Quirinal residence, and as a corrupt governor of Africa Nova.[56]

Perhaps what we have in such passages are examples of the famous Sallustian *inconcinnitas*:[57] this is usually seen at the level of the individual sentence, in constructions like 'pars ... alii', where the failure to complete the expected lexical pattern is, we feel, the result of a conscious artistic decision. Syme characterised the effect of these disruptions as a deliberate attempt to wreck 'the rhythm, balance and elaboration of the long and convoluted sentence ... in an age saturated and nauseated with political oratory'.[58] If our analysis of Sallust's expositional style is accurate, however, this wilful refusal of a periodic structure at the level of the sentence may be related to a pervasive unwillingness to fashion his material into coherent sequences at higher levels of discourse. One example of this from the *Bellum Catilinae* comes when, at the end of that work, after giving a brief

[55] *BJ* V.1.
[56] See McGushin 1977, 21.
[57] Ibid., 14f.
[58] Syme 1958, 135.

description of the battle in which Catiline is killed, the narrative simply ends, without warning and with no explanatory comment from the writer. A recent commentator, McGushin, offers the following explanation:

> It might not be over-fanciful to suggest that the inconclusiveness of Sallust's description is meant to underline the inconclusiveness of fratricidal strife, the shadow of which lay over Rome at the time of writing.[59]

Perhaps this was indeed what Sallust meant to suggest; but even allowing for the proximity of his audience to the time of the conspiracy, it must remain doubtful whether Sallust in fact made it sufficiently clear that this was the correct inference. If it is permissible to question the extent to which Sallust had mastery over his material in the narratives, the question arises more readily of the more intractable material in the prefaces.

Related to all this is the question of the sources of the ideas expressed in the preface to the *Bellum Catilinae*, in the attempt to assimilate Sallust's preface to previous examples of the *exordium*, much effort has been made to locate direct written sources for it: two of the chief candidates have been Isocrates and Posidonius, but Polybius, Plato, Panaetius, Cicero (*De Republica*), Dicaearchus and others have all, singly or in combination, been proposed as major direct influences at one time or another. As McGushin points out, 'the variety of sources, the inability to adhere exclusively to one major source, invite caution ... [Rather] all the concepts which Sallust borrows from the framework of his basic theme were widely known and widely expressed.'[60] But what was Sallust's part in this process? Although the individual elements of the preface may have been commonplace in themselves, he does not write as if a coherent argument composed of these individual elements was something he could rehearse with confidence. In the search for the origin of statements in the preface, what has perhaps been overlooked is the consciousness of a writer (in his first public work, in a kind of historiography virtually without precedent in Latin) trying to articulate for himself an authorial persona, and the relationship between historical events and the public and private values of historiography, in a way which will also convince his audience. As I have suggested already, these issues are handled with much more confidence in his second monograph, in which, of course, the problem of a lack of precedent are considerably diminished.

One indication of the level of confidence, or feeling of authoritativeness in the preface is the unevenness in tone of voice. This is,

[59] McGushin 1977, 289.
[60] Ibid., 293f.

again, an example of a problem in the relationship between 'seeing and saying' that we outlined earlier;[61] we can see this specifically in the vacillation between different forms of the subject; in particular, Sallust uses the form 'it seems to me' whenever he makes a statement justifying his action in writing history (at a.3, 2.9, 3.2, 4.2). The form represents here a degree of authorial confidence midway between the untroubled manner in which he adduces the more obvious commonplaces, in the third person, and the strained humility of the first person voice (in 3.3-4.5), where he attempts to persuade us of his impartiality. But this oscillation in turn creates difficulties for the preservation of the impression of *auctoritas* in the narrative.

The problems thus created are only resolved by Sallust after the end of the formal preface;[62] first, a lengthy sketch of his arch-villain Catiline, directly after the preface, distracts attention from the comparatively feeble persona of the author; second, by reviewing the former glory and subsequent decline of public morality since the foundation of Rome, he eventually offers the reader a clear idea of the way in which the events of his narrative should be understood.

Livy

By contrast with both Tacitus and Sallust, Livy draws attention to himself straightaway: of the fourteen instances of the first-person verb, six come in the first sentence. He seems to have recognised that he could make a virtue of the necessity to write in the first person, by creating in the authorial persona itself a model of the kind of reader he would wish his audience to imitate:

> et legentium plerisque haud dubito quin primae origines proximaque originibus minus praebitura voluptatis sint, festinantibus ad haec nova quibus iam pridem praevalentis populi vires se ipsae conficiunt: ego contra hoc quoque laboris praemium petam, ut me a conspectu malorum quae nostra tot per annos vidit aetas, tantisper certe dum prisca illa tota mente repeto, omnis expers curae quae scribentis animum, etsi non flectere a vero, sollicitum tamen efficere posset.[63]

> (And I do not doubt that to most readers the earliest origins and the period immediately succeeding them will give little pleasure, for they will be in haste to reach these modern times, in which the might of a people which has long been very powerful is working its own undoing. I myself, on the contrary, shall seek in that an additional reward for my toil, that I may avert my gaze from the troubles which our age has been witnessing for so many years, so long at least as I am absorbed in the

---

[61] Above, pp.46ff.

[62] *BC* I.4-5.

[63] *Praef.*, I.4-5. Livy's claim to veracity arises almost *en passant*, perhaps indicating a desire to seem not to protest the claim too much.

recollection of the brave days of old, free from every care which, even if it could not divert the historian's mind from the truth, might nevertheless cause it anxiety.)

Later on, there is a clear invitation to the reader to interpret the work in this way also:

> ad illa mihi pro se quisque acriter intendat animum, quae vita, qui mores fuerint, per quos viros quibusque artibus domi militiaeque et partum et auctum imperium sit ...

> (Here are the questions to which I would have every reader give his close attention, what life and morals were like; through what men and by what policies, in peace and in war, the empire was enlarged and established ...)[64]

It is hard to suppress the suspicion that the apparent candour with which Livy appeals to the reader may have been encouraged by a critical appreciation of Sallust's first preface. In this connection, Ogilvie noted that Livy's omission of the theme of *ambitio* constituted a rebuke to Sallust.[65] The point is, however, that Livy did not actually omit this idea, but he included it and developed it in a subtler and more effective way than his predecessor. The theme of the writer's achievement is introduced at the outset, but in the form of a denial that this is any concern of the writer:

> facturusne operae pretium sim si a primordio urbis res populi Romani perscripserim nec satis scio nec, si sciam, dicere ausim, quippe qui cum veterem tum volgatam esse rem videam, ...

> (Whether I am likely to accomplish anything worthy of the labour, if I record the achievements of the Roman people from the foundation of the city, I do not really know, nor if I knew would I dare to say so, since I can see that the theme is not only old but hackneyed ...)[66]

'Why mention the idea in the first place, then?', we might ask, and in fact there is a much clearer implication of the writer's ambition at I.3-4: in this passage and again at I.9-10, Livy goes on to suggest a particular idea of the nature of his achievement (as he wishes the reader to see it) in a series of images of and references to size and 'monumentality', which effectively equate the idea of literary greatness with the very size of his work (as both task and product).

---

[64] Ibid., I.9.
[65] R.M. Ogilvie, *A Commentary on Livy Books 1-5* (Oxford, 1965), 24.
[66] *Praef.* I.1-2.

et si in tanta scriptorum turba mea fama in obscuro sit, nobilitate ac
magnitudine eorum me qui nomini officient meo consoler. Res est
praeterea et immensi operis, ut quae supra septingentesimum annum
repetatur et quae ab exiguis profecta initiis eo creverit ut iam
magnitudine laboret sua.

(And if in so vast a company of writers my own reputation should be
obscure, my consolation would be the fame and greatness of those whose
renown will throw mine into the shade. Moreover, my subject involves an
immense amount of work, seeing that it must be traced back over seven
hundred years, and that starting out from slender beginnings it has so
increased now as to labour under its own magnitude.)

The phrases *tanta scriptorum turba* and *nobilitate ac magnitudine*
refer literally to *novi ... scriptores* in the preceding sentence. The first
of them seems, however, to draw attention to itself as over-
emphasising the notion of quantity for the purposes of the immediate
context. In the second phrase, we are explicitly given to understand
magnitudine in the sense of 'greatness of worth', yet *turba*, as a
description of these writers, seems to imply most readily a lack of
individual distinction, rather than an abundance of talent. The real
function of these phrases, I submit, is to prepare the reader for the
references to the size of Livy's undertaking (*immensi operis ...;
magnitudine laboret sua*) in the next sentence, so that in *magnitudine*
we have, as it were, a central ambiguity (greatness of size, greatness of
value) supported by other words referring to or suggesting the size of
the work.

In I.9-10 this 'mass' is given a shape: Rome's declining greatness is
assimilated to the collapse of some kind of edifice

labente deinde paulatim disciplina velut desidentis primo mores
sequatur animo, deinde ut magis magisque lapsi sint, tum ire coeperint
praecipites, donec ad haec tempora quibus nec vitia nostra nec remedia
pati possumus perventum est.

(Then let him note how, with the gradual relaxation of discipline, morals
first gave way as it were, then sank lower and lower, and finally began
the downward plunge, which has brought us to the present time, when
we can endure neither our vices nor their cure.)

This metaphor anticipates that in the passage immediately following
where Livy's work will be depicted as a monument on which instances
of human conduct are inscribed:

Hoc illud est praecipue in cognitione rerum salubre ac frugiferum, omnis
te exempli documenta in inlustri posita monumento.

(What chiefly makes the study of history profitable and wholesome is

that you behold examples of every kind of human conduct as if they were
set forth upon a shining monument.)

Here, in addition to the traditional claim for the value of *historiae* as
sources of right conduct, Livy offers first, in the image of
monumentality, a summation of the earlier claims for his work (on the
basis of its size and the labour involved in writing it) and second, in the
order in which the metaphors of the two passages appear, the more
ambitious suggestion of the reconstruction – via the reading of his own
work – of Roman greatness.

Conclusion: critical evaluation and the contexts of belief

The act and art of serious reading comport two principal motions of
spirit; that of interpretation and that of valuation (criticism, aesthetic
judgement). The two are strictly inseparable. To interpret is to judge.[67]

In a sense, the ancient 'act and art of serious reading' was an
extreme example of this definition, in that the act of interpreting
historiographical content was, as we saw, straightforwardly and
explicitly an act of moral judgement. On the other hand, the ethical
judgement involved in seeing historical events as the result of virtue
and vice was, for the ancient reader, primarily an interpretive act; the
criteria of aesthetic judgement were regarded as quite separate, as is
shown by two tendencies in the structure of ancient criticism of
historiography.

First, there is the tendency in both criticism and theory to separate
considerations of content (*res*) from those of form (*verba*). This division
occurs in the general arrangement of Lucian's treatise, where the first
part is devoted to advice on research into material, and the second to
the composition of the text. The division reflects Lucian's assumption,[68] which we noted earlier, that there is no difficulty for a good
historian about seeing what was significant and then saying it in the
appropriate way. Accordingly, he divides failed historians into two
classes;

they have no eyes for the noteworthy; nor, if they had eyes, any adequate
faculty of expression.[69]

Livy presents this as a traditional distinction in historiographical
evaluation:

---

[67] G. Steiner, 'Viewpoint: a new meaning of meaning', *TLS*, 8 Nov. 1985, 1262.
[68] *Hist. Conscr.*, 56.
[69] Ibid., 32.

dum novi semper scriptores aut in rebus certius aliquid allaturos se aut
scribendi arte rudem vetustatem superaturos credunt.

(New writers invariably believe that they will either offer some new
material or else surpass their uncouth predecessors in literary skill.)[70]

And Dionysius of Halicarnassus' essay on Thucydides is also divided
between comment on the historian's scrupulousness in research and on
his formal qualities. Dionysius' essay, in fact, especially exemplifies
the second tendency in ancient criticism relevant here. For Dionysius,
an historian himself, writing about an historian to an historian (Q.
Tubero), Thucydides' most distinctive quality was not (as it is in
modern accounts of ancient historiography) his single-minded pursuit
of facts, but his stylistic and structural idiosyncrasy.[71] This is typical of
the greater interest shown by critics of *historiae* in form than in the
accuracy or interpretation of content. Though Quintilian remarks
briefly on Clitarchus' failure to observe the first law of history
(*Clitarchi ... fides infamatur*),[72] his comments on Herodotus,
Thucydides, Livy and Sallust are all to do with structure and style.[73]
    What are the implications of this lack of critical interest in factual
accuracy for our understanding of the status of these texts in
antiquity? It is tempting to see it as an indication of a different view of
historiographical content from the one outlined above, whereby the
recognition of *historiae* as presenting *res gestae* becomes simply a form
of lip-service to an outmoded ideal, the 'real' view of historiography
being more like Cicero's, in his letter to Lucceius:

> ... the regular chronological record of events interests us as little as a
> catalogue of historical occurrences; but the uncertain ... fortunes of a
> statesman ... give scope for suspense, delight, annoyance, fear and hope;
> should [this] end in some striking consummation, the result is a complete
> satisfaction of mind which is the most perfect pleasure a reader can
> enjoy.[74]

Doesn't this kind of statement make the ancients' view of *historiae*
look, much more than I have acknowledged, like their view of those
genres which related *res fictae*, such as epic or tragedy?
    Such an argument seems to me ultimately unhelpful to the task of
describing the status of *historiae* in antiquity. In so far as it depends
especially on the predominant ancient interest in the form and style of
historiae, it invokes a false equation of 'literature' (a modern category

[70] *Praef.* I.2.
[71] *On Thucydides*, 21.
[72] *Inst. Orat.*, X.1.75.
[73] X.i.32, 73-5, 101f.
[74] *Ad Fam.*, V.12.5.

in any case) and fiction. In fact, the evaluation of some *non-fiction* in terms more usually associated with literary (or in Aristotelian terms, 'poetic') texts, among which fiction may predominate, did not present much difficulty in antiquity, nor does it today.

In the *Poetics*, Aristotle distinguishes between history and poetry on the basis that the former narrates what happened in chronological series, the latter narrates the kind of thing that would happen probably or necessarily, in sequence. The distinction is made on the *a posteriori* basis of the examination of individual works. Therefore, when he mentions the possibility of a work which relates an actually-occurring probable sequence of events, the criterion of probable sequence means that the author of such a work is a 'maker' (*poiêtês*), rather than an historian.[75] But Aristotle was not here describing the usual method of classifying texts in antiquity. Unlike Aristotle, readers would not normally wait until after they had analysed a work before deciding whether it was history or poetry: the question was decided in advance on the basis of the influences on reception outlined above. Nor was Aristotle's method adopted by historians themselves. Polybius and Diodorus, for example, thought organicity was a virtue of their histories; Polybius, because one can thereby understand 'the comprehensive scheme of events and how it led up to the end';[76] Diodorus, because it 'facilitates the reading and contains such recovery of the past in a form that is perfectly easy to follow'.[77] They had no misgivings as to the possible distortion of the events they related in this way, since, like Lucian,[78] they saw no such problem in sorting the trivial from the significant. The predominant ancient critical interest in the form and style of *historiae*, meanwhile, did not presuppose an underlying scepticism about the content of these texts because the separate consideration of the two meant that the former was not assumed to affect the status of the latter unduly except where the author was thought to have a personal interest in the facts.

The same kind of text is familiar to readers today. For instance, American literature of recent years has produced a number of books whose subject has been real-life murders and murderers[79] – books like Norman Mailer's *The Executioner's Song* and Truman Capote's *In Cold Blood*, which present vivid detailed narratives of their grisly events and the circumstances surrounding them. Capote's book is, he says, 'a true account of a multiple murder and its consequences'.[80] Now, such a claim does not usually mean that we would read this kind of text in the

[75] 1451b.
[76] I.4.3, 7-11.
[77] I.3.8.
[78] Above, pp.49-40.
[79] I owe this example to Pratt 1977, 92-7.
[80] Ibid., 92, n.4.

same way that we would read a *history* (something entitled, perhaps *Urban Homicide in America, 1945-1970*), asking questions like: where is the evidence that these events took place in the way that the author says they did? What are his sources? Has he included all the relevant information? Even if we do wish to ask such questions, we will not find the answers to them in Capote's book – it is simply a narrative of events. But though we might wish to ask such questions at some point, our 'act and art of serious reading' depends only in small part on the answers to them. We still notice important 'non-literal' meaning in the events of, say, a moral or psychological nature, and we may certainly still evaluate the way in which the story is told – in terms of clarity, narrative continuity, and even, as in Cicero's letter to Lucceius, in terms of suspense and organicity. This kind of reading is not confined to a tiny percentage of literary works today:

> as a glance at today's best-seller lists can show, nonfictional narratives – memoirs, survival-stories, travel-tales and the like – are as much a part of the public's literary preference as fiction.[81]

It is, finally, as a member of this class of texts that I think the reader in antiquity regarded *historiae*. The conditions of reading (cultural presuppositions, knowledge of the genre, the writer's *auctoritas*, and the narrative manner of speaking) gave the reader no sufficient reason to disbelieve what he read in these texts, unless he himself knew of an alternative version. But his lack of knowledge, and the lack of evidence and analysis in the text itself meant that he could not use historical categories as his main evaluative criterion. Consequently, the critical discussion of *historiae* in antiquity did not include, as it has done for us, a strong inclination toward discoveries or new approaches, for those were not at stake, or not at stake to the same extent. And in the general absence of this critical orientation, it was the 'art of serious reading' that the ancient reader exercised on the evaluation of narrative form.

Bibliography

Auerbach, E. 1953. *Mimesis. The Representation of Reality in Western Literature* (Princeton).

Barthes, R. 1977. 'Introduction to the structuralist analysis of narrative', in Stephen Heath, ed., *Image, Music, Text* (Glasgow), 79-124.

Beard, M. and Crawford, M. 1985. *Rome in the Late Republic* (London).

Culler, J. 1975. *Structuralist Poetics: structuralism, linguistics and the study of literature* (London).

Hopkins, K. 1978. *Conquerors and Slaves* (Cambridge).

[81] Ibid., 96.

—————— 1983. *Death and Renewal* (Cambridge).
Janson, T. 1964. *Latin Prose Prefaces* (Stockholm).
McGushin, P. 1977. *C. Sallustius Crispus: Bellum Catilinae, a commentary* (Leiden).
Momigliano, A. 1981. 'The rhetoric of history and the history of rhetoric: on Hayden White's tropes', in E.S. Shaffer, ed., *Comparative Criticism*, 3 (Cambridge), 259-68.
Pratt, M.L. 1977. *Toward a Speech Act Theory of Literary Discourse* (Bloomington, Indiana).
Rambaud, M. 1946. 'Les prologues de Salluste et la démonstration morale dans son oeuvre'. *Rev. Ét. Latines* 24, 115-30.
—————— 1953. *L'Art de la déformation historique dans les Commentaires de César* (Paris).
Scholes, R. and Kellogg, R. 1976. *The Nature of Narrative* (Oxford).
Stern, J.P. 1973. *On Realism* (London).
Syme, Sir Ronald 1958. *Tacitus* (Oxford), 2 vols.
White, Hayden 1973. *Metahistory* (Baltimore).
—————— 1978. *Tropics of Discourse* (Baltimore).
—————— 1980. 'The value of narrativity', in W.J.T. Mitchell, ed., *On Narrative* (Chicago).
Wiseman, T.P. 1979. *Clio's Cosmetics: three studies in Greco-Roman literature* (Leicester).
—————— 1981. 'Practice and theory in ancient historiography', *History* 66, 375-93.
Woodman, A.J. 1978. 'Theory and practice in ancient historiography', *Bull. Council University Classics Depts.* 7, 6-8.

3

Livy and the Invention of History

Giving up the normative ideal of progress has a significant cost, however.
Uncertainty is part of the price.

David Hoy, 'Jacques Derrida', in Quentin Skinner, ed.,
The Return of Grand Theory in the Human Sciences
(Cambridge, 1985), 43.

In history, beginnings and endings are important. A proper preface wins the reader's confidence and locates the story in its context of time; how the text ends, as John Henderson shows us in his own essay, determines how we read it. Between the beginning and the ending, the history must be story-shaped if it is to persuade, but it is on the basis of the scope of the story as a whole that modern critics make their judgements. Livy's monumental history of the Roman Republic up to his own day provides a perfect illustration of the uncertainty to which they are reduced when the simple question 'At what point did Livy's history end?' remains a mystery (for only a fraction of the original 142 books now survive intact). Livy 'probably died pen in hand, the work closing with Drusus' death' (in 9 BC), says A.H. MacDonald in the *Oxford Classical Dictionary*; Henderson gives us a collage of other proposals, in a striking demonstration of the extent to which presuppositions based on not much more than surmise have formed scholarly views about the nature and purpose of the work, and so of its proper use as a quarry for historical evidence. How much, too, scholarship of the most impeccably traditional kind ('philology') is itself entirely vulnerable.

Livy in fact presents the dilemma posed by all ancient writers, and especially historians, whose work is only partially preserved. Oddly enough, this is the case with all four of the great Roman historians – Sallust, Livy, Tacitus, Ammianus Marcellinus. Yet scholars cannot resist the imposition of their own order; they feel more secure if loose ends are tied up, uncertainties resolved, even where there is no direct evidence for the preferred solution. Tacitus must have finished the

64

Annals with the death of Nero (another missing ending); Ammianus must have telescoped two centuries into his missing books – or written two histories perhaps. Once settled, their work can be neatly filed away for use as a 'source', according to the documentary model we all learned as students.[1]

Such self-serving is exposed in Henderson's essay and rejected in favour of leaving Livy as he is, in a state of uncertainty. The disadvantages of such an approach are obvious: it is likely, for a start, to engender hostility among traditional scholars – 'at present, historians are quite willing to listen to neighbors in the social sciences, but the less manageable contributions of literary critics and philosophers are often met with extreme suspicion if not active resistance.'[2] People do not like having their honest efforts undermined. A deeper problem is that deconstruction, like extreme forms of cultural relativism, can hardly help being self-contradictory, for if no claim can be made to correctness then why write at all? The very act of writing presupposes a degree of authority which it explicitly disclaims. Must it be thought of, then, as a form of play, for it is certainly playful? The notion of undecidability, whether as used by Derrida or Kristeva, can likewise seem simply like a dead end. If we really cannot know anything, why bother? Yet if the result is uncertain, or 'as yet unnameable',[3] the danger to traditional scholarship, and to the concept of history itself, is all too obvious: 'sometimes Foucault and Derrida, like Nietzsche or even Heidegger, look wistfully for a "beyond", but generally their point is that there is really no such thing as "history".'[4] Peradotto's 'vacuum of discredited humanistic values' points up the real nature of the threat posed by deconstruction to the professional expertise of the academic world, and thus explains part of the reason for the hostility it often encounters.

---

[1] And rightly so, for how else could we have formed our judgement? See G.R. Elton in *The Practice of History* (1967).

[2] Dominick LaCapra, *History and Criticism* (Ithaca, NY, 1985), 73.

[3] J. Peradotto, *Arethusa* 16 (1983), 20, citing Derrida. Play: J. Derrida, 'Structure, sign and play in the discourse of the human sciences', in R. Macksey and E. Donato, *The Languages of Criticism and the Sciences of Man: the structuralist controversy* (Baltimore, 1970), 247-65; in theology – the writings of Dan O. Via Jr., e.g. *Kerygma and Comedy* (Philadelphia, 1971) and D. Crossan, e.g. 'Parable, allegory and paradox', in D.Y. Hadidian, ed., *Semiology and Parables* (Pittsburgh, 1976), 247-81, esp. 271f. ('Allegory as play').

[4] Hoy in Skinner 1985, 49.

Livy and the Invention of History
John Henderson

The Seminar. The Ancient History Seminar. Thus far, Herstory (Cameron; King). Coming, History (History as texts? Is 'history as text' to mean 'how to process texts to write history', to mean just that? Just that?). Herein, Story. The writer of this text would like to begin – to have begun – with the claim that his title is 'The Invention of History', but that's his Story. What Averil Cameron has (had) in mind for my title – which *is* hers – may provide us with an ending. But that's her Story.*

How important beginnings, and endings, are to narratives remains to be seen: whether they should relate is a big question and a small story:

'Bus.
Platform.
Bus platform. That's the place.
Midday.
About.
About midday. That's the time.
Passengers.
Quarrel.
A passengers' quarrel. That's the action.
Young man.
Hat. Long thin neck.
A young man with a hat and a plaited cord round it. That's the chief character.
Person.
A person.
A person. That's the second character.
Me.
Me.
Me. That's the third character, narrator.
Words.
Words.
Words. That's what was said.
Seat vacant.
Seat taken.
A seat that was vacant and then taken. That's the result.
The Gare Saint-Lazare.
An hour later.
A friend.
A button.

* And this is her paper: it's as delivered in January 1985 at ICS, all but. The discussion afterwards *was* interesting and lively but I stick by what I said.

Another phrase heard. That's the conclusion.
Logical conclusion.[1]

A question, our question, would be whether 'Logical Analysis' can escape (re-)narrativisation by its readers. And so with 'Rhetorical Analysis', too, as will be seen.

A 'collection' of epigraphs – scissors-and-paste compilation, a history of puns:

> Whereas one used to relate the history of tradition and of invention, of the old and the new, of the dead and the living, of the closed and the open, of the static and of the dynamic, I undertake to relate the history of the perpetual difference ...[2]

> The 'new approach' or the latest formula may well prove a disappointment and send one gladly back to Hippolyte Taine ...

> Livy does not invent on a large scale. He feels bound to follow what he regards as an adequate source.[3]

> If then Livy went beyond the annalistic tradition in featuring or starring Camillus in the decision on Rome's future, he must not be credited with that invention. For him it is too bold. It belongs to the poet, whose right, whose poetic duty, and whose invariable attitude was to see history not as an impersonal process, but as a succession of events shaped by the deeds, the words, and the individual fortunes of great men. The invention belongs to the poet ...[4]

> Les historiens ... n'expliquent pas les événements, quoi qu'ils pensent; ils les explicitent, ils les interprètent: l'historicité est invention.[5]

> The real value of history lay in inventing ingenious variations on a probably commonplace theme, in raising the popular melody to a universal symbol and showing what a world of depth, power and beauty exists in it.[6]

> In general there has been a reluctance to consider historical narratives as what they most manifestly are: verbal fictions, the contents of which are as much invented as found and the forms of which have more in common with their counterparts in literature than they have with those in the sciences.[7]

---

[1] Queneau (trans. Wright) 1958, 60-1 'Logical Analysis'.
[2] Foucault in Leitch 1983, 153.
[3] Syme 1945, 106.
[4] Skutsch 1968, 13. See Skutsch 1985, 5f. for summary (and, inevitably, slightly revised nuance).
[5] Veyne 1983, 195.
[6] Nietzsche in White 1978, 54.
[7] White 1978, 82.

History, so considered (i.e. à la Arendt), is a fictive substitute for authority
and tradition, a maker of concords between past, present and future, a
provider of significance to mere chronicity. Everything is relevant, if its
relevance can be invented ...[8]

That's the end of the epigraph(s).

A programmatic 'periocha' is expected in this genre, the genre of the
seminar paper, to serve as epigraph. 'History as text' means, means to
me, in general the TelQuel/Barthes/Foucaulti (see White) thesis that
History is a Discourse of traditional scholarship practising willed-
wilful imposition as an institution, installing the trope of wilful
imposition in the academy of culture ... But herein, a more specific
subject.

History is Text because texts end ... Without the sense of an ending
there is no writing history. Modern history-writing would like to shrug
off narratological shop-soiling. History would like to be a plot found
outside language, in the world; it would like to be a 'plot' only by an
epiphenomenal accident; it would not like to submit to the indignities
of iterability, of being the always already written, of re-presenting the
repertoire of narratives in its culture, condemned to find its
explanatory power, its insight, its persuasiveness, attractiveness,
fascination the product of its conformity with fictional patterns: the
world 'must not be' story-shaped. The Historian hero(ine) *will* escape
Vladimir Propp, Gérard Genette, Tzvetan Todorov ... Classical
history-writing is not subject to such counter-dependency, perhaps.

I want to raise the question of the teleology of the classic historical
text. For this purpose Livy will epitomise what I hereby designate the
'millesima pagina' complex:

> uester porro labor fecundior, historiarum
> scriptores? perit hic plus temporis atque olei plus.
> NULLO QUIPPE MODO MILLESIMA PAGINA SURGIT
> OMNIBUS et crescit multa damnosa papyro;
> sic INGENS rerum numerus iubet atque operum lex.[9]

In his discussion of narrative plot, Kermode has asked us to 'suppose,
for instance, that it is a thousand-page novel ...'[10] but what I would
point to in Juvenal's classic caricature of the historian is the phrase
nullo modo.

---

[8] Kermode 1966, 56.
[9] Juvenal, *Satire* 7.98ff.
[10] Kermode 1966, 45.

The expert in antiquity on the subject of monu-mentality/brevity –
Martial – neatly fingers the problem of Livy:

pellibus exiguis artatur LIVIUS INGENS
QUEM MEA NON TOTUM BIBLIOTHECA CAPIT.[11]

But so does Livy himself in his prefatory phrase *immensum opus*.[12]

Just what are the relations between the classic historian's definitive
history, his stake in finitude and in the infinite? Is the open-ended
necessarily inconclusive? *res est praeterea et immensi operis ... ut iam
magnitudine laboret sua.*

Luce suggests, defensively enough, that 'the scale on which Livy
chose to narrate the history of Rome undoubtedly proved to be as
important a determinant in his selection of sources as any other ...'[13]
And we should ask what else may be involved in the traditional remark
'The sheer scope ... is formidable'[14] – more, that is, than a rhetorical
commonplace of the ancient historian, or the ancient historian's work
she is writing about (OgLIVY, *Livy 1-5*, 26, ' "The magnitude of the
undertaking": ... A second reason for bridling at the prospect of writing
Roman history. Not merely have so many important men turned their
hands to it before but the task is daunting in itself. This view seems
unique to Livy' – until you consult the Addenda in the revised edition
ad loc. and are shown that this 'magnitude' is a commonplace, in
ancient historians of Rome).[15]

What are the monumental history's limits? Sallust died in the course
of writing *Historiae* V; Tacitus evidently completed his thirty books of
Historiae and *Annales*, though Augustus seems to have eluded him:
the ends of both Tacitus' works have none the less perished ... And
Livy? Livy was known in 142 books to the tradition which resulted in
the *Periochae* – *if* the *explicit* in the majority of its MSS's *omnium
librorum* is accurate (books 136-7 have just been elided from the
Periochae and many of the later *Periochae* have barely come into
being). We have nothing of Livy's own narrative beyond book 45 except
some short quotations.

---

[11] Martial, *Epigrammata* 14.190, Titus Liuius in membranis (cf. 186 *immensum
Maronem*, 188 on Cicero and 192 on Ovid, *Metamorphoses*).
[12] Livy, *Praefatio* 4, cf. 4.4.4 *in aeternum urbe condita, in immensum crescente*, 5.7.10,
6.23.7, 26.27.1, 28.28.11.
[13] Luce 1977, 173.
[14] Ogilvie in *CHCL* II.458.
[15] Ogilvie 1965, 26.

The end of monumental narrative may be thought through a variety of models.

Briefly – since 'Livy after all was an Augustan'[16] – the *Aeneid*. Epic poets at Rome are finished by their poems. 'Virgil [is] describing the progress of Aeneas from the broken city of Troy to a Rome standing for empire without end (*imperium sine fine*) ... And in the journey of Aeneas the episodes are related internally; they all exist under the shadow of the end.'[17] The *Aeneid* is unfinished, whether or not unfinishable: but it scarcely lacks its end, either in the sense of its last lines in linear order or in the sense that its structuring on the archê/telos of post-Actian re-vision is inconclusive. Though and because Virgil did not see the saecular games, his poem's 'renovations' of the Roman past were firmly tied to the ordering of the Roman present through Augustus.[18] Lucretius' description of the atomic *elementa* in flux in his exemplary scriptural *elementa* could ex hypothesi never be completed. Ovid's *Metamorphoses* constantly mutated form, metamorphosed, under revision. Valerius Flaccus is impeccably partial. The lyric poet Statius finished the Civil War epic 'for' Vespasian who finished the Civil War, but his *Achilleid* was cut short of its ambitions by Titus' inglorious early death/by the assassination of Domitian/by Statius decease – 'stuck at the first turn' (*Silvae* 4.7.23). To prove the rule, Silius, after terminating his epic non-poem after contracting an incurable disease starved himself to death. More interestingly Lucan was more directly killed by the *immensum ... opus* (1.68) of his own poem. If the telos of the *Bellum Civile was* Cato's triumph over Caesarism in his suicide at Caesar's final military victory, what stopped him getting to this transfiguration was precisely Caesar-ism: in the last lines of book 10 the Caesarian monster Scaeva resurrects himself to wall in the poem, prematurely, come back from the apparently dead to besiege Lucan – what stopped the poet reaching the transcendance of Stoic martyrdom was Scaeva – and, outside the text, the inescapability of the realities of the triumph of the Caesars. As Julius is penned in the palace at Alexandria by his own *bellum civile*, it burns down the largest library in the world: all those books lost to the world. And Caesarism destroyed the end of Lucan's book, too – if Lucan had wished the end to be the assassination

---

[16] Stadter 1972, 288.

[17] Kermode 1966, 5.

[18] Ibid. 1966, 11. Death as the (in)complete is the edge of writing, e.g. van Heurck in Ecker 1985, 106 – as we are told in an editorial footnote, I think – ' "Types of Death" is the title of (Ingeborg) Bachmann's projected novel trilogy, left uncompleted at her death' ... We supply 'completed *by* her death' too fast, see Rajan 1985 (announced as forthcoming), 'distinguishing between the incomplete poem and the unfinished poem, Professor Rajan sees the unfinished poem as remaining in dialogue with its own dissensions ...'

of Nero, Caesar made it the Pisonian fiasco. Lucan, remember, is that scandal – the epic poet who began writing epic with his whole adult life apparently stretching out before him, as before his Emperor. The case of Ennius, at length. Closely analogous to Livy's, or so it is agreed:[19] the *Annales* appear to have been written in the 170s BCE in five triads of books to book 15; 'the original conclusion to the *Annals*' was the fall of Ambracia, the triumphal return of Fulvius Nobilior, the foundation of the Temple of the Muses and the 'tired old horse' simile as sphragis. Ennius was thus completing the *Annales* down to 185/4 BCE around 161 BCE (Varro has Ennius say in book 12 it was 172 BCE);[20] Pliny suggests in his phrase *sextum decimum adiecit annalem* an appendix, a revised 'plan' and (?) a supplement … in the form of a sixth triad of books, on the Istrian War to 171 BCE written to … the end of perEnnius' life, traditionally accepted as 169 BCE.[21] Two points here: (1) the effect of re-vision is to deplete any finitude; (2) the monumental writer *writes on*, his work's trajectory crosses its archê without reaching its telos: it could not be the case, to overstate, that the vision of Ennius in the mid 170s BCE, incorporated the annals of 169, 170, 171, etc.

The Livian 'loop' is, by comparison with Ennius, accepted by most scholars to operate on a far more extravagant scale (recognised especially by Syme: 'He had now to deal with events that had occurred since he began his work.')[22]

One more final monument of narrative, *the* monument to narration, Proust: 'For a decade and a half critics tried to judge the whole from a few parts … So Proust had to serve as the sole qualified guide to his own uncompleted work … The opening sections, he insists, give a distorted impression of the whole. Everything hangs on the conclusion (… It looks almost like a conspiracy against readers).'[23]

Most Livian scholars agree that he started writing after Actium and 'published' his first pentad around 27-25 BCE. What was the telos that allowed him to start? First, a fantastic possibility: 'Livy's original plan may have been to carry his History down to the death of Augustus.'[24] In one version of revisionist zeal for order Livy is actually allowed a

[19] Skutsch 1968, 18f; Jocelyn 1972; 1020f; Gratwick in *CHCL* II.60f; cf. Sheets 1983, 22.

[20] Varro ap. Gellius, *Noctes Atticae* 17.21.43.

[21] Pliny, *Nat. Hist.* 7.101 *Q. Ennius T. Caecilium Teucrum fratremque eius praecipue miratus propter eos sextum decimum adiecit annalem …*

[22] Syme 1959, 62.

[23] Shattuck 1974, 10. Call this the Joycean 'conspiracy' – will 'Work in Progress' ever (have) turn(ed) out 'Finnegans Wake'?

[24] Laistner 1963, 80.

plan for 150 books with five triads of decades, 1-30, 31-60, 61-90 Marius and Sulla, 91-120 Pompey and Caesar, plus a projected 30 books on Augustus.[25] An obsolescent view, dare I say it, next: 'In Livy's original plan the goal was evident: Actium, the end of the Civil Wars, and the Triumph of the young Caesar. Reaching that limit in the composition of his histories, he decided to go further (one may conjecture). He added the supplement of 9 books (i.e. books 134-142).'[26] The consensus is that Livy's plan was to write *Ab Urbe Condita* to the Death of Cicero in 43 BCE: 'The last book in Livy's original plan seems to have been book 120, which included an epitaphion for Cicero.'[27] An attractive notion, inversion of Thucydides, where the epitaphios ends the first year of the narrative – as Dionysius complains, the Halicarnassian; the Birth of the Historian is the Death of the Orator; the Birth of Republican History is the Death of the Theorist of its Writing (Livy is 'flesh of Cicero's theory of historiography').[28] A haunting notion, too – Seneca the Elder, as well, offers the Death of Cicero as the moment terminating the repertoire for declamatory invention ...

So: 'Books 121-142 were held back for some reason or other and not given to the world till later',[29] and 'These books were written as a supplement to Livy's great work, somewhat in the manner of books 16-18 of Ennius' *Annals*'.[30] 'An afterthought to the original plan and may also have been too politically controversial to be published in Augustus' lifetime ... An "appendix".'[31] It is an axiom that Livy's narrative from 42-9 BCE in books 121-142 represents a second phase of writing.[32]

The 'subtitle' to *Periocha* 121 is the evidence: '(*liber*) *qui editus post excessum Augusti dicitur.*' Speculation has ensued. We may 'suspect' that Livy left 121-142 for after Augustus' death with 'prudence' ... because of the 'resolute independence in his writing'.[33] More soberly, for instance speeches *by* Augustus in Livy, in Livian style, might have to wait for deification – the price of immortality sticking at death?[34]

[25] Wille 1973, 117.
[26] Syme 1959, 38.
[27] Woodman 1977, 34.
[28] Walsh in Dorey 1966, 119.
[29] Syme 1959, 39.
[30] Stadter 1972, 299.
[31] Ogilvie in *CHCL* II.458. His last word (?), Ogilvie 1984, 119, 'On the whole, I am now convinced that Livy's final plan was 150 books, which, as Luce has argued, were structured in units of 15 and written in units of 5.' How difficult a task it is to epitomate one's view of Livy's 'whole' history.
[32] Luce 1977; Wille 1973; Crosby 1978.
[33] Walsh in Dorey 1966, 120.
[34] Syme 1959, 72.

And so forth.[35] NB: (1) Syme warns that Klotz improbably read *dicitur* as *dicitur a Livio*,[36] (2) Walsh naughtily writes 'We are told that 121-142 were not published until after Augustus' death'.[37]

As always Syme is scrupulous. 'The fragility of this testimony will be borne in mind' ('If the superscription of Book 121 is to be accepted and utilised (and that is a large question) ...').[38] We now have a new edition of the *Periochae*: Jal finds the subtitle we 'want' in 4/24 of his collated MSS (one of those 4 lost and witnessed by Pithou's dubious 'notes'); he prints the subtitle in his text but *with* the comment 'Nous ne croyons guère nous-même, tout en le maintenant dans notre édition, à son authenticité'.[39] Jal also points out that almost all editors before O. Jahn omitted the subtitle.[39] The subtitles to books 109-116 make an interesting comparison: *'qui est ciuilis belli primus, secundus, tertius* etc. etc. (so most of Jal's MSS). Syme[40] accepted books 109-116 as a Livian unit and detected a Livian Preface in *Periocha* 109's talk of *causae ciuilium armorum*. This has been resisted by others.[41]

Jal's Introduction helpfully points out that the *Periochae* are themselves a text ('Le travail de l'épitomateur')[42] and we need to learn to read this unfamiliar genre with some expertise, I think, if we are to feel at all comfortable with the standard treatment of the 'subtitle' to 121: are they 'summaries'? 'resumés'? abridgements, précis, indices ...? ('Nature et style des *Periochae*';[42] Fornara has a useful sketch.)[43] No escape from textuality, no end to the will to impose documentary status on writing: History.

If the *Periochae* do follow Livy to his last book, the end was 9 BCE, Death of Drusus, Tiberius' brother and Claudius' father, given an elogium by his brother and then by Augustus. Syme saw this as *the* place to stop: 'This was the culmination of the grandiose Augustan plan of conquest in central Europe' ... 'He *had* to stop. The year 9 BC was the ideal date ... Melancholy but proud commemoration of the Emperor, dynasty, Claudia virtus ...' 'The year 9 BC therefore appears

---

[35] One speculation: I hear Scots self-deprecation in the scholarship here, e.g. Ogilvie in *CHCL* II 459f, 'like most Roman men of letters, he was a provincial and retained something of a provincial austerity in his attitude to life.' Many men of Roman letters in the UK seem so.

[36] Syme 1959, 38.

[37] Walsh 1961, 8: contrast Walsh 1974, 9, '... which he is said to have held back ...'.

[38] Syme 1959, 72, 39.

[39] Jal 1984, cxx.

[40] Syme 1959, 32.

[41] By Stadter 1972; Wille 1973; Luce 1977; Crosby 1978; Walsh 1961 etc.

[42] Jal 1984, lxvii, lxxix.

[43] Fornara 1983, 191f (a quote from 200, 'Sub specie aeternitatis, history has altered but little').

to be both a necessary and an attractive terminal date.'[44] With
characteristic rigour Syme savages the cliché scene of Livy expiring
Pen-in-Hand and we are left with the vision of Livy making sure he lives
out his days with (1) Books 121-142 safely stashed away and 1-120 his
'monument', (2) nothing after 9 BCE given the Livy treatment. And why
not?

We must learn to read subtitles "superscriptions"? 'subtleties'? ...) of
Periochae (= ?), themselves *made* – as it has often enough been argued –
from 'Epitomes' *made* from Livy's narrative, if we are to see that
narrative's end. *How* unsatisfactory is such a formulation: 'The decision
by Livy to write a history of Rome from the foundation of the city can
reasonably be explained by the circumstance that the republic, as
traditionally conceived, *had come to an end*, for better or for worse'?[45]
How important is the end to Livy's history? How teleological *is* (his)
historical narrative?

'History never goes beyond this level of very simple explanation; it
remains fundamentally an account, and what is called explanation is
nothing but the way in which the account is arranged in a comprehensible plot.'[46] If history *is* narrative, it's plot. Plot brings with it
implications of causality, closure, teleology. If history aims to resist
emplotment, to remain 'story' (in Forster's sense, say, 'The succession of
"and then ..." ', the pure line of mutation), reading practices always
seem to detect/construct 'plot' (Forster's "That's why/So ...", the structured symmetry of relations between initial and final states). Post-hoc-
ergo-propter-hoc-ism, for instance, always seems to defy the purity of
mutation (cf. Rimmon-Kenan 17: read 'The king died and then the
queen died.' Does it not narrativise?)[47]

History is narrative which insists that its 'That's why/So ...' follows
from verisimilitude, from reference *from* the specific event *to* forms of
explanation authorised by our cultural codes (norms of explanation,
common sense, historical sense, as of period ...). But history is narrative, is articulated as that. Its 'That's why/So ...' also follows from the
functional or structural needs of the plot. Historical narrative is the
struggle, the name of that struggle between (1) the linear chains of the
text and (2) the reverberations of the cultural codes, the reader's
image-repertoire.

---

[44] Syme 1959, 67, 70f.
[45] Fornara 1983, 73.
[46] Veyne 1984, 87 (a quote from 83, 'History is one of the most harmless products ever
elaborated by the chemistry of the intellect').
[47] Rimmon-Kenan 1983, 17.

I here abuse, by re-using, Barthes' taxonymy from *S/Z*.[48] (1) The line, the syntagmatic line, re-solves into the hermeneutic voice, voice of truth and the prohaeretic, voice of the empirical. The hermeneutic narrative works from the proposal of enigma, through disclosure, to closure in final re-velation: the end governs the show. The prohaeretic narrative makes itself 'real', loads the interplay between free choice by individual characters, 'their' decisions, and on the other side the various forms of teleological determinism forcing the narrative towards its predestined end. Prohaeresis enforces constant revision, constant structuration and re-constructuration. (2) The image-repertoire of a narrative consists in the regulation of its paradigmatic equivalences, its symbolic work (as A to B so X to Y) and its referential imbrication with those cultural codes of authority, commonsense, les maîtres de vérité ...

In the interweaving of these properties of narrative the text achieves its precarious difference – its generic typing and its specific, the difference which would make its identity. In our preference for the paradigmatic (for (2) above) we will find emphasis on the multiple readings of the disjoined and overdetermined 'poetic' work *in* the text and *between* the text and our world. In our obedience to the syntagmatic (1) we will submit willingly/wilfully to the orders of the text, subjected to the teleology of desire, reading on through the crises which are the nodes of the plot, searching for the single thread, looking for the end ...

To bring this problematic of reading, of reading narrative, this problem of textuality to bear on Livy as monumental historian is to interrogate the expert judgments: 'Rhetorical training allowed Livy to cope with the great undifferentiated mass of Roman historical happenings, and, philosophically speaking, to make sense of it.'[49] 'But his rhetorical power does not take control of the whole with the authority of a panoptic vision.'[50] 'It is thus possible to visualise events in the framework of human motivation, and beyond this the historian can ascribe a particular sequence of happenings only to chance or divine agency.'[51] 'The great bulk of the history, as well as the huge time-span covered, militate against any easy conception of the whole.'[52] Etc.

This is indeed the ace played by the Epitomators of Antiquity – e.g. Florus, *Praef.* 3, 'The very vastness of the subject (The History of Rome) is a hindrance to the knowledge of it' ... Florus aims to help 'by

---

[48] Barthes 1975.
[49] Ogilvie in *CHCL* II.462.
[50] Walsh in Dorey 1966, 117.
[51] Walsh 1982, 1066.
[52] Luce 1971, 265.

76   *John Henderson*

displaying the ... greatness (of the Roman People) all at once in a single view'.[53]

How could *Livy* structure *his* work as a single view? Does *his Praefatio* map out the project (of 1-120, see esp. Crosby on *Praef.* 9)?[54] Thus, 'Livy had his cohesive vision to lend shape to his writing'.[55] But does e.g. book 31, *Praef.* 2 announce with its phrase *perscripturum res omnes Romanas* a revised, open-ended goal 'beyond book 120'? An opening of the end, its pre-deletion? The moment of the *Praefatio* to the histories is foregrounded in the reading experience by the 'primacy effect' (first impressions last longest);[56] this is, however, ying to the 'recency effect's' yang of retrospective re-structuration, adaptation to the latest up-dating, retroactivity ...[57] However we regard the teleological strength of the *Praefatio* for 1-120, we come up against the Livian 'loop' and know that *this* is one preface which cannot be written 'last', if Livy's books 1-142 are (to be) considered a single project: 'The length of his history and the amount of sheer labour expended upon its composition also suggest that he started early and pursued his goal with extraordinary tenacity and single-mindedness.'[58] Such a view must tell less than, e.g., 'He did not have a well-articulated, consistent system of thought on the subject. On some points he had come to hold quite [NB: fudge] settled views; others he found difficult and problematic, and appears to have been wrestling with them in the course of his history.'[59]

An author who begins a book in his thirties and is still writing it into her sixties if not seventies *must*, we could propose in the name of 'Life', revise the conception of the work: 'Proust often treated writing as a continuation of life by other means ... As in life itself, the scope of action and reflection encountered in the *Search* exceeds the capacity of one mind to hold it all together at one time' (Proust, who published his work serially, and insisted on the strength of its ring-structure, though only 60 per cent was published in his lifetime ...).[60]

Mustn't Livy's *History* be troped on the 'organicist fallacy' – the *Urbs'* Birth, Efflorescence, Decline (in short, the *Aufstieg und Niedergang der römischen Welt*) a story of its writer's 'life'? In Proust, the long

[53] Fornara 1983, 191f.
[54] Crosby 1978.
[55] Walsh in Dorey 1966, 116.
[56] Livy 31.1.2 *nam etsi profiteri ausum perscripturum res omnes Romanas in partibus singulis tanti operis fatigari minime conueniat* ...
[57] Rimmon-Kenan 1983, 120.
[58] Usher 1969, 166.
[59] Luce 1977, 233.
[60] Shattuck 1974, 12f; cf. Docherty 1983 *passim*, esp. 172f.

decline of Marcel *is* the successful writing of his novel: the author's ruination *is* the structuring of the *Search*. Livy's old age qualifies him to write the History of the End; the writer of the *Urbs* finally writes the entropic narrative of the *Orbis* (the End of all Histories, cosmocracy in cataclysm ...), writes up as world-famous author-ity. The history is (to be) a monumentum to its author, the ultimate patriot: 'Livy's life flows in a hidden stream'.[61] Livy is the Palinurus of the Augustan mission, drowned in the self-suppressing script of *imperium*, prime exemplum of *deuotio*, 'suicidally' embracing anonymity for the national synthesis ... As monumentum the *Ab Urbe Condita* is being read teleologically: we are looking to the end, à la Herodotus.

A prohaeretic reading may start from the *Praefatio* to book 31, 5:

> iam prouideo animo, uelut qui proximis litori uadis inducti mare pedibus ingrediuntur, quicquid progredior in uastiorem me altitudinem ac uelut profundum inuehi, et crescere paene opus quod prima quaeque proficiendo minus uidebatur ...

This is the historian's version of the Tristram Shandy paradox ('The more I write the more I shall have to write').[62] As events unwind with the writing of the text, the enunciation of historical narrative re-winds itself: as the historian approaches her own time, the pressure of the enunciation increases and history becomes slower ...[63] Livy must leave source-books for 'life', for life, as he writes on: 166-191 BCE fill 25 books at 3 years per book; 91-43 BCE take 72 books at one and a bit years per book; 43 BCE itself took 3 books (118-120: you see, Livy never got over Cicero's end?). A contract is negotiated between writer and reader from the *Preface* on, to delay (with Camillus and Fabius Maximus ...), not to thirst for the end, to learn from the narrator's pessimism *not to finish*. Leave him to approach his paper-suicide in solitude![64] For whatever reason, only one quote is preserved from antiquity for Livy 134-142; *conceivably* even the epitomators or *Periochae* tired at 142, well before 'the end' – in what we have of the *Periochae* 'the editors' industry flagged and failed'[65] or however else we should explain that lacuna for books 136-7 and the attendant progressive brachylogy of the last score or so of our *Periochae* ... On a

[61] Syme 1959, 52.

[62] Cf. Waugh 1984, 71, 'The subject of the novel becomes the battle between the chronological duration of the "writing" and that of the events in "history", and the battle between these and the real and implied duration of the reading', 142f.

[63] Barthes 1981, 5f; Genette 1980, 86f. Would 'zero degree' history be the 'one year, one book' of Caesar's *Commentarii* and (?) Pollio's *Historiae* (Zecchini 1982, 1286)?

[64] Gabba in Millar & Segal 1984, 79f, 'But Livy's pessimism does not appear only in the preface ... As far as his attitudes and sentiments are concerned, he seems to belong to a category of losers.'

[65] Syme 1959, 52.

monumental scale, the plot between the writer and reader seems to ensure that if life does spare the writer to finish his History and the peradventures of accident spare his book's material survival, still readers will not spare sufficient life to reach the end. So much for Sallust, just *so* must for Livy, and *so much* for Tacitus ...

On the one hand, the seamless endlessness of the monumental history which readers will not finish, whether or not the writer finished writing it, shrugs off attempts to read the 'denotation' of the work; instead insisting on the connotations of monumentality itself, which then becomes its denotation (in the double-declutching shift of Barthesian myth-production).[66] Livy's history is the authoritative machine for the recovery of the Roman past, the authorised 'renovation' of *imperium*, the reordering enabled by the new order (cf. in stone the Fasti Triumphales' physical completeness with Balbus' triumph? The force of the Elogia pageant fixed in the Forum of Augustus?). From such a point of view the historian is (to be) the institutionalised functionary: clerk of the court.[67] His disqualifications to write history – lack of political, military experience, lack of senatorial dignity, lack of aristocratic shares, etc. etc., are plenary qualifications for Livy the court functionary of the *pax Augusta*, the eunuch of Livia (e.g. the term *augustus* is similarly (dis-)qualified ...).[68]

The authority of the project is invested in its 'panoramic'/'synoptic'/ 'comprehensive' powers, its willed/wilful mastery, the assurance with which its re-vision of the story of Rome structures its view 'from the centre' round the archê/telos of its plot. For instance, the Justice of the History of the Victors must be teleologically differentiated from the Force used by the Victims through a final (re-)distribution of a meaning immanent in events from the beginning ... The end must justify, is what justifies, the means (*uis* v. *uis→ius/uis,* or rather *uis uersa*).

If we accept an 'original plan' for the *Ab Urbe Condita* of culmination

---

[66] Barthes 1973, 114f.

[67] Barker 1984, 4f on Pepys' 'discourse of the ... clerk' is suggestive here: 'no doubt attenuated. That is part of its charm and is certainly the stylistic register which has characterised its reproduction and transmission in the history of writing ... a text whose regularities, it is said, are determined only by the pattern of the empirical, whose transcription it is ... Don't plainness of style and the epistemological naïvety it suggests thus function as a guarantee of profound identity, allowing us across a gulf which we call history but which by the very nature of this particular claim to intelligibility is nothing more than the deployment of sameness along a chronological axis ... the a-libi-dinous (a-Livy-dinous?) justification of reading "for information sake" ' (sic).

[68] Cf. Moretti 1983, 13, 'What is at issue once more is the orientation of the historian's gaze: whether one should look only at what is behind the masterpiece, unilaterally emphasizing a break, a rupture of the historical tissue – or whether, by showing the consequences of every great work, one should accentuate its function as a genuine producer of historical "stability".'

in the Death of Cicero and 43 BCE in 120 books, we thereby position books 121-142 and 42-9 BCE as the 'supplement'.[69] In the Derridean critique, the 'supplement', in 'completing' the corpus, undoes and figures the undoing of the corpus: supplements are revisionary ratios.[70] Let us see. 'History itself, like the Roman state, had been brought back into the right and traditional path. In the briefest of Roman definitions, the Republic consisted in the government of annual consuls chosen by election':[71] thus *History* continued until 14 CE. Similarly, e.g. Woodman agrees to read the emphases in the *Periochae* on Augustan *bella* in books 121-142 and their reticence on 'political history' as a return to the plot of books 1-50, revised by Augustus' representation as *dux* and *imperator*.[72] And, as we've seen, 9 BCE is read by Syme as the culmination of the plot of Augustan military conquest, the end of the cosmocratic narrative and its narration.[73]

Such revisionary alteration in the end of history, of the *History*, retrojects back through the corpus; undoing, for example, the narrator's reticences in his struggle with the Struggle of the Orders, its order, and amplifying his abstemious intrusions into the long pageant of *res domi* and *res foras*; and so on. Most obviously, the 'organic' troping of history is transcended – or trounced: in place of the *Aufstieg und Niedergang* culminating in the Epitaph to the Republic there unfolds the story of the Survival of the Republic through the kiss of life at Actium ... to the prospect of the Augustan Empire as a dynastic inheritance (an alteration vastly closer to inversion than, say, the shift in import undergone by the Temple to Mars Ultor between its being vowed in 42 and finished in 2 BCE; think of the bemusement of C. Sosius as he watched the story of his re-vision of the Temple of Apollo in turn re-vised by post-Actian history and the politics of the Palatine – Such is Life).

The 'shifters' – the *hic-nunc-nos* of narrative[74] – in Livy orient his readers in a ratio between text and life, rendering all formalist readings of the *History* false-naive. Given the 're-vision' of the *Ab Urbe Condita* in books 121-142, we will see the scope of these 'shifters' rippling out to include much more than the classic grammatical categories which invoke the plenitude of presence – way beyond the sense of the *Preface*'s *nostra tempora*, for instance, we will subsume the terms *augustus, princeps*, and, yes, *consul* and *imperium* and so forth

---

[69] Stadter 1972, 229, Syme 1959, 38: their word, now mine.
[70] Derrida 1976, esp. 269f. (Cf. 6f, 'The End of the Book and the Beginning of Writing').
[71] Syme 1959, 62.
[72] Woodman 1977, 38.
[73] Syme 1959, 68.
[74] Barthes 1981, 6f.

and find them hollowed out and re-filled with a different sense by time's reflex, the sense of difference as past defers to the returning view. Names, too, of course – Brutus, Romulus, Horatius, yes and Liuius – have acquired and shed significances under the shadow of the cancelled end to *History*, its cancellation (cf. *spolia opima*, and the insertion at 4.19ff for its effect just within the first pentad).

The structure of 1-120, once 'supplemented', will have lost its 'centre' with its end: 'The structure is that by which the end is made present throughout the work. The analyst of structure has the task of displaying the work as a spatial configuration in which time past and time future point to one end which is always present.'[75] It is indeed this notion of the 'centre', *the* formalist proposition, the prop of formalism, which the Derridean project has worked to undo: if the archê/telos frame a centre whose function is to support the structure, the system, so that 'centre' is '(an) invariable presence – eidos, archê, telos, energeia, ousia (essence, existence, substance, subject), alêtheia, transcendality, consciousness, God, man, and so forth',[76] then discovery – uncovering/recovering – of play in the signifier(s) will always already have de-centred the signified centre.[77] The Livian 'loop' creates a slip-knot of signification along which the signifiers 'run'; its revisionary supplementarity is that of the extra piece in the jigsaw – to use the old historiographical cliché – which in making us repeat, but with de-compositional ends in view, the specific and synoptic checking of fit through the whole set problematises the concepts of wholeness, fit and set into undecidable volatility.[78]

Is the *Ab Urbe Condita* the story of Roma? Of the Respublica? Of? Or? Is book 1 a pre-face to the story of Roma as Respublica – does Roma become Roma *with* the *respublica libera* in book 2?[79] Is book 1 a part of or apart from the history of Roma? So many questions. If the end is the second Brutus, the Second Triumvirate, the end of duly elected consuls, then book 1 is an 'archaeologia', apart from the text – pre-history, pre-face. If not, if History continues through Actium, through to the 'restoration' of consular elections in 23 BCE, will book 1 have become a part of the narrative of Roma as history? In which case, the force of the 'restitution' of the *respublica libera* may turn its original foundation out as the politicking man-oeuvre of the first Brutus, legitimate heir of the Tarquin tyrants, thereby undoing the Augustan façade ...

---

[75] Culler 1975, 243.
[76] Derrida 1978, 279f.
[77] Leitch 1983, 36.
[78] On the notion of 'decomposition' see Ulmer 1985, 51f.
[79] Livy 2.1.1, *liberi iam hinc populi Romani res pace belloque gestas ... peragam*, 7, *libertatis autem originem inde ... numeres ...*

Once the History of Rome becomes the narrative of *dominatio*, whether by *reges*, by *princeps* or by *consules*, we are well on the way to the schema of Tacitus' *Annals* 1.1, perhaps, and the 'anti-Tite-Live chez Tite-Live'. At least we shall be revising our view of the systematic trend from Livian decade to Livian decade towards a structuring around the careers of their dominant personalities – e.g. 'These later books of Livy ... reflect exactly the political realities of the Clst BC, so different from its predecessor'.[80] Once Augustus is allowed to supplement the progression of Marius/Sulla and Pompey/Caesar, we'll look back at Coriolanus and Camillus, Papirius Cursor and the rest to see that they are precisely not 'so different' from what preceded and what followed; that Livy's Roma was always dominated by *principes*, whatever the constitutional conditions ... Thus the 'constitution' is de-constructed by its 're(con)stitution' by Augustus and the *respublica* becomes part of the façade, parergonal ornament, and not the 'centre' constitutive of Roma(n History).[81]

If books 1-5 are a 'mythical' pre-face to the 'History' of books 6-120: are 1-120 but an Annalistic *Periocha* pre-fatory to 121-142, the 'Historia' of Livy's own re-searches into his own life-time? In that case, we find another discouragement to teleological readers of Livy from actually proceeding towards the end: as Syme puts it, 'The real history (after 27 BCE) is secret history'.[82] Dio also sees a watershed in History with the arrival of 'Augustus' in 27 BCE: history is henceforth only possible after the death of the Emperor.[83]

Is there an uncanny fit between that *Periocha* 121 subtitle, (liber) *qui editus post excessum Augusti dicitur*, and the anecdote in Seneca, *Contr.* 10, *Praef.* 8 (1-7: 'I'm bored and ashamed of all this' – i.e. this is the last book of *Controversiae*, the end is in sight – 'It's not relevant to describe Livy's son-in-law, he was only listened to for Livy's sake. Scaurus? The fire was kind to him ... Labienus (Rabienus?)? Ferocious, Pompeian and had the honour of having book-burning *invented* to deal with him. What a good job for all that it was only *invented* after Cicero ... a good job, that is, that these punishments only started when genius had ceased ... The judge of Labienus later saw his own writings burned ... Labienus didn't take this insult lying down – he walled himself up *in monimenta* ... *maiorum suorum* ...):

---

[80] Woodman 1977, 34.
[81] On the slide in the notion of 'ornament' concepts (as cosmos/cosmos ...) see Ulmer 1985, 40f.
[82] Syme 1959, 69.
[83] Dio 53.19.3, cf. Fornara 1983, 89.

meminimus aliquando, cum recitaret historiam, magnam partem illum libri conuoluisse et dixisse 'haec quae transeo post mortem meam legentur'?[84]

Such an understanding of the passing of the right to write contemporary history may perhaps account altogether for the subtitle? But, then again, Livy may have shared this understanding with Seneca, and Labienus (?), so it still *may* be that something in a Livian *Praefatio* to book 121 'lies' behind the (Epitomators'/*Periochae*'s) subtitle? If so then scholars should still be obliged to suggest what kind of something this might have been: Labienus precisely did *not* write down in his history 'This is not to be read until after my death or the Emperor's, whichever comes first'!

I've been privileging syntagmatic readings of Livy, Livy read as the Augustan orderly ordered to find order and stamp it on the past, ordering his readers to read in an orderly fashion. But Livy's repertoire of decades and pentads, books and years, careers and episodes also invited disjunctive and so paradigmatic interpretation. A 'poetic' reception of the Livian text will stress the proportionality invoked by story pattern, by thematic or imagistic parallelism, in short by the work of textuality and intertextuality. To read of Manlius Capitolinus *is* (not) to read of Catiline, Camillus *is* specified as a Scipio (manqué), an Augustus (with warts); Coriolanus *is*, in turn, diacritically diagrammed against Camillus (is he not?) ... As the metaphoricity endemic to narrative gathers monu-mental mo-mentum, the multiplicity of readings tends toward the infinite, the inconclusive. Such response to episodic 'units' framed from the text, the text *as* frame, feeds back to the decentred reception of Livy as 'Livy the Declaimer'.

The refusal of structure, of system; the pleasures and frissons of ad-hoc-ism; Livy as the stylist without a subject, the orator without a brief, the colour-by-numbers scene-painter – these traditional views stress Livy's role in History Writing, in the History of Writing History, as exemplary model of rhetorical *inventio*, the aggregational and agglutinative craft of eloquence proceeding and parading without recourse to any 'epistème' to handle the 'collection' of data presented him by his genre. Still the coding is referential,[85] privileging explanation in the form of likelihood or rationalisation according to the moral/aesthetic/'cultural' schemata of contemporary, i.e. post-Actium,

---

[84] Cf. but contrast the story of Pollio and Plancus in Pliny, *Nat. Hist.* 1, *Praef.* 31, *nec Plancus illepide cum diceretur Asinius Pollio orationes in eum parare quae ab ipso aut liberis post mortem Planci ederentur, ne respondere posset, 'cum mortuis non nisi laruas luctari'.*

[85] Barthes 1981, 5f.

Roma. This 'History Man' sinks to a ramble recounting of stories of incidental chronicity in which interlocking plots are mirages, puns, metafictional demonstrations, no more, that 'history' thinks itself into plots, whether independently of or by human design.[86]

Nevertheless, the formula 'Livy and the *Inventio* of History' is not an end but only an invitation to (re-)narrativise. The post-hoc-ergo-propter-hoc-ism of reading practices will militate against any such collapse of the syntagmatic and we may with definitional certainty assert that a stereographic reading of the narrative is always already plotted into the configurations of the Livian

Bibliography

Barker, R. 1984. *The Tremulous Private Body. Essays on subjection* (London).
Barthes, R. 1973. *Mythologies*, trans. A. Lavers (London).
———— 1975. *S/Z*, trans. R. Miller (London).
———— 1981. 'The discourse of history', trans. S. Bann, in E. Shaffer, ed., *Comparative Criticism. A Yearbook* 3 (Cambridge), 7-20.
Briscoe, J. 1971. 'The first decade', in Dorey 1971, 1-20.
———— 1975. rev. Wille 1973, *Journ. Rom. Stud.* 65, 224-25.
———— 1978. rev. Luce 1977, ibid. 68, 227-28.
Burck, E. 1966. *Vom Menschenbild in der römischen Literatur* (Heidelberg).
———— 1971. 'The third decade', in Dorey 1971, 21-46.
CHCL II. *Cambridge History of Classical Literature* II (1982), ed. E.J. Kenney and W.V. Clausen.
Crosby, T. 1978. 'The structure of Livy's *History*', *Liverpool Classical Monthly* 3, 113f.
Culler, J. 1975. *Structuralist Poetics: structuralism, linguistics and the study of literature* (London).
Derrida, J. 1976. *Of Grammatology*, trans. G.C. Spivak (Baltimore).
———— 1978. *Writing and Difference*, trans. A. Bass (London).
Docherty, T. 1983. *Reading (Absent) Character. Towards a theory of*

[86] Waugh 1984, 48f (on Malcolm Bradbury's *The History Man*). There is a good deal of confusion, punning even, in the controversies over Livian structure. Besides the work already noticed see (1) On the book as a 'unit': Suits 1974, 257f. (Briscoe 1978, 228, 'It is quite possible that he ended each book at an appropriate place determined at the time he wrote it'; (2) The 'episode': Luce 1971, 265f. (Ogilvie in *CHCL* II.461, 'Livy's aim was to construct a meaningful series of scenes', 462, 'his art of creating coherent episodes'; Woodman 1977, 35, 'Livy constructs a narrative of successive episodes', etc. etc.); (3) The 'career': Burck 1966, 354f.; (4) The 'pentad'/'decade'/'pentekaidekad': Burck in Dorey 1971, 21, '(The third decade) a *hen kai holon* with the telos of the Roman final victory' (Briscoe 1975, 224, 'This merely reflects the way in which the text of Livy was transmitted in Antiquity' or 'Livy himself planned and executed his work in groups of 5-10 books, the books being divided at significant points'). See esp. the controversy over book 10 <—> book 11, Syme 1959, 30; Briscoe in Dorey 1971, 1; Stadter 1972, 293 ... Much of this work of de-termination is flawed by wilful/willed mastery of textuality, finally, though many of the scholars have successfully positioned Livy between love and life.

84 *John Henderson*

characterization in fiction (Oxford).
Dorey, T.A., ed. 1966. *Latin Historians* (London).
——— 1971. *Livy* (London).
Ecker, Gisela, ed. 1985. *Feminist Aesthetics*, trans. H. Anderson (London).
Fornara, C.W. 1983. *The Nature of History in Ancient Greece and Rome* (Berkeley and Los Angeles).
Gabba, E. 1983. 'The Historians and Augustus', in Millar and Segal, 1984, 61-88.
Genette, G. 1980. *Narrative Discourse*, trans. J.E. Lewin (Oxford).
Gratwick, A.S. 1982. 'Ennius' *Annales*', *CHCL* II, 60-76.
Jal, P. 1984. *Abrégés de Livius, de l'histoire romaine de Tite-Live*, t. 34.1-2 (Paris: Budé).
Jocelyn, H.D., 1972. 'The poems of Quintus Ennius', in H. Temporini, ed., *Aufstieg und Niedergang der römischen Welt* (Berlin) I.2, 987-1026.
Kermode, F. 1966. *The Sense of an Ending. Studies in the theory of fiction* (Oxford).
Laistner, M.L.W. 1963. *The Greater Roman Historians* (Berkeley and Los Angeles).
Leitch, V.B. 1983. *Deconstructive Criticism. An advanced introduction* (New York).
Luce, T.V. 1971. 'Design and Structure in Livy: 5.32-55', *Trans. Am. Philol. Ass.* 102, 265-302.
——— 1977. *Livy. The composition of his history* (Princeton).
Millar, F. and Segal, E., eds. 1984. *Caesar Augustus. Seven aspects* (Oxford).
Moretti, F. 1983, *Signs Taken for Wonders* (London).
Ogilvie, R.M. 1965. *A Commentary on Livy books 1-5* (Oxford).
——— 1982. 'Livy', *CHCL* II, 458-66.
——— 1984. 'Titi Livi Lib. XCI' *Proc. Camb. Philol. Soc.* 210, 116-25.
Queneau, R. 1958. *Exercises in Style*, trans. B. Wright (London).
Rajan, R. 1985. *The Form of the Unfinished. English Poetics from Spenser to Pound* (Princeton).
Rimmon-Kenan, S. 1983. *Narrative Fiction: Contemporary Poetics* (London).
Shattuck, R. 1974. *Proust* (London).
Sheets, G. 1983. 'Ennius Lyricus', *Illinois Classical Studies* 8,22-32.
Skutsch, O. 1968. *Studia Enniana* (London).
——— 1985. *The Annales of Quintus Ennius, edited with an introduction and commentary* (Oxford).
Stadter, P.A. 1972, The structure of Livy's *History*', *Historia* 21, 287-307.
Suits, T.A. 1974. 'The structure of Livy's thirty-second book', *Philologus* 118,* 257-65.
Syme, Sir Ronald. 1945. rev. W. Hoffmann, *Livius und der zweite punische Krieg, JRS* 35, 104-8.
——— 1959. 'Livy and Augustus', *Harvard Stud. Clas. Philol.* 64, 27-87.
Ulmer, G.L. 1985. *Applied Grammatology. Post(e)-Pedagogy from Jacques Derrida to Joseph Beuys* (Baltimore).
Usher, S. 1969. *The Historians of Greece and Rome* (London).
Veyne, P. 1983. *L'Elégie érotique romaine. L'amour, la poésie et l'occident* (Paris).
——— 1984. *Writing History*, trans. M. Moore-Rinvolucri (Manchester).
Walsh, P. 1961. *Livy. His historical aims and methods* (Cambridge).
——— 1966. 'Livy', in Dorey 1966, 115-42.
——— 1974. *Livy. Greece and Rome New Surveys in the Classics* 8 (Oxford).

———— 1982. 'Livy and the aims of "historia": an analysis of the third decade', in H. Temporini, ed., *Aufstieg und Niedergang der römischen Welt* (Berlin), II.30.3, 1058-74.

Waugh, P. 111984. *Metafiction. The theory and practice of self-conscious fiction* (London).

White, H. 1978. *Tropics of Discourse. Essays in cultural criticism* (Baltimore).

Wille, G. 1973. *Der Aufbau des livianischen Geschichtswerks* (Amsterdam).

Woodman, A.J. 1977. *Velleius Paterculus. The Tiberian Narrative (2.94-131)* (Cambridge).

Zecchini, G. 1982. 'Asinio Pollione: Dall'attivita politica alla riflessione storiografica', *Aufstieg und Niedergang der römischen*, II.30.3, 1265-96.

4

Dio on Augustus

There is no such thing as politically innocent historiography.

Hayden White, 'Rhetoric and History', in H. White and
F.E. Manuel, eds., *Theories of History* (Los Angeles, 1978), 24.

Scholars writing about the history of Greece and Rome are highly unlikely as a group to give up their traditional concern with literary sources and adopt a wholly deconstructionist or synchronic approach. The nature of their subject and their relative lack of source material together place an importance on the Greek and Latin historians themselves, not paralleled in the case of modern history. Even the most determined adherent of statistical or quantitative method, for instance, must nevertheless turn repeatedly to literary sources to supplement his often patchy and unsatisfactory documentary evidence, for there are very few if any subjects in ancient history on which it is possible to construct a satisfactory argument without recourse to literary sources.[1] There are even fewer subjects in ancient history on which there is sufficient non-literary evidence available for 'hard' history to be possible (if it is possible at all); simply because of the general lack of evidence in comparison with what modern historians can take for granted, the amount of interpretation even in the most traditional and rigorous ancient history is extremely high. Perhaps this is precisely why the techniques of source-criticism, the analysis and ranking of sources in terms of their reliability, are so well developed in our field, and will continue to be the basic tool, despite the challenge presented by literary theory to the standard distinction between primary and secondary sources.[2] It is the same dilemma that we encountered with John Henderson's essay (Chapter 3 above): since to use all sources as if they were on an equal level, or to use all their statements without differentiation is a nonsense, those critics who

---

[1] I remember a series of lectures given by Sir Ronald Syme in Oxford about 1960 on exactly this theme – a diversion for the lecturer, and instructive for the student audience, but a *jeu d'esprit* all the same.

[2] For which see e.g. P. Veyne, *Les grecs ont-ils cru à leurs mythes?* (Paris, 1983), 14.

argue against traditional source criticism must still, at least if we take the extreme position, also utilise it themselves.

Nor do the sources 'speak for themselves'. If for us the concept of a value-free history is a chimera,[3] so is the idea of a value-free source, for these 'sources', in our field, are largely also histories, and as prone to personal, political and ethical bias as our own (indeed, in the latter case even more so). To analyse these underlying influences in a given author has therefore been and will continue to be a major task. It is what ancient historians generally mean by 'historiography', and it can have two kinds of result – to help the understanding of why and how the writer in question wrote as he did, both as an individual and in relation to his cultural context, and to act as a preliminary to the use of his work in our own historical reconstructions. The former question may also be extended to the history of later readings of the work, and later uses. It is very different from source-criticism (*Quellenkritik* in the narrower sense, that is, the tracking down of the authorities 'used' by the author in question), which can be a narrow and mechanical exercise. John Rich's discussion shows, among other things, how futile it can also be in certain circumstances. Nevertheless, if practised properly it must remain an essential part of the other.[4]

Cassius Dio is, as it happens, both a writer who is very much the product of his age and a major source for us on earlier Roman history, especially the reign of Augustus and the beginnings of the empire. John Rich shows us how an understanding of Dio as a political philosopher and moralist, and a refusal to see him only in terms of this or that source, will help us to read and reconstruct that history better.

Dio on Augustus

J.W. Rich

1. Introduction

In both his career and his writings Cassius Dio is the supreme instance of a man who was at once a Greek and a Roman. Dio's family belonged to the aristocracy of Nicaea in Bithynia. His father entered the senate and reached the consulship. Dio himself achieved the relatively rare feat for the son of a provincial senator of maintaining, indeed

---

[3] Though still the avowed aim of some: see e.g. T.D. Barnes, *Constantine and Eusebius* (Cambridge, Mass., 1981), v, 274-5 (a work to be built on 'a basic framework' of 'underlying facts', 'less subjective' than most histories of Constantine, based on 'precious nuggets of information'.

[4] The major exponent of historiography, and indeed the history of historiography, in our own day was Arnaldo Momigliano, who was also resolutely opposed to the disconnection of history from events.

improving on, his father's status: his distinguished career culminated
in a second consulship in 229. However, he did not lose touch with his
provincial origins: it was to Bithynia that he retired after his second
consulship.[1] Dio's chief work was a huge history of Rome, of which
about a third survives intact and the rest in epitomes.[2] Dio wrote in
Greek, and his history is one of the last products of the renaissance of
Greek literature under the Roman Empire. Like the other writers of
that epoch, Dio formed his style on that of the classical Greek authors.
He took Thucydides as his chief model, a conventional enough choice at
the time. Dio's debt to Thucydides' abstract and antithetical manner is
marked and direct verbal borrowings are numerous; moreover,
Thucydides' influence was not merely stylistic, but affected Dio's whole
cast of thought.[3] However, the standpoint from which Dio wrote was
that of a Roman of the senatorial class. His identification with Rome
was complete, and his values and preoccupations are those of a senator
living at a time when that class was under threat from hostile
emperors, encroaching *equites* and mutinous armies. The genre of
historical writing to which Dio's work belongs is also Roman: Dio
revived the tradition of annalistic histories of Rome, in abeyance since
Tacitus, and was the first since Livy to attempt what had once been the
main type of Roman historical writing, the history of the city from its
foundation to the writer's own day.[4] Thus in Dio's work the Greek and
Roman historical traditions are fused.[5]

Dio has not generally received much credit for originality. Many
scholars still approach his history with the assumptions of traditional
source-criticism: on this view, Dio normally followed a single source
and his own contribution mainly consisted of selecting the source to be
followed and adding rhetorical embellishment. Millar, whose
admirable study remains the standard work on Dio, is vigorously
opposed to conventional source-criticism, but holds that Dio only once,
in his treatment of Augustus' establishment of monarchy in books

[1] On Dio's career see Millar 1964, 5-27, 204-27; Letta 1979; Barnes 1984; Ameling
1984. For the failure of most provincial senators to transmit their status to their sons see
Hopkins 1983, 120-200.

[2] The best preserved part of the history covers the period dealt with in this paper; it
survives intact for 69-5 BC and with gaps for AD 4-14.

[3] On Dio's debt to Thucydides see briefly Millar 1964, 42, 76, 177; Flach 1973a, 130-1.
Some of the verbal borrowings were collected by Litsch 1893 and Kyhnitzsch 1894.

[4] A contemporary of Dio's, Asinius Quadratus, wrote a history of Rome in Ionic Greek
in fifteen books, covering the period from the foundation to Severus Alexander (*FGH* 97);
the priority cannot be established with certainty, but it seems most likely that Asinius
was prompted by Dio's example to attempt a work of the same kind but on a smaller
scale.

[5] See further Millar 1964, 174-92, an excellent discussion of the blend of Greek and
Roman in Dio, and Flach 1973a, locating Dio in the tradition of senatorial
historiography. Gabba 1959, and 1984, 70-5, stresses Dio's links with earlier Greek
writers on the Roman empire.

52-53, aspired to analysis and interpretation, and elsewhere did not rise above the level of mere narrative.[6] I shall try to show that these verdicts do not do justice to Dio. His methods were more complex than the proponents of source-criticism suppose, and he was not a mere narrator but an interpretative historian. One must not exaggerate. Dio is often slapdash and inaccurate, and his thought is generally scarcely less mediocre than his style. But he used ideas to shape his history more than any but the greatest of ancient historical writers.

Dio's treatment of Augustus has received a good deal of discussion. Some scholars hold that Dio was markedly more favourable to Augustus the ruler than Octavian the faction-leader.[7] Manuwald, who has recently published a valuable monograph on the topic, rejects this view, and claims that there are inconsistencies in Dio's treatment of Augustus throughout his career, most of which he explains in terms of the use of different sources.[8] In what follows I hope to show that, although there are inconsistencies in Dio's treatment of Augustus, they are less important than has commonly been supposed and mostly arise not from the combination of sources but from ambivalences in Dio's own attitudes and aims as a historian. In much of his work Dio's stance is that of the cynical observer of human affairs, exposing men's pretences and laying bare the realities of power. There was ample precedent for this in the Roman historical tradition, but Thucydides' influence was strong here and it was often in Thucydides' terms that Dio formulated his perceptions of the conflict between appearance and reality and the unchanging character of human nature.[9] This was, however, only one side of Dio. There was also the rhetorician, eager to show off his skills, and the political moralist, who sought to draw from the past lessons about how emperors should conduct themselves.

I shall proceed by briefly examining Dio's treatment of each phase of Augustus' career. First, however, it is necessary to say a little more about Dio's methods of work.

2. *Dio's methods*

In two passages Dio tells us something about his methods.[10] In a

---

[6] Millar 1964, 55-60, 73-118. For his views on traditional source-criticism see 34-5, 84-5.

[7] Notably Tränkle 1969; Stekelenburg 1971, 121ff.

[8] Manuwald 1979. The strengths and weaknesses of Manuwald's work are admirably assessed by Pelling 1983. See also Roddaz 1983 in substantial agreement with Manuwald.

[9] E.g. the antithesis *logôi ... ergôi* ('ostensibly ... but in reality'), as much a favourite with Dio as with his master (Nawijn 1931, 343, 490), and Dio's distinctions between alleged reasons and real motives for wars (frag. 43.1-3; 46.35.2; 48.45.4ff.; 50.1.1ff.) For Dio's use of the concept of human nature see 36.20.1 (echoing Thuc. 3.82.2); 52.18.1 and 55.14.4 (both echoing Thuc. 1.76.2); further instances in Nawijn 1931, 62, 853.

[10] On Dio's methods see Vrind 1926, 321-7; Millar 1964, 32-46.

fragment from the preface he claims that 'I have collected (?) virtually all the information recorded by anyone about them (*sc.* the Romans), but have not included it all in my history but only what I have selected'.[11] Much later he tells us that 'I spent ten years in collecting all the achievements of the Romans from the beginning to the death of (Septimius) Severus, and another twelve in writing my history: subsequent events will be recorded to wherever it may be possible'.[12] The dating of the 22 years in which 'the bulk of the history was composed is controversial. In my view they are best taken as starting in or soon after 201.[13]

In collecting all his material before beginning to compose Dio was following a well established ancient practice, though it may be doubted whether anyone else took it to such an extreme.[14] On recent events Dio could draw on his own experience or oral evidence, but for most of his work he was almost entirely dependent on literary sources.[15] Thus his chief occupation during the ten years in which he gathered his material will have been reading. Dio no doubt exaggerated its extent, but we must accept that he read widely: presumably he worked as hard in these years as in the twelve years of writing. He cannot have relied solely on his memory during the great programme of reading, but must constantly have taken notes, probably on parchment or papynes. We must imagine him working like the elder Pliny, who, according to his nephew, 'never read a book without making excerpts'.[16] Both at this

---

[11] Frag. 1.2. The first verb is lost; I here accept the supplement proposed by Millar 1964, 33.

[12] 72.23.5 (the passage survives only in Xiphilinus' epitome).

[13] So Vrind 1923, 166-7; Bowersock 1965, 470-3; Birley 1971, 8. A starting point *c.* 194-7 (so Schwartz 1899, 1686; Gabba 1955, 297-9; Millar 1964, 28-32) implies that the ten years of gathering material ended some years before Severus' death on 4 February 211, in contradiction of Dio's statement that he covered Roman history up to Severus' death. Letta 1979 and Barnes 1984 argue for a starting point in 211 or later, but this view does not adequately account for Dio's statement (72.23.3) that it was the success of his work on the wars at the beginning of Severus' reign that prompted him to embark on the Roman history, and makes it hard to see why Dio restricted himself in his period of gathering material to events up to the death of Severus.

[14] Lucian, *Hist. Conscr.* 47-8; Avenarius 1956, 71-93. No parallel for such a long period of collecting material is known (the 22 years in Dion. Hal., *Ant. Rom.* 1.7.2 are simply the period of Dionysius' residence in Rome, all of which could be represented as a preparation for his history).

[15] Cf. Millar 1964, 35-7.

[16] Pliny, *Ep.* 3.5.10. A number of ancient writers distinguish two phases in composition, first, the assembling of material in the form of a rough draft (*hypomnema*) and second, the turning of the draft into a finished literary product (Avenarius 1956, 85ff.). Dio's notes may be taken as the equivalent of this draft. Too much has sometimes been made of Lucian, *Hist. Conscr.* 47-8, which prescribes a three-stage procedure, distinguishing the amassing of the material from the compiling of the *hypomnema* (e.g. Pelling 1979, 94-5; Barnes 1984, 252). The tripartite procedure is hard to parallel and there is no warrant for applying it to Dio.

stage and when writing up he probably made much use of slave and freedman assistants.[17]

It is natural to suppose that during the twelve years of composition Dio, while sometimes referring back to the original sources, worked mainly from his notes. If so, he was following a procedure different from that of many ancient historians. A number of historians can be shown to have followed a main source so closely that they must have written with the text open before them, for example Livy and Diodorus.[18] But this need not trouble us: there is no reason to suppose that ancient historians all worked in the same way, any more than their modern counterparts. Pelling has recently argued that Dio too wrote with the text of one main source before him, using this for the basis of his narrative and much of his material, but from time to time supplementing it from his notes on other writers. However, it is hard to see why Dio should have devoted so much effort to preliminary reading if, when he came to write up, he was prepared to follow a single source as closely as Pelling supposes.[19]

It might be expected that differences in historians' methods would be reflected in the finished product. A historian who worked mainly from notes drawn from a variety of sources would enjoy greater freedom than one who closely followed a main source – freedom in the selection and shaping of material, and, if he chose, in explanation and interpretation. To my mind, this greater independence of treatment is precisely the distinctive quality of Dio's history.

It is therefore quite mistaken to try to apply traditional source-criticism to Dio. Any one passage may draw on several sources (although, of course, it need not do so); interpretative and thematic links may be Dio's own. All we can do is to consider what kinds of sources Dio is likely to have consulted. He will certainly have read widely among earlier historians. On the triumviral and Augustan periods historians whom he may have consulted include Pollio, Messalla Corvinus, Dellius, Nicolaus of Damascus, Livy, the elder Seneca, Cremutius Cordus and Aufidius Bassus. Somewhere among writers such as these he must have found the material which enabled him to form a view of Augustus' career very different from the regime's

[17] Cf. Pelling 1979, 95.

[18] On their methods see respectively Luce 1977, 139-229; Hornblower 1981, 18-39. Neither author is comparable to Dio. Diodorus was a mere compiler. Whereas Dio was abridging, Livy was usually writing on the same scale as his amplest sources, and in most of the sections where we can observe him at work his main source, Polybius, was incomparably superior to the alternatives. The usual view that his techniques remained the same elsewhere in his work may be mistaken.

[19] Pelling 1979, 91-5. Pelling based his case chiefly on the doctrine (propounded by Schwartz 1899, 1697-1714, and subsequently canonical) that Livy was Dio's main source for the late Republic and the triumviral period, but this has now been exploded by Manuwald 1979, 168-254, who demonstrates that, unlike Dio, Livy adhered to the official line of the Augustan regime on the triumviral period.

official line; but there is no warrant for supposing that at any point Dio selected one writer as his principal guide.[20] How far he drew on other sorts of writing it is difficult to say. He certainly consulted some memoirs: Augustus' *Autobiography* is one of the only two sources he names.[21] He may have used other biographical material too, although perhaps not Suetonius' life of Augustus.[22]

3. *From republic to monarchy*

The establishment of the Principate plays a part of the greatest importance in Dio's history. In his terms the transition is from democracy to monarchy: following the standard usage of his day Dio uses 'democracy' and its cognates simply of republican as opposed to monarchical government,[23] and he rightly insists that, despite Augustus' claims, the regime which he established was in fact monarchy. Augustus' establishment of monarchy gives rise to lengthy excursuses which occupy much of books 52 and 53. It also helps to determine the economy of the whole work: the first forty of the eighty books are devoted to Rome under the kings and the 'democracy'; books 41-50 cover the transitional years 49 to 31, when various leaders were struggling for supremacy; the last thirty books cover the 'monarchy', starting in book 51 from Actium.[24]

Not only is the establishment of monarchy heavily stressed in Dio's account, but the preceding years are dominated by its approach. We cannot say how far back this went since Dio's account of the period before 69 BC is lost; however, he later makes Agrippa say that Cinna, Pompeius Strabo, the younger Marius and Sertorius were all aspiring to supreme power.[25] He portrays the struggles of the late republic as mainly for personal power.[26] Pompey chose not to impose himself as monarch when he had the opportunity on his return from the East, but soon came to regret his decision.[27] By contrast, Caesar was aiming at

[20] As Millar 1964, 85 observes, he may have found Cremutius Cordus particularly congenial. However, Manuwald 1979, 254-7 shows that we cannot say whether his history continued beyond the civil wars to cover the reign of Augustus.

[21] 44.35.3. The citation is incorrect: presumably Dio's notes got muddled.

[22] Manuwald 1979, 258-68, criticising Millar 1964, 85-6.

[23] Cf. de Ste. Croix 1981, 614-15. The word *demokratia* came to be used for any internally self-governing republic, whether democratic or oligarchic, in the Hellenistic period, and was the regular term used by the Greek writers of the Principate for the constitution of the Roman Republic. The development was made possible by the fact that *demos*, like our 'people', is ambiguous: it may denote either the whole people of a state or the masses as opposed to the upper class. Dio normally uses *demos* for the Latin *populus* and *plethos, okhlos* or *homilos* for *plebs* (Fechner 1986, 198-205).

[24] Cf. 51.1.1; 52.1.1; below, n.68.

[25] 52.13.2.

[26] I am very grateful to Dr. A.W. Lintott for allowing me to see his excellent study of Dio's treatment of the late Republic, which has long awaited publication in *ANRW*.

[27] 37.20, 50.6.

monarchy from the time of his dream at Gades during his quaestorship.[28] Even Cicero was aspiring to the leadership.[29] The goal of Cato, the only politician not out for his own advancement, was to prevent tyranny and defend liberty; Dio's concept of 'democracy' as meaning simply 'republican government' leads him to present Cato, preposterously, as the champion of the people, even a 'lover of the people'.[30] In the civil war of 49-48 both Pompey and Caesar were fighting for the supreme power and the whole empire would be subject to the victor.[31] After Caesar's murder, the struggle resumed. Brutus and Cassius, like Cato, were 'lovers of the people', fighting for democracy and liberty,[32] but Antony, Octavian and Lepidus each sought the supremacy for themselves.[33] Philippi decided the issue between monarchy and democracy; subsequent battles were merely about who should rule.[34]

Most of these claims were not original to Dio, but they provide the framework for an interpretation of the history of the period which was very much his own. Dio's account of the relations between Pompey and Caesar illustrates this well. He holds that Caesar sought throughout to undermine Pompey's position in pursuance of his goal of supreme power, while from 60 a prime factor in Pompey's conduct was his perception that his power was not as great as he had hoped and Caesar's was growing. Dio gives us elaborately worked out accounts of the motives of Caesar, Pompey and Crassus at the formation of the First Triumvirate and of Pompey in 56,[35] attributing to the protagonists generalised reflections on human behaviour of the kind of which he was fond.[36] At two points above all Dio diverges from the rest of our tradition, and in both cases it seems most likely that Dio himself was responsible. First, he gives an account of the events of 56-55 in which the Conference of Luca is not mentioned and the candidature of Pompey and Crassus for the consulship of 55 is treated as a combination against Caesar.[37] It is hard to believe that he found anything like this in any of the sources he consulted. Rather, it is the extreme case of Dio's methods leading him astray: at some point either in the note-taking or the composition stage he overlooked Luca and

[28] 36.43.3-4; 37.22.1, 37.3, 52.1-2, 54-56; 38.34.3; 41.24.2; 42.8,2 etc. Cf. Pelling 1982, 146-7.

[29] 36.43.4-5; cf. 38.11.2. Dio's view of Cicero was perverse but original; cf. Millar 1964, 46-55.

[30] 37.22.1-4, 57.3; 43.11.6; cf. 38.3.1.

[31] 41.17.3, 53-6.

[32] 47.38.3, 42.3-4.

[33] 44.34.5-6; 45.4.3, 11.2; 46.32.1, 34.4, 46.3, 54.4; 47.1.1, 18.2; 48.1.2; 50.1.1; 51.15.3 etc.

[34] 47.39.1-3.

[35] 37.54-6; 39.25-6.

[36] 37.55.2-3; 39.26.1-2.

[37] 39.24-34.

developed instead his own version of events in terms of Pompey's fear of Ceasar's growing power. Secondly, in his final summing up the traditional judgement is reversed. According to the tradition, Caesar could not brook a superior or Pompey an equal, but Dio has it that 'Pompey wished to be second to no man and Caesar to be first of all'.[38] Dio's version is in agreement with his overall view of their relations. We should conclude that Dio amended the version that he found in his sources to bring it into line with that overall view.

Nowhere does Dio set his stamp more firmly on his account of events than in his treatment of the early career of Octavian. This has been carefully analysed by Manuwald.[39] As he shows, Octavian is more to the fore in Dio's account than in the other extant versions.[40] Like his rivals, Octavian is represented as setting his sights from the start on monarchy and pursuing this goal with consummate duplicity, to which Dio draws attention at every opportunity. His treatment of the events of August to November 43 may serve as an example. Octavian marched on Rome to secure his first consulship 'pretending to be compelled by his soldiers', and, after it had been conferred, he thanked the troops sincerely but expressed feigned gratitude to the senate.[41] The senate then sent him out against Antony and Lepidus unaware that he had already come to an agreement with them. He nominally accepted the command but in fact took no action against them, not because he felt any compunction about breaking his agreement but because he saw that for the time it was in his interest to collaborate with them.[42] The accord which the three then made was merely a pretence: each of them fully intended to renounce it when the time was ripe.[43] Unfortunately, Manuwald draws the wrong conclusion from his analysis. For him Dio's account derives in the main from a lost source and his own contribution amounts to little more than some touching up. It was, indeed, not novel to claim that Octavian had been motivated throughout by the desire for dominance,[44] and most of Dio's interpretations of individual episodes can be paralleled in our other sources. But Dio's account as a whole presents us with a coherent and powerful interpretation which gives the narrative shape and which, in its view of individuals' motivation and fondness for analyses of motives and generalisations, shows close correspondences

---

[38] Lucan, 1.125-6; Flor., 2.13.14; Dio, 41.54.1.

[39] Manuwald 1979, 27-70.

[40] In addition to the instances collected by Manuwald 1979 see 47.20.3-4, 21.2.

[41] 46.43.6, 47.1. In the first passage, as often, Dio uses the convenient indicator of irony, *dethen* ('forsooth').

[42] 46.52.1-3. A similar explanation of Octavian's collaboration with Brutus is given at 45.14.2-3.

[43] 46.54.4, 56.4; 47.1.1.

[44] Note especially Tac., *Ann.* 1.10.1.

with the rest of Dio's history. This must be the work not of a 'source' but of Dio himself.[45]

Dio repeatedly expresses his approval of the change from 'democracy' to monarchy. Monarchy was the best form of constitution, at any rate for a state as large as Rome had become. Such a state could not be governed with 'moderation' (*sophrosyne*) under a 'democracy', and without moderation there could not be harmony. The alternative to monarchy was thus ruin.[46] Dio is strongly critical of Caesar's murderers: their action was both a crime, punished by God, and a political misjudgement, since Caesar's monarchy was better for Rome than the 'democracy' they sought to restore.[47] These views had a long pedigree,[48] and by Dio's time it would perhaps have been impossible to take any other position.

Dio does, however, have much that is favourable to say of the republican leaders, and in this too he was in the mainstream of the historical tradition. He was following tradition when he extolled Cato's virtues (Cato was, he tells us, virtually alone among his contemporaries in still displaying 'moderation') and described Brutus and Cassius as behaving well in Asia. More striking is his account of Philippi, in which he draws a much stronger contrast between the idealism of Brutus and Cassius and the unscrupulous ambition of their opponents than is to be found in any other version. Brutus and Cassius were reluctant to begin battle not just for prudential reasons but because as 'lovers of the people' they did not wish citizens' blood to be shed. The speeches to the troops made on their side dwelt on freedom and 'democracy'; their opponents offered, besides vengeance on Caesar's murderers, the property of their enemies, rule over men of their own race and a donative of 20,000 sesterces. They had any old password, but Brutus' was 'Freedom'.[49] None of this indicates any wavering in Dio's preference for monarchy over 'democracy', which he reasserts here.[50] Dio's version is the product simply of his keenness to expose the pretences of those who sought power. He is ready to make his rhetorical point even at the cost of some distortion of the facts, as when he omits to point out that Brutus and Cassius too gave donatives at Philippi.[51]

Dio favoured monarchy but not despotism, and this leaves its mark on

[45] Pelling 1983, 222-3.

[46] 44.1-2; 47.39.4-5; 53.19.1; 54.6.1; 56.44.2; cf. 52.15.5-16.4. The ambivalence towards monarchy which Manuwald 1979, 8-26 detects and explains in terms of different sources is largely non-existent. Dio's use of *douleia* ('slavery') and its cognates of the Romans under monarchy (46.32.1, 34.4; 50.1.2) is merely realist, not disapproving. On Dio's views on 'democracy' and monarchy see now Fechner 1986.

[47] 41.63.5; 44.1-2; 48.1.1.

[48] E.g. Tac., *Hist.* 1.1.1., 16.1; Jos., *AJ* 19.162; Sen., *Ben.* 2.20.2; Flor., 2.14.6; App., *BC* 4.133.

[49] 47.38.3-5, 42.3-43.1. For a review of the treatment of Brutus and Cassius in the sources, see Rawson 1986, and also Fechner 1986, 111-28.

[50] 47.39.4-5.

[51] App., *BC* 4.100, 118.

his treatment of Pompey and Caesar. In the period of their struggle it is Pompey, not Caesar, whom he associates with his ideal of the good ruler. Thus he tells us that Pompey declined extravagant honours because he knew that when conferred on the powerful they had the appearance of being extorted,[52] and in his final summing up that 'Pompey was anxious to be honoured by men of their own free will, to be their leader by their consent and to be loved by them, whereas Caesar did not mind if he ruled over the unwilling, issued orders to men who hated him and conferred his honours himself'.[53] However, when he comes to Caesar's dictatorship, he blithely contradicts himself: Caesar is now the exemplar of the good ruler. He never misses an opportunity to dilate on Caesar's clemency towards his opponents; Caesar's persistence in it shows, he holds, that it was not simply prudential but arose from his innate goodness.[54] He represents Caesar as making a reassuring speech to the senate on his return to Rome in 46, in which he promises to be not a tyrant but a leader, protector and father,[55] and his words are borne out by his subsequent conduct.[56] Thus Brutus and Cassius were not true liberators, but the murderers of the state's leader and protector.[57]

In this part of his work, then, both sides of Dio are on view, the hardheaded student of *Machtpolitik* and the political theorist, keen to expound his views of how Rome should best be governed and ready to find exemplars in the characters of his history. It is in this light that his treatment of Octavian's rise to power should be judged.

It is a mistake to regard Dio's account of Octavian as negative or hostile. If he had been hostile, he would not have been so vague in his allusion to Octavian's alleged attempt to assassinate Antony[58] or denied the rumour of his involvement in the deaths of Hirtius and Pansa.[59] In seeking to establish monarchy Octavian was, in Dio's view, acting in Rome's best interests. His criticism is reserved for Caesar's murderers and, in a striking passage, the senate. They were to blame,

---

[52] 37.23. Dio puts the same doctrine into the mouth of Maecenas (52.35.1-2). Note also his explanation of Pompey's feigned reluctance to assume the pirate command in terms of the jealousy which would be aroused if he sought it openly (36.24.6, 26.1-2).

[53] 41.54.1.

[54] 41.62-3; 42.6.3, 27.4, 50.2, 55.3; 43.12-13; 44.45-7 etc.

[55] 43.15-18. No other extant writer mentions Caesar addressing the senate at this point (Plut., *Caes.* 55.1 reports a speech to the people boasting of his victory), and Millar 1964, 81 may be right that Dio had no authority. However, Caesar must have made a speech to the senate on his return, which may well have included words of reassurance, and Dio may have found a record of it in his sources.

[56] 43.18.6. Dio does subsequently criticise Caesar for arrogance and accepting excessive honours, but puts the chief blame on those who conferred the honours (43.42ff.; 44.3ff.).

[57] 44.2.5; cf. 44.48.1-2.

[58] 45.8.2. Cf. Cic., *Fam.* 12.23.2; App., *BC* 3.39; Suet., *Aug.* 10.3.

[59] 46.39.1.

he says, for the disasters which befell Rome in 43, culminating in the proscriptions; instead of seeking to further their own cause by support-ing now one leader and now another they should have chosen one man of the best intentions as their leader and stuck to him.[60] Although he does not say so explicitly, it is clear that Dio thinks that their choice should have fallen on Octavian. Dio's vivid portrayal of Octavian's duplicity and undeviating pursuit of power is not intended to show disapproval. This is Dio the realist, seeking to expose the gap between appearance and reality and lay bare the true springs of men's actions.

However, if Dio was untroubled by Octavian's goal, the violence which he used in its pursuit was a different matter. There was no virtue by which Dio set greater store in a ruler than clemency. The clemency of Augustus was celebrated in official propaganda, but there was a wide gap between the propaganda and the facts. For Dio this was not merely an academic question. He had been present in the senate when Septimius Severus had menacingly commended the cruelty of Sulla, Marius and Augustus as safer than the mildness of Pompey and Caesar.[61] In his narrative Dio follows two different strategies for dealing with the problem. Usually he makes no attempt to disguise Octavian's harshness.[62] He reports that on various occasions he spared only a minority of his opponents,[63] and draws attention to some instances where claims of mildness were made unjustly by him or on his behalf.[64] However, on the proscriptions he takes a different line, seeking to exculpate Octavian and drawing near for the only time in his account of his rise to the official view. Octavian, he claims, took part in them just because he was sharing power; that such conduct was not in his nature was shown by the fact that he did nothing comparable when he became sole ruler; he saved many, was harsh to those who betrayed their friends and lenient to those who protected them.[65] We shall see that this problem continued to trouble Dio, and he was still wrestling with it when he came to compose his final verdict on Augustus.

4. The establishment of monarchy

According to Dio, the process by which monarchy was established at Rome went as follows. The struggle for power was decided at Actium on 2 September 31; Octavian was now the master of the Roman

---

[60] 46.34.

[61] 75.81.1.

[62] 46.48-9; 48.14.3-5; 49.12-4-5; 51.2.4-6, 16.1.

[63] 48.14.3, 5; 49.12.4; 51.2.4. Contrast Augustus' own claim to have spared all who asked for pardon (*RG* 3.1; cf. Vell. 2.86.2).

[64] 46.49.5; 52.42.8.

[65] 47.7. Dio does not go so far as to claim that Octavian tried to prevent the proscriptions (so Vell. 2.66.1; Suet., *Aug.* 27.1). Suetonius alleges that once he had begun he was the worst of the three.

world.[66] On his return to Rome in 29 he deliberated with his closest associates about whether to retain the monarchy. Agrippa urged him to restore 'democracy', Maecenas argued for monarchy and Octavian came down in favour of Maecenas' view.[67] In 27 he announced his resignation. This was a deliberate ploy, designed to secure men's apparent consent for his rule. The senate protested as anticipated, and Octavian agreed to accept the supreme power, pretending to do so only because compelled. In order to seem 'democratic' and avoid the appearance of monarchy, he accepted only powers that were limited in extent and time, although in reality his power was complete and permanent. He then received various honours including the name Augustus.[68]

The debate between Agrippa and Maecenas is the most remarkable of the debates held in private which are an unusual feature of Dio's history (serious historians had long confined speeches to public occasions).[69] Like other Greek historians under the empire, Dio felt free to invent the content of a speech, but it is not clear whether he was prepared to write a speech without evidence that one had been made. In any case, he must have had evidence for the Agrippa-Maecenas debate. He must have read in his sources not just that, as Suetonius says, Augustus thought of restoring the republic after his defeat of Antony,[70] but also that Agrippa urged him to do so. That Augustus' principal associate was opposed to the establishment of monarchy would, if true, be a fact of considerable importance. Dio was not so frivolous as to invent such a claim merely so that he should have a spokesman for 'democracy'.[71] It is, however, in one sense to his discredit as a historian that he accepted the truth of the

---

[66] 51.1.1.

[67] 52.1-41.

[68] 53.2-20. Dio is inconsistent about the precise point at which monarchy began, identifying it variously with Actium (50.1.2, 51.1.1, 56.30.5), the debate of 29 (52.1.1), and the settlement of 27 (53.17.1, 19.1; contrast 53.2.6, 12.1, where he speaks of it as confirming an already established monarchy). These inconsistencies are best seen as the product simply of sloppy writing on Dio's part (Pelling 1983, 223, against Manuwald 1979, 77-100).

[69] Dio's other private debates are: Pyrrhus and Fabricius (frag. 40.33-38), Cicero and Philiscus (38.18-29) and Augustus and Livia (55.14-21). Herodotus gives many such debates, and in Thucydides there is the Melian Dialogue (note also Thuc. 3.30, 113). Their absence from later serious historians, as opposed to romantic writers like Curtius Rufus, may be due not so much to qualms about evidence as to the fact that it was to public occasions that formal oratory was appropriate.

[70] Suet., *Aug.* 28.1. Millar 1964, 105, thinks that this passage may be Dio's only evidence, but see above, n.22.

[71] So Millar 1964, 105-6. *Contra* Millar, there is no conflict between the role assigned to Agrippa here and Dio's statement at 54.29.3 that he helped him to establish the monarchy as if he were really an enthusiast for autocracy (cf. 52.41.1: Agrippa helped Augustus put Maecenas' recommendations into effect as zealously as if they had been his own). Flach 1973a, 136, takes the reference to the Agrippa/Maecenas debate in Donatus Auctus, *Vita Vergilii* 78 (Diehl 1911, 37) to derive from a source earlier than Dio, but it is more likely that the Renaissance scholar who composed the passage was drawing on Dio (Manuwald 1979, 23).

story and included the debate. The writer who had so effectively exposed Octavian's unscrupulous and unswerving pursuit of power now invites us to believe that, when the prize was won, he considered giving it up. Dio the realist had to give place here: the rhetorical and didactic opportunities of the debate were too good to miss.

Agrippa argues that 'democracy' is the best form of constitution, and that installing monarchy at Rome would be difficult, dangerous and personally unrewarding. Maecenas' much longer speech, which Dio clearly intends us to find convincing, opens with general arguments in favour of monarchy and a demonstration that it is in Octavian's personal interest to retain power (52.14-8). Maecenas then passes to advice on how to rule, designed to show that it would be possible for Octavian to rule successfully despite the difficulties and dangers pointed out by Agrippa. This advice, which takes up the greater part of the speech, falls into two parts: specific administrative proposals (52.19-33) and more general guidance for the ruler's conduct (52.34-40). Dio comments afterwards that Augustus put some of Maecenas' suggestions into effect and left the rest for his successors. Many of the administrative proposals do not correspond either to the practice of previous reigns or of Dio's own time. It is clear that at least some of these were intended by Dio as suggestions for reform which he would have liked to see implemented in his own day. Their general tenor is to the advantage of the senate.

It is unfortunate that modern discussion has concentrated almost exclusively on these suggestions for administrative reform. The result has been that 52.19-40 has been regarded as a kind of political pamphlet unrelated to its context; many scholars have supposed that it was a later insertion or that Dio changed his plan in the course of composition.[72] This is mistaken. Maecenas is not Dio, and his whole speech belongs in its dramatic context as a refutation of Agrippa.[73] Thus, for example, the financial proposals respond to objections raised by Agrippa,[74] and in the section about senatorial and equestrian appointments Maecenas seeks throughout to show that his proposals will ensure the emperor's security, because he is answering Agrippa's argument that good men cannot safely be promoted.[75] Many of Maecenas' proposals do correspond to the practice of Augustus or subsequent emperors; thus one of the functions of the section dealing with administration is to give an analysis of the problems facing Augustus and of the imperial system as it evolved under him and his

---

[72] Bleicken 1962 and Millar 1964, 102-18 remain the best discussions. Recent treatments include Espinoza Ruiz 1982; Roddaz 1983, 75-84; Zawadski 1983.
[73] Cf. McKechnie 1891.
[74] 52.6, 27-9.
[75] 52.8.

successors.[76] Furthermore, the speech does not exist in isolation from the rest of the history. There are frequent points of contact, not only with the institutional excursuses in the account of the settlement of 27, but with the narrative of Augustus' reign: as we shall see, Dio regularly draws attention to aspects of Augustus' conduct which conform to Maecenas' prescriptions.

The function of the Agrippa-Maecenas debate is complex and many-sided. But above all it enables Dio to present his most extensive statement of the political creed which he asserts at so many points in his history, that the best form of government for Rome was one in which one man had a monopoly of power but ruled with moderation and in partnership with the senators, using them to administer his empire and consulting them about his decisions.

Throughout his extended account of the settlement of 27 Dio insists, as in his narrative of Octavian's rise to power, on the contrast between his claims and his true intentions. He stresses that the resignation and the subsequent acceptance only of limited powers were a pretence intended merely to make it *appear* that men freely consented to Augustus' rule and that his position was not monarchical.[77] Dio did not, of course, originate this interpretation. Tacitus encapsulates it in a phrase ('he accepted everything ... under his rule under the name of *princeps*')[78] and Dio will have consulted sources, lost to us, which recounted the resignation of 27 as a sham. However, the way in which he elaborates the theme and extends it, through excursuses on institutions, into an analysis of the whole imperial system is all his own,[79] is a trace too of Dio's capacity to distort the facts to make his point. Thus he reports the doubling of the praetorians' pay immediately after the agreement to continue in power and before the division of the provinces with the comment 'so eager was he in reality to establish monarchy',[80] although in fact this probably came about in association with the division of the provinces.

As before, Dio does not imply any disapproval by his emphasis on the gap between appearance and reality in the conduct of Octavian/ Augustus.[81] In drawing attention to it so strongly he is simply carrying out his historian's duty of laying bare the truth about men's actions. It is, in fact, clear that he fully approves of the settlement of 27. He reasserts here his view that monarchy was the best form of government for Rome,[82] and he can only have applauded Augustus'

[76] Cf. Hammond 1932, who spoils his case by arguing that this is the speech's only function.
[77] See especially 53.2.6, 11.1-12.3, 13.1, 16.1.
[78] *Ann.* 1.1.1.
[79] Cf. Millar 1964, 93-100.
[80] 553.11.5.
[81] *Contra* Millar 1964, 102: 'Dio's attitude of mixed acceptance and indignation'.
[82] 53.19.1.

attempt to give his monarchy a 'democratic' guise. He had made
Maecenas urge that the emperor should erect just such a façade, and
we shall see that one of Augustus' greatest merits in Dio's eyes was his
success in somehow combining monarchy with 'democracy'.

5. *The reign of Augustus*

Dio gives a relatively small-scale account of Augustus' reign,
sandwiched between his generous treatments of the settlement of 27,
seen as inaugurating the reign, and Augustus' death and obsequies. He
was to follow the same practice in his account of subsequent reigns,
using biographical techniques in the extended opening and closing
sections.[83] Great as its value is for us as evidence, this section of his
work is not a success as a piece of historical writing. The annalistic
framework prevents him from bringing out clearly many of the
important developments of the reign, and he often gets bogged down in
trivia. This is in striking contrast with the narrative sweep of much of
his account of the Late Republic and Civil War periods and his success
in imposing his own interpretations on those events. The difference is
of course largely in the events themselves and in the nature of the
evidence for them, and Dio himself was well aware of the difficulty of
writing imperial history.[84]

Dio continues to insist, where appropriate, on the contrast between
the appearance and the reality of Augustus' power. Later renewals of
his powers were accompanied by the same pretence of unwillingness;
the distinction between the *fiscus* and the *aerarium* was unimportant;
Augustus already enjoyed greater power than the office of dictator
conferred and so in 22 BC sensibly avoided the odium of the name; the
decree of AD 13 by which the decisions of his *consilium* gained the force
of *senatusconsulta* gave him powers which in reality he possessed
already.[85]

Among the mass of material which Dio has set down from a wide
variety of sources there are a number of items which do not redound to
Augustus' credit. One of the most striking is the story of Licinus, the
procurator of Gaul: when Augustus found out about his extortion,
Licinus told him that he had been amassing the money for him, handed
it over and so got off.[86] Dio does not conceal that Augustus had his
personal weaknesses: thus the inconsistency between his stance as a
moral reformer and his own numerous liaisons sometimes caused him
embarrassment.[87] But Dio's view of Augustus as a ruler is almost

[83] Questa 1957; Millar 1964, 40, 61.
[84] 53.19; 54.15.1-3.
[85] 53.22.2-4; 54.1.5; 55.6.1, 12.3; 56.28.1, 3.
[86] 54.21.
[87] 54.16.3-6. His affair with Terentia: 54.19.3; 55.7.5.

entirely favourable; for him, Augustus was a model emperor both at home and abroad.

Indeed, Dio's conception of Augustus' imperial policy was a remarkable feat of mental dexterity, for he managed to persuade himself that Augustus, who was in fact the greatest conqueror in Roman history, had consistently both preached and practised a policy of not expanding the empire and so was an exemplar of the policy which, as is clear from the later part of his work, he himself favoured.[88]

In his account of Augustus' conduct of domestic affairs the qualities which Dio finds admirable are those which senators had always valued in emperors and which he had alrady delineated in the speech of Maecenas.[89] Thus Augustus consulted senators in advance about his legislative proposals, either through his *consilium* or by other means, brought all kinds of business before the senate, was diligent in his attendance and sought to make its debates free.[90] He did not disdain to appear in court, both as a witness and in support of his friends.[91] Men were allowed to speak frankly before him and he welcomed advice.[92] Insults to his friends Appuleius and Maecenas were checked but not punished.[93] L. Sestius was honoured for his devotion to the memory of Brutus.[94] He would not allow men to call him 'master', hated flatterers and declined some honours.[95] He tried not to give way to anger.[96] Some of what he was obliged to do as a ruler and legislator caused offence, but in his later years he grew milder and increasingly unwilling to offend senators.[97] In much of this Dio was simply following his sources, whose prejudices he shared. However, he made his own contribution as well. Some of the judgements are his own, as on the trial of Nonius Asprenas: Suetonius cites this as an instance of Augustus' scrupulousness in balancing his obligations to his friend against his desire not to interfere in the course of justice, and the same was probably true of Dio's source; Dio misses the point and adduces Augustus' willingness to appear on Nonius' behalf as an example of his wish to be 'democratic'.[98] This is one of a number of passages where Dio uses the theme of Augustus' moderate and 'democratic' behaviour to

[88] 53.10.4; 54.9.1; 56.33.5-6, 41.7; cf. 52.37.1 (Maecenas's advice). Cf. Brunt 1963, 172, 174-5; Millar 1964, 67, 82, 141-3, 149.

[89] On the virtues of emperors see Wallace-Hadrill 1981, 1982.

[90] 53.21.3-6, 33.1; 55.4.1, 25.4-5, 34.1-2; 56.28.4-6. Cf. 52.31.1-2, 32.1-2 (Maecenas' advice); 56.40.3, 41.3 (Tiberius' obituary). Brunt 1984 defends the accuracy of this account of Augustus' dealings with the senate.

[91] 54.3.1-3; 55.4.2-3.

[92] 54.3.3; 55.4.3, 7.3; 56.43.1-2. Cf. 52.33.6-7; 56.41.8.

[93] 54.30.4.

[94] 53.32.4.

[95] 54.13.1, 27.2, 35.2-3; 55.9.2, 12.2, 4. Cf. 52.35; 56.41.8.

[96] 54.3.6, 27.4; 55.7.1-3; 56.43.3.

[97] 54.19.1; 55.5.3, 12.3; 56.25.4.

[98] 55.4.3; Suet., *Aug* 56.3 (supplying the name).

link disparate material, not following a source but imposing his own interpretation.[99]

Perhaps the most important of all the imperial virtues in the eyes of senators was clemency, and, as we have seen, the conduct of Octavian on this score during his rise to power had given Dio some difficulty. Nor were matters altogether plain sailing even after the attainment of monarchy, for real or alleged conspirators met punishment. Dio reported a number of these episodes, insisting that it was always impossible to determine the truth about allegations of conspiracy against emperors.[100] However, he found a congenial opportunity for treating the subject at length in the story that Augustus pardoned the conspirator Cinna on the advice of Livia. This provides the occasion for another closet debate like that between Agrippa and Maecenas: a brief dialogue between Augustus and Livia is followed by a lengthy speech by Livia arguing that clemency is more likely to ensure a security than punishment. Dio represents her argument as being borne out by the sequel, for, he assures us, the pardon so endeared Augustus to everyone that there were no more conspiracies against him.[101] This time we have positive evidence that the claim that such a discussion took place was not just invented by Dio, for the story is also given by Seneca.[102] However, as with the Agrippa-Maecenas debate, his acceptance of the story and decision to accord it such extensive treatment constitute another victory for his desire to show off and to edify over his historical judgement. But, just like the Agrippa-Maecenas debate, the episode is not to be seen as a pamphlet divorced from its context. Some of Livia's arguments take up points which Dio makes elsewhere,[103] and the incident as a whole helps Dio to reach his final, favourable verdict on this aspect of Augustus' conduct. This emerges clearly from the conclusion of Livia's speech, which, as we shall see, is echoed in the final verdict: 'in this way you will be held to have committed all your acts of harshness under compulsion, ... but, if you persist in your old policy, you will be thought to have done them by inclination.'[104]

---

[99] 53.33.1-2; 54.3.1-2; 55.4.1-2 (the courtroom illustrations will have been linked in Dio's source, as in Suet., *Aug.* 56.3-4, but Dio himself probably made the connection with the reform of senate procedure.

[100] 54.3.4-8, 15.1-4; 55.4.3, 10.15. The speculations of Millar 1964, 87-90 and Manuwald 1979, 100-30 about the character of Dio's sources for this material are unconvincing (cf. Pelling 1983, 224).

[101] 55.14.1-22.2.

[102] *Clem.* 1.9. It is uncertain whether Seneca is Dio's source. They differ on the date, and Seneca devotes most space to Augustus' conversation with Cinna, which Dio does not mention, but such differences could have been the product of Dio's adaptation. See further Manuwald 1979, 120-7; Giua 1981.

[103] E.g. men's inclination to think that conspiracy charges are trumped up (52.31.9-10; 54.15.2; 55.18.5-6); the good ruler compared to a doctor (54.17.1-2, 18.1, 20.3; 56.39.2; Giua 1983, 440 n.3).

[104] 55.21.4.

6. Dio's final judgement on Augustus

Dio's lengthy treatment of Augustus' death and obsequies (56.29-47) includes two retrospects of Augustus. The first is Tiberius' funeral oration (56.35-41). This, of course, gives us not Dio's views, but views which he deemed appropriate to the speaker.[105] Thus the speech includes various claims which are in direct conflict with Dio's narrative, for example, that Augustus resorted to arms at the start of his career to avenge his father and help the people in their necessity, that he pardoned the majority of his opponents, and that his resignation in 27 BC was sincere and his subsequent acceptance and renewals of power were made under compulsion.[106] However, even when the views are not Dio's own, they reflect his perspective, as when Tiberius concedes that Augustus made temporary alliances with Antony and Lepidus while always intending to break them,[107] and Dio's own values are reflected in the praises of Augustus' conduct as sole ruler.[108]

In the second retrospect (56.43-5) Dio describes the Romans' reaction to the loss of Augustus and adds comments of his own:

(43.1) Not many felt real grief for him at the time, but later they all did. For he was accessible to all alike, aided many with money, showed great honour to his friends and was overjoyed when they spoke their mind freely. ... (3) They remembered these qualities of his and also that he did not get uncontrollably angry with those who had injured him, and kept faith even with those who did not deserve it. ... (4) They missed him greatly for these reasons and because, mixing monarchy with democracy, he both preserved their freedom and gave them order and security as well, so that they lived, untroubled either by the licence of democracy or the oppression of a tyrant, enjoying freedom and moderation in a monarchy without fear, under kingly rule yet not enslaved, governed democratically yet without discord.

(44.1) Those who remembered his deeds in the civil wars attributed them to the force of circumstances and based their judgement of his true inclination on his conduct after he attained undisputed possession of the supreme power. It is true that there was a vast difference, (2) as anyone may confirm by examining his acts individually. I would sum them all up by saying that he put an end to all civil strife and transformed the

---

[105] Dio was, as usual, following the historiographical doctrine which had long been dominant, that speeches need not be authentic but should be appropriate to the speaker and the situation (see Walbank 1965, 5, 18-9). The recent discussions of Tiberius' speech by Manuwald 1979, 133-40 and Giua 1983 are unsatisfactory: Manuwald supposes that Dio was closely following a source, while Giua oddly thinks that Dio's real views are to be found in the speech and not in his narrative. A minor but unexplained puzzle is that Dio disregards the immediate context, making Tiberius speak as though his succession and Augustus' apotheosis had already been decided (56.35.2, 41.9).

[106] 56.36.2, 38.1-2, 39.4-6. See further Manuwald 1979, 136-9.

[107] 56.37.1-3.

[108] 56.40-1.

constitution in the best possible way and greatly strengthened it, so that if excessive violence was sometimes employed, as is apt to happen in exceptional circumstances, one might more justly blame the circumstances themselves than him.

(3) An important reason for the high esteem in which he was held was the length of his reign. The majority and the more able of those who had known the democracy were dead. (4) Their successors had no personal knowledge of it, and, having been brought up largely or entirely under the existing regime, did not just acquiesce in it because it was what they were used to, but favoured it because they saw that it was better and freer from fear than that of which they had heard.

(45.1) They knew all this while he was alive, but realised it more fully after his death. It is the tendency of human nature not to notice its happiness in times of prosperity so much as it misses it in adversity. This is what happened with Augustus: it was when they discovered how different Tiberius was that they regretted him. (2) Men of sense were able to foresee the changed circumstances at once, for the consul Pompeius, when he went to meet the procession bringing Augustus' body, was hurt in the leg and had to be carried back with the body, and an owl sat on the roof of the senate-house again at the first senate meeting after his death and uttered many ill-omened cries. (3) So great was the difference between the two that some suspected that Augustus had chosen Tiberius as his successor, although well aware of his character, expressly in order to enhance his own glory.

This passage has attracted a good deal of discussion because of the delicate problem of its relation to Tacitus. Tacitus too casts his retrospect of Augustus in the form of a statement of the Romans' opinions about him (*Ann.* 1.9-10) and there are a number of close parallels between this section of Dio and the opening chapters of the *Annals*.[109] However, there are also important differences between Tacitus and Dio. Tacitus reports that different views were current about Augustus' career among 'men of sense'. Some took a favourable view of his aims and conduct in the civil wars and praised his government as sole ruler. Others were hostile to Augustus: throughout the civil wars his real motive had been greed for power, and every phase of his career had been marked by violence and cruelty. Tacitus does not say what he himself thinks; however, he reports the second view at greater length, and it is clear that it is this that has his sympathy, though he is not to be taken as agreeing with it in full. Dio, on the other hand, reports only views favourable to Augustus and explicitly states his agreement. The contrast which he makes is not between opposing views of Augustus but between the imperfect understanding of their loss which the Romans felt at the time and the full realisation which they attained when they experienced the rule of Tiberius.

---

[109] Goodyear 1972, 155 tabulates some of the main parallels.

There has been general agreement among scholars that Tacitus and Dio were here following a common source, and controversy has centred on the question which version is closer to the original.[110] In my view the possibility that Dio was drawing on Tacitus himself deserves to be taken seriously: it seems unlikely that he omitted Tacitus from his extensive programme of reading and, as we have seen, Dio was capable of considerable reshaping of his material. Whatever Dio's source or sources were, his version bears his own hallmark. The rhetorical elaboration of 43.4 with its Thucydidean echo[111] and the generalisation about human nature at 45.1 are both typical of Dio. At some places where Dio recalls Tacitus, whether he is drawing on him or using a common source, the lameness of Dio's version betrays his own handiwork. Thus, if Augustus' position was strengthened by the fact that few could now remember the republic (44.3-4), it will, as in Tacitus, have been because men did not miss what they had never known. Dio's elaboration that they perceived the superiority of the new regime spoils the point: those who had known the republic would have been no less well placed to discern that.[112] The 'men of sense', whose rational views are contrasted in Tacitus with the idle matters which excited the wonder of the majority, undergo a bizarre transformation at the hands of the superstitious Dio (45.2).[113] It seeme to me most likely that it was Dio himself who introduced the rather feeble contrast between the Romans' attitudes to Augustus at the time of his death and after they had had experience of Tiberius, as a substitute for a contrast of favourable and unfavourable views such as we find in Tacitus.[114]

Dio here took what he found in his source or sources and made use of it for his own purposes with his usual freedom, probably writing with just his notes in front of him. By the time that he came to write, he may well have forgotten the discordant note which had been struck in the tradition. Whereas Tacitus used the device of reporting the views of

[110] Tacitus closer to the original: Schwartz 1899, 1716; Tränkle 1969; Flach 1973b, 126-38. Dio closer to the original: Klingner 1954, 3-26; Syme 1958, I.273, II.690-1; Goodyear 1972, 155-6; Gartner 1975, 140-6; Manuwald 1979, 140-67 (a revised version of Manuwald 1973); Roddaz 1983, 85-6. For Tacitus as a possible source of Dio see Questa 1963, especially 63ff.; Solimeno Cipriano 1979. See also Giua 1983, 450-6; Pelling 1983, 225; Mehl 1981.

[111] The concluding phrases echo Thuc. 2.40.1.

[112] Cf. Pelling 1983, 225. In this passage two points are combined which are made separately by Tacitus (*Ann*.1.2.1, 3.7). This may as easily be the product of conflation by Dio as of dispersion by Tacitus (so Syme, loc.cit., n. 110).

[113] Tac., *Ann*. 1.9.1-3. Dio's first work had been on the dreams and portents which led Severus to hope that he might become emperor (73.23.1). He frequently reports portents, and both asserts himself and attributes to the protagonists belief in their predictive value. Cf. Liebeschuetz 1979, 227-9.

[114] The contrast may have been suggested to Dio by the allegation that Augustus had made Tiberius his successor for the sake of the unfavourable comparison (45.3; cf. Tac., *Ann* 1.10.7; Suet., *Tib*. 21.2-3).

contemporaries to avoid stating his own opinion, Dio's chief purpose was to make explicit his own judgement of Augustus. He has nothing to say here on the question of Augustus' motives during his rise to power, which was one of the principal issues in dispute between Tacitus' 'men of sense': Dio had already made it abundantly clear that he believed that Augustus had been motivated throughout by the desire to rule, and, unlike those to whom Tacitus attributes this opinion, he did not regard this as reprehensible. His concern here was to show how Augustus measured up to what he required of an emperor. As in the Agrippa-Maecenas debate and the narrative of Augustus' reign, the criteria which he used were those that the senatorial class had traditionally employed in assessing emperors' merits. The most important requirements were that emperors should respect what was now a much restricted concept of 'freedom' and should show clemency.

As far as 'freedom' was concerned, Dio gave Augustus his enthusiastic approval. In the narrative of his reign he had represented Augustus as behaving in this regard in complete conformity with the prescriptions for an ideal emperor which he had put into the mouth of Maecenas, and he reasserts this view here, when he accounts for the Romans' grief in terms of Augustus' merits as an emperor (43).[115] He begins by mentioning a number of aspects of Augustus' conduct which a Latin writer might have subsumed under the general heading of 'behaving like a citizen' (43.1).[116] These lead up to the claim that the regime was an ideal blend of monarchy and 'democracy', a striking new twist to the ancient doctrine of the 'mixed constitution' (43.4).[117] There is a formal inconsistency here with the earlier passages in which he had spoken of Augustus as creating only the semblance of 'democracy';[118] Dio's focus was now on Augustus the ideal emperor, not on the contrast between appearances and reality in his affairs. The contradiction is unimportant: Dio's words here are not to be taken as qualifying his view that real power rested exclusively with the emperor.

As we have seen, Augustus' record on clemency had been a source of difficulty to Dio throughout. The solution he adopts here (44.1-2) is the one for which he had prepared us in his treatment of the proscriptions and the pardon of Cinna, that Augustus' record as sole ruler showed that

[115] Manuwald 1979, 25, 141-5 is wrong to read the passage not as expressing Dio's own views about Augustus' qualities but as merely reporting views held at the time.
[116] Cf. Wallace-Hadrill 1982.
[117] This passage appears to be the only instance of this version of the 'mixed constitution' (though cf. Tac., *Agr.* 3.1): Aalders 1968, 120; Nippel 1980, 24. The commoner notion of monarchy as 'true democracy' was put into Maecenas' mouth by Dio (52.14.4); for this see Starr 1952/3; de Ste. Croix 1981, 323.
[118] See above, nn. 77, 85. A similar inconsistency occurs at 55.4.1, where he speaks of Augustus as wishing 'to be democratic'.

clemency was his true nature.[119] However, his language betrays his embarrassment: here alone he uses the device of reporting the view of Augustus' contemporaries as a means of avoiding making his own view explicit. He represents them as accepting, as Livia had hoped, that Augustus' harsh deeds in the civil wars had been performed under compulsion, but limits himself to the more cautious claim that 'one might more justly blame the circumstances themselves than him'. Once again, comparison with Tacitus suggests that Dio handled his source freely. The argument from necessity figures in Tacitus as a justification not for Augustus' harshness to his opponents but for his original resort to arms.[120] Tacitus makes those favourable to Augustus assert that after he became sole ruler a 'few matters were still dealt with by violence so that there might be quiet for the rest'.[121] This recalls Dio's language at 44.2, but that refers primarily to the civil war period, and Dio has chosen his words with such studied vagueness that it is left unclear whether he thinks any acts of violence occurred during the period of sole rule.

7. Conclusion

Two main themes run through Dio's account of Augustus. The first is the singlemindedness with which he pursued supreme power from the start of his career and the consummate duplicity which he deployed both in its pursuit and, after he had achieved his goal, in making it appear that his rule had men's free consent and was republican in character. The second is his excellence as a ruler. There is no fundamental conflict between these two themes, for Dio did not disapprove of Augustus' aspiration to monarchy or of his duplicity in this cause. However, a number of contradictions do occur, of which Dio's equivocations over Augustus' record on clemency are the most notable. To a great extent these are the product of the tension between two different facets of Dio's persona as a historian – the realist seeking to expose the truth about men's nature and actions and the political moralist who saw in Augustus the embodiment of the ideal emperor.

Bibliography

Aalders, G.J.D. 1968. *Die Theorie der gemischten Verfassung im Altertum* (Amsterdam).

[119] See above at nn. 65, 104; so also 56.38.1. For the contrast between Augustus' conduct in the civil wars and as emperor see Seneca, *Clem.* 1.9-11, who, however, takes his record as emperor not as revealing his true nature but as 'exhausted cruelty'.

[120] Tac., *Ann.* 1.9.3. Dio put this argument in the mouth of Maecenas (52.18.1) and Tiberius (56.36.2), using the same word *ananke* as at 55.21.4 and 56.44.1, but it is clear that he himself regarded it as merely a pretext.

[121] Tac., *Ann.* 1.9.5: *pauca admodum vi tractata quo ceteris quies esset.*

Ameling, W. 1984. 'Cassius Dio und Bithynien', *Epig. Anat.* 1, 123-38.
Avenarius, G. 1956. *Lukians Schrift zur Geschichtsschreibung* (Meisenheim).
Barnes, T.D. 1984. 'The composition of Cassius Dio's *Roman History*', *Phoenix* 38, 240-55.
Birley, A. 1971. *Septimius Severus* (London).
Bleicken, J. 1962. 'Der politische Standpunkt Dios gegenüber der Monarchie. Die Rede des Maecenas, Buch 52, 14-40', *Hermes* 90, 444-67.
Bowersock, G. 1965. rev. Millar 1964, *Gnomon* 37, 469-74.
Brunt, P.A. 1963. rev. H.D. Meyer, *Die Aussenpolitik des Augustus und die augusteische Dichtung* (Cologne, 1961), *Journ. Rom. Stud*, 53, 170-6.
———— 1984. 'The role of the senate in the Augustan regime', *Class. Quart.* 34, 423-44.
Diehl, E. 1911. *Die Vitae Vergilianae und ihre antiken Quellen* (Bonn).
Espinosa Ruiz, U. 1982. *Debate Agrippa-Mecenas en Dion Cassio* (Madrid).
Fechner, D. 1986. *Untersuchungen zu Cassius Dios Sicht der römischen Republik* (Hildesheim/Zurich/New York).
Flach, D. 1973a. 'Dios Platz in der kaiserzeitlichen Geschichtsschreibung', *Antike und Abendland* 18, 130-45.
———— 1973b. *Tacitus in der Tradition der antiken Geschichtschreibung* (Göttingen).
Gabba, E. 1955. 'Sulla "Storia romana" di Cassio Dione', *Riv. stor. ital.* 67, 289-333.
———— 1959. 'Storici greci dell'impero romano da Augusto ai Severi', ibid., 71, 361-81.
———— 1984. 'The historians and Augustus', in F. Millar and E. Segal, eds., *Caesar Augustus: Seven Aspects* (Oxford), 61-88.
Gärtner, H.A. 1975. *Beobachtungen zu Bauelementen in der antiken Historiographie besonders bei Livius und Caesar* (Wiesbaden).
Giua, M.A. 1981. 'Clemenza del sovrano e monarchia illuminata in Cassio Dione, 55, 14-22', *Athenaeum* 59, 317-37.
———— 1983. 'Augusto nel libro 56 della Storia Romana di Cassio Dione', ibid., 61, 439-56.
Goodyear, F.R.D. 1972. *The Annals of Tacitus, I: Annals I.1-54* (Cambridge).
Hammond, M. 1932. 'The significance of the speech of Maecenas in Dio Cassius, Book LII', *Trans. Am. Philol. Ass.*, 63, 88-102.
Hopkins, M.K. 1983. *Death and Renewal* (Cambridge).
Hornblower, J. 1981. *Hieronymus of Cardia* (Oxford).
Klingner, F. 1954. 'Tacitus über Augustus und Tiberius. Interpretationen zum Eingang der Annalen', *Sitz. Akad. Wien* 7, 1953 (Munich) (repr. Klingner, *Studien zur griechischen und römischen Literatur*, Zurich and Stuttgart, 1964, 624-58).
Kyhnitzsch, E. 1894. *De contionibus, quas Cassius Dio historiae suae intexuit, cum Thucydideis comparatis* (Diss. Leipzig).
Letta, C. 1979. 'La composizione dell'opera di Cassio Dione: cronologia e sfondo storico-politico', in *Ricerche di storiografia antica I: Ricerche di storiografia greca di età romana*, Biblioteca di studi antici 22 (Pisa), 117-89.
Liebeschuetz, J.H.W.G. 1979. *Continuity and Change in Roman Religion* (Oxford).
Litsch, E. 1893. *De Cassio Dione imitatore Thucydidis* (Diss. Freiburg).
Luce, T.J. 1977. *Livy: the composition of his History* (Princeton).
Manuwald, B. 1973. 'Cassius Dio und das "Totengericht" über Augustus bei Tacitus', *Hermes* 101, 352-74.

—— 1979. *Cassius Dio und Augustus* (Wiesbaden).
McKechnie, P. 1981. 'Cassius Dio's speech of Agrippa: a realistic alternative to imperial government', *Greece and Rome* 28, 150-5.
Mehl, A. 1981. 'Bemerkungen zu Dios und Tacitus' Arbeitsweise und zur Quellenlage im "Totengericht" über Augustus', *Gymnasium* 88, 54-64.
Millar, F.G.B. 1964. *A Study of Cassius Dio* (Oxford).
Nawijn, W. 1931. *Index Graecitatis* (vol. 5 of U.P. Boissevain, ed., *Cassii. Dionis Cocceiani Historiarum Romanarum quae supersunt*, Berlin, 1895-1931).
Nippel, W. 1980. *Mischverfassungstheorie und Verfassungsrealität in Antike und früher Neuzeit* (Stuttgart).
Pelling, C.B.R. 1979. 'Plutarch's method of work in the Roman Lives', *Journ. Hellenic Stud.* 99, 74-96.
—— 1982. rev. G. Zecchini, *Cassio Dione e la guerra gallica di Cesare* (Milan, 1978), *Class. Rev.* 32, 146-8.
—— 1983. rev. Manuwald 1979, *Gnomon*, 55, 221-6.
Questa, C. 1957. 'Tecnica biografica e tecnica annalistica nei ll. LIII-LXIII di Cassio Dione', *Studi Urbinati* 31, n.s. B 1-2, 37-53.
Questa, C. 1963. *Studi sulle fonti degli Annales di Tacito* (Tome).
Rawson, E. 1986. 'Cassius and Brutus: the memory of the Liberators', in I.S. Moxon, J.D. Smart, A.J. Woodman, eds., *Past Perspectives* (Cambridge), 101-19.
Roddaz, J.M. 1983. 'De César à Auguste: l'image de la monarchie chez un historien du siècle des Sévères. Réflexions sur l'oeuvre de Dion Cassius, à propos d'ouvrages récents', *Rev. Et. Anc.* 85, 67-87.
Ste. Croix, G.E.M. de 1981. *The Class Struggle in the Ancient Greek World* (London).
Schwartz, E. 1899. 'Cassius' (40), Pauly-Wissowa, *Realenzyklopädie* 3. 1684-1722 (repr. in Schwartz, *Griechische Geschichtsschreiber*, Leipzig 1957, 394-450).
Solimeno Cipriano, A. 1979. 'Tacito fonte di Cassio Dione?', *Rend. Accad. Napoli* 54, 3-18.
Starr, C.G. 1952/3. 'The perfect democracy of the Roman Empire', *Am. Hist. Rev.* 58, 1-16.
Stekelenburg, A.V. van 1971. *De Redevoeringen bij Cassius Dio* (Delft).
Syme, Sir Ronald 1958. *Tacitus* (Oxford), 2 vols.
Tränkle, H. 1969. 'Augustus bei Tacitus, Cassius Dio und dem älteren Plinius', *Wien. Stud.* 82, 108-30.
Vrind, G. 1923. *De Cassii Dionis vocabulis quae ad ius publicum pertinent* (The Hague).
—— 1926. 'De Cassii Dionis Historiis', *Mnemosyne* 54, 321-47.
Walbank, F.W. 1965. *Speeches in Greek Historians*, The Third J.L. Myres Lecture (Oxford) (repr. Walbank, *Selected Papers* Cambridge, 1986, 242-61).
Wallace-Hadrill, A., 1981. 'The emperor and his virtues', *Historia* 30, 298-323.
—— 1982. 'Civilis princeps: between citizen and king', *Journ. Rom. Stud.* 72, 32-48.
Zawadski, R. 1983. 'Die Konzeption der römischen Staatsverfassung in der politischen Doktrin des Cassius Dio', *Anal. Cracov.* 15, 270-318.

5

Reading Female Flesh: *Amores* 3.1

Beauty is the lover's gift.

Congreve, *The Way of the World*.

We are least willing to give up the habits we have the most lovingly treasured. Reading the Augustan elegists as love poets, and using their poems as a window into the life of society women in the Rome of Augustus is one of them. It lets us think the Romans are like us, not all serious, grand and noble like Virgil, but prone to romantic passion, liable to make mistakes, even rather absurd. The knowledge that this poetry is deeply in debt to Hellenistic models does not appear to have shaken our propensity to take it at face value in any very serious way, to judge not just from the books on Roman women which make it their starting point but also from prevailing literary interpretations, as Maria Wyke shows in her essay. On this view, the detection of parallels between the elegists and their models becomes an important academic exercise, which nevertheless affects the assessment of the Latin poems themselves only when it is felt to have been taken to excess. It thus exposes the fact that the basis of judgement is the modern assumption that the highest form of literary achievement lies in originality; by this standard, however, ancient writers become immediately problematic, and invite an inescapably patronising kind of critical judgement.

The Roman love poets are particularly in danger of misinterpretation. In British schools at the moment, the love poems of Catullus – the short ones of course – are often a student's first introduction to Latin poetry, and make an immediate appeal which simply sidesteps the real interpretative issue. The same student a few years later will probably expect Ovid's *Ars Amatoria* to provide a titillating read instead of a clever twist on the practice of writing love-poetry as well as the values of the solemn Augustan regime.

For all the striking impressions that Roman love elegy at the end of the republic and the beginning of the empire may make on a modern reader, however, there is little sign that male attitudes to women had really changed. In certain ways a few women at the top levels of Roman

society behaved in freer ways, and in some respects their legal position
improved by modern standards;[1] but the same stereotypes and the
same male expectations on the whole prevailed, at least to judge from
the literature of the end of the first century, which displays a degree of
misogyny as striking as any of the affective sentiments that modern
readers find in the love poets.[2] This situation of conflicting and uneven
evidence is familiar to anyone who tries to study ancient women; thus
scholars in this instance turn from the literary texts to legal evidence
or to philosophical writers and moralists such as Plutarch and
Epictetus;[3] a similar apparent discrepancy between different kinds of
source material exists in the case of women in the classical Greek
period, where the evidence of Athenian law as revealed in the works of
the orators appears at odds with the portrayal of women in Greek
drama. All this is well known, yet it continues to call forth a mass of
writing on the subject mostly directed at defending one position or
another. For if not all, then certainly the majority of the practitioners
write from a feminist standpoint, and often enough with an overt
purpose.

One of the later chapters in this volume (Sr. Charles Murray, on
'History and Faith', Chapter 7 below) raises in acute form the same
problem of how far a historian can or should be engaged with his
material, that is, committed to a certain point of view. The feminist
theologians, of course, are doubly engaged and thus present a
particularly interesting example (p.175 below); moreover, they can find
in Christian writing and doctrine a persistent image of women also
enshrined in Christian practice which their own commitment to the
feminist position forces them to deconstruct (see also Cameron,
Chapter 8 below).

A crucial task in any attempt to resolve these problems must be a
closer reading of the literary source material, above all when it
actually consists of works of 'literature'. By this I mean to make a
utilitarian distinction between the conventional use of the term
'literary sources' by historians to denote texts written by individual
authors or collective groups of texts such as the Hippocratic corpus,
discussed by Helen King (Chapter 1 above), whatever their nature, in
distinction with epigraphic (inscriptional), legal or other documentary
material and a narrower and conventional definition of 'literature' to
mean imaginative fictions both in poetry and in prose; I do not mean to
prejudge a general definition of literature. Maria Wyke is not primarily

---

[1] See recently E. Cantarella, *Pandora's Daughters* (Eng. trans., Baltimore, 1986),
135ff. and (much better) Jane Gardner, *Women in Roman Law and Society* (London,
1986).

[2] Cantarella, 143ff.

[3] In general see the chapter by P. Veyne in P. Ariès and G. Duby, eds., *A History of
Private Life* (Eng. trans. Cambridge, Mass. 1987).

concerned to argue this or that case about the social role of Augustan women, but rather to show how at least some of the texts commonly used for that purpose might in fact be read. It could be argued that such a reading of Ovid's portrait of Elegy and Tragedy in *Amores* 3.1 does not license us to read all Roman elegy in this way, since in the first place Ovid comes late in the sequence of Augustan elegists and is a writer both peculiarly conscious of the tradition already established and ready to capitalise on it; moreover, here he quite clearly writes about poetry, not about women, real or otherwise. Yet, as Maria Wyke shows here, this poem can nevertheless point to better ways of reading those elegies which do seem to be 'about' real women.[4] A similar point is made about some of the evidence commonly used in studies of women in early Christianity in my own chapter (below, Chapter 8), where again a realist approach to the source material has on the whole prevailed, at least outside criticism of the Gospels themselves (for which see Murray, Chapter 7 below).

Is Roman poetry particularly in need of this kind of literary analysis? It would seem so, to judge from the consensus of modern views outlined by Wyke. Greek literature has certainly, and for recognisable reasons, attracted a far less realist criticism in recent years, both in general and in particular on its presentation of women. That is not to insist that realist criticism is wrong, but rather that its present dominance in Latin literary study would probably be easier to justify if it were in fact tempered by a more serious and continuing challenge from other quarters. The evident presence of that hostility which we have already noted towards 'modern' critical approaches (above, p.2) is not after all a healthy situation, and it certainly does not help historians to use literary texts with any confidence. 'The poet's task – is to invent a reader':[5] just so, and the reader's task is to read well.

Reading Female Flesh: *Amores* 3.1

Maria Wyke

I. Liberated ladies

Augustan elegy has set a seductive trap for historians of women's lives in antiquity. For, written in an autobiographical mode, it appears to confide to its readers a poet's personal confession of love for a woman

---

[4] See further Wyke, 'Written women: Propertius' *scripta puella*', *JRS* 77 (1987), 47-61.
[5] W.J. Ong, *Interfaces of the Word* (Ithaca, NY, 1977), 76ff.

114   *Maria Wyke*

who is not his wife.[1] Read uncritically, such love poetry has been
employed to confirm the existence in Augustan Rome of a whole
movement of sophisticated and sexually liberated ladies, as in J.P.V.D.
Balsdon's study *Roman Women: their history and habits* (1962) and,
more recently, Sarah Pomeroy's *Goddesses, Whores, Wives and Slaves*
(1975).[2] Propertius' Cynthia, Tibullus' Delia and Nemesis, at times
even Ovid's Corinna, have been extracted from their poetic world to
become representative of a cultured society 'où l'émancipation
féminine se traduit avant tout par la recherche d'une liberté dans
l'amour'.[3] Working from a different perspective, Ronald Syme has
suggested a more cautious assessment of the elegiac heroine's place in
history. Although proposing that Ovid's poetry has much to offer the
historian, Syme does not himself employ the *Amores* as source
material for the construction of an Augustan demi-monde. Yet he still
sets out the social conditions in which he sees elegy's ladies operating;
a post-war period which would have witnessed a number of women
reduced to a marginal existence through calamity or a love of
pleasure.[4]

    Literary critics have recognised that other prominent features of
Augustan elegy conflict with its apparently autobiographical narrative
structure. Not only is elegy's personal confession of passion articulated
in a manner which is highly stylised and conventional, but Hellenistic
and Roman traditions for erotic writing also contribute clearly to the
formation of the world in which the elegiac hero and heroine move.
Once recognised, such discrepancies undermine any attempt to
construct a simple relation between elegiac verse and the world in
which it was composed.[5] Augustan elegy has therefore been identified
as political fiction. But the representations of women which occur in it
have not been subjected to the same rigorous critical scrutiny. Most
commonly, critics recognise the presence of considerable artifice in the
elegiac texts, yet continue to treat their female figures as belonging to
a special category of discourse; a window onto the reality of female
lives at Rome. The reader is allowed to move along an unobstructed
pathway from woman of fiction to woman of flesh.

    An early example of the critical strategies employed to isolate the
elegiac *puella* from poetic artifice and to safeguard her status as a
living individual can be found in Jean-Paul Boucher's *Études sur
Properce: problèmes d'inspiration et d'art* (1965). There, despite his
considerable interest in the impact of Hellenistic literary practices on

[1] For 'the seductive trap of confessional poetry' and the misunderstandings such
poetry generates see respectively Bright 1978, 99 and Veyne 1983, 10.
[2] Balsdon 1962, 191-2 and 226; Pomeroy 1975, 172.
[3] Fau 1978, 103 and cf. Grimal 1963, esp. his chapter 'L'Amour et les poètes'.
[4] Syme 1978, 200-3.
[5] See e.g. Du Quesnay 1973, 2; Veyne 1983, 11-12; Griffin 1985, ix.

the Propertian corpus, the author concluded his studies by trying to construct a plausible portrait of a Roman woman out of Cynthia's poetic characteristics. A chapter entitled 'Poésie et vérité' conveniently provided a bridge between formalistic accounts of Propertian poetic techniques and romantic readings of the narrative's heroine. Thus, to read the titles Cynthia, Delia, Nemesis and Corinna as pseudonyms of living individuals, the textual characteristics of a fictive female are frequently disengaged from their context in a poetry-book and reshaped into the detailed portrait of a girl-friend by whom the text was inspired. A physique has been constructed for Cynthia: 'She had a milk-and-roses complexion. Her long blonde hair was either over-elaborately groomed or else, in less guarded moments, it strayed over her forehead in disarray ... Those attractive eyes were black. She was tall, with long slim fingers.'[6] So constructed, Cynthia is then positioned in the social formation of the Augustan epoch; the female beloved is read as referring out of the poetic sphere to a specific 'emancipated' woman of the late first century BC. Out of the elegiac text is born the historical reality of a liberated lady.

The difficulty involved in assimilating *all* the written women of elegy to living, liberated ladies has been recognised, however, and the procedure has not therefore always been adopted uniformly. For, at least in the case of the *Amores*, its inappropriateness has been generally acknowledged. Most commentators would agree with the view that the Ovidian Corinna does not have 'un carattere precisamente individuabile ed è priva di autenticità, perché in realtà non esiste'.[7] Corinna's status as a particular Augustan girl-friend has been challenged largely because the text in which she is portrayed is read as a mischievous travesty of earlier love elegy. The Tibullan corpus has been classified as manifestly more 'sincere', yet Nemesis too has aroused some suspicion and one critic has proposed that both Nemesis *and* Delia be regarded as essentially literary creations because their separate characteristics satisfy the demands of a poetic polarity; Delia is goddess of Day, Nemesis daughter of Night.[8] But in *The Latin Love Poets: from Catullus to Horace* (1980), Oliver Lyne questioned the need for any of these concessions to poetic artifice. He found no compelling reason to doubt that Nemesis and Delia were pseudonyms of particular women and even attempted tentatively to reappropriate Corinna for realism by drawing attention to a physique which John Sullivan had earlier assembled: 'physically she was *candida* with rosy cheeks, tall and dignified ... with small feet and an

[6] Sullivan 1976, 80 and cf. Boucher 1965, 468-9.
[7] Bertini 1983, xvi. Cf. for instance Grimal 1963, 156; Bright 1978, 104; Barsby 1979, 15-16. The question of whether Corinna had an identity independently of the elegiac text is insoluble for Du Quesnay 1973, 2-3 and of no literary interest for Sullivan 1961, 522-8.
[8] Bright 1978, 99-123.

abundance of fine closely-curled hair.'[9] The fabric of a poetic text is again turned into a mistress's flesh.

The general hazards of such a critical enterprise, of reading liberated ladies out of literary discourses, have not gone unobserved. For example, the publication of Paul Veyne's work *L'Élégie érotique romaine: l'amour, la poésie et l'occident* (1983) has been welcomed for the unrelenting pressure with which it points to the artifice of elegy's narrator and narrative subject (lover and beloved), and for the timely warning it thereby gives to all those Anglo-Saxon classicists set on reviving the practice of reading elegy as an expressive and realistic representation of its authors' lives and loves.[10] But love poetry continues to be beset by Romantic theories of literary production: in the introduction to his collection of essays *Latin Poets and Roman Life* (1985), Jasper Griffin pictures Augustan poetry in terms of emotional truths and erotic realities to be glimpsed behind a thin coating of conventional poetic devices. Poetic artifice can now be readily accommodated to autobiographical narratives for it simply raises the realities of Roman life to the level of idealised art: Cynthia is a profit-making courtesan over whom the heroines of myth cast a glittering sheen; stylised depictions of female nakedness constitute transposed reflections of encounters with professionals in Rome.[11]

Such conflicting or inconsistent readings of elegy's female figures have an established place in twentieth-century classical scholarship and are clearly not yet resolved. Ever since the call in the 1950s for a clear account of the respective roles played by *realer Wirklichkeit* and *dichterischen Spiel* in the production of the elegiac text,[12] reading elegy's written women has been exposed as a problematic practice. For example, Hans-Peter Stahl's recent contribution to the literature on the Propertian corpus, *Propertius: 'Love' and 'War'* (1985), reveals the critical inconsistencies which are often at work. Stahl recognises that Cynthia possesses 'literary' qualities, admits nevertheless that his own work is constructed from a naïve standpoint, and leaves it to his reader to draw an appropriate line between Augustan reality and elegiac literariness. But the structure of his book does not otherwise assist such an enterprise. For neither recognition nor admission appears until the last footnote of Stahl's fifth chapter, while throughout the main text frequent reference is made to two formative experiences of love and war in Propertius' life – a torturing love for Cynthia and the massacre of Perusia. The reader of Stahl's book is actively directed to

---

[9] Lyne 1980, 239-40 argues that 'a reasonable picture does emerge from the poems' of Corinna and draws attention to, but does not quote, the physique assembled by Sullivan in 1961, 524 n.5. For a living Corinna cf. Fau 1978, 112 and Green 1982, 22-5. See also the more cautious arguments of McKeown 1987.

[10] F. Cairns, *TLS*, 4 October 1985, 1118.

[11] Griffin 1985, 139 and 110.

[12] Most notably by Allen in 1950a and 1950b.

look out of the Propertian corpus to the realities of a woman's love-life in Augustan Rome.

Thus despite accounts which foreground the artifice of elegiac poetry, many critics still read out from the female subjects of its discourse to specific liberated ladies. Romantic approaches to literary eroticism are both persistent and pervasive. Within the arena of this debate elegiac representations of the female form deserve particular scrutiny, since the critical strategy of reading written women rests referentially on the construction of an Augustan girl-friend and her body out of the anatomy of poetic texts. Within the confines of this article I propose, therefore, to examine a single poem, *Amores* 3.1, because it constitutes a point in the corpus of Augustan elegy where the text itself signals demonstrably and humorously that the female form can bear a reading as political fiction. But the physique there assembled incorporates many attributes of the elegiac *puella* and is located in a poem which encourages its readers to look out to other modes of representing the female form and back at the role of the *puella* in articulating elegy's poetic and political concerns. So *Amores* 3.1 may also provide clues to the operations of female representation elsewhere in love elegy and have important implications for reading Cynthia, Delia, Nemesis and Corinna.

I also propose, in the course of investigating the narrative methods of *Amores* 3.1, to employ the term 'The Elegiac Woman'. As a means of signifying singly or collectively the representations of women in the elegiac corpus, it functions as a useful corrective practice. While the titles Cynthia, Delia, Nemesis and Corinna are all available to be read as proper names or pseudonyms, the term 'The Elegiac Woman' constantly identifies elegy's female figures not as girl-friends but as narrative subjects. It also draws attention to the bond between those written women, their common generic ancestry and their life in a cycle of poetic eroticism.[13]

II. Elegia

The scene of *Amores* 3.1 is set in the vicinity of a cave.[14] The narrator (as poet) recalls his encounter there with two writing-practices in female form; Elegia and Tragoedia. He describes their appearance and comportment and a debate in which each woman advocates her own mode of poetic production, denigrating or dismissing the other. Eventually the narrator adopts Elegia, however temporarily, as his Muse. Thus the third and final book of Ovid's *Amores* gets under way.[15]

---

[13] The term was deployed in this way in Wyke 1984.

[14] References to and quotations from the *Amores* follow Kenney 1965.

[15] The question of what relationship holds between the first and second editions of the *Amores* does not have a substantial bearing on my readings of 3.1. Cameron 1968 argues that the second edition constitutes little more than a shortened version of the first.

Female flesh as poetics

The manner in which Ovid has here depicted female flesh – as if poetic genres were proud possessors of a human anatomy – has been cited by a Romantic critic as an example of how poets' encounters with naked prostitutes at Rome are raised to the level of art by the application of a thin brushstroke of mythology or allegory. 'The picture of a Roman man about town, running an eye over the girls on offer in some louche establishment' is often visible beneath a dignifying veneer of appropriate poetic devices.[16] Others have read the female flesh with which Elegia is endowed rather differently: 3.1 has readily been accepted by some commentators as depicting not a prostitute but an elegiac poetics. The poem is one of a whole series scattered throughout the corpus of Augustan elegy which maps out a debate over styles of writing. On this occasion, however, the terrain is not Helicon's slopes, but female physiques.[17] It is worth dwelling for a moment on the second of these approaches to *Amores* 3.1, since critics are so rarely prepared to read female flesh as poetic fiction. Clearly that practice is acceptable here because the flesh is labelled 'Elegy'.

Amores 3.1 is viewed as principally concerned with a stylistic contrast first expounded in the polemical works of Callimachus as an opposition, in poetic practices, between the *lepton* and the *pachu*. The Latin literary-critical terminology for this *Stilkampf* was then established in 'neoteric' poetry, further developed in Virgil's *Eclogues* and frequently deployed in the Propertian corpus.[18] In the context of 3.1, the advocacy of Fine Poetry is constructed round the dramatic device of a contest between two women. But, entitled Elegia and Tragoedia, these women have only a precarious signification as individuals, so that a catalogue of their physical features functions more importantly as a catalogue of stylistic practices. The attributes of poetic genres are made flesh and women are displayed as modes of male discourse. Every aspect of Ovid's women – their shape, comportment and speech – is constructed in accordance with a Callimachean apologetics, and everywhere the reader is required to unite these women with issues of poetic production: 'The point throughout depends on the simple device of treating these two personifications as human beings and at the same time as poetic genres.'[19] Thus even the cave before which the women come to play out their struggle for an author reproduces the topography of the poetic programme with which Propertius introduced *his* third poetry-book,

[16] Griffin 1985, 105.
[17] See especially Schrijvers 1976. Cf. Reitzenstein 1935; Wimmel 1960, 295-7; Berman 1975, 14-20.
[18] See Wimmel 1960, *passim*. On the Propertian corpus cf. Quadlbauer 1968 and 1970.
[19] Lee 1962, 169. Cf. Bertini 1983, 227.

thereby setting out Ovid's work for comparison.[20]
The narrator describes the first woman's approach:

> uenit odoratos Elegia nexa capillos,
> et, puto, pes illi longior alter erat.
> forma decens, uestis tenuissima, uultus amantis,
> et pedibus uitium causa decoris erat. (3.1.7-10)

> (She came – Elegy – her scented curls bound up,
> and, I suspect, one foot longer than the other:
> well-formed, finely dressed, a lover's look,
> imperfect movement occasioning elegance.)

Elegia is endowed with the body of the Elegiac Woman: 'Mademoiselle Elégie ressemble à tout point à la bien-aimée chantée par les poètes élégiaques.'[21] The hairstyle, outline, dress and expression catalogued in the hexameter verses 7 and 9 all reproduce attributes ascribed elsewhere to elegy's beloveds. When Cynthia first makes a physical appearance in the Propertian corpus, her hair is elaborately styled and perfumed, her dress is of fine Coan silk, and she possesses an ornamented *forma* (1.2.1-8).[22] The affinity between Elegia and the Elegiac Woman is disclosed, moreover, by the reappearance of Elegia's attributes in the two poems directly following *Amores* 3.1, where physical features are assembled for an Ovidian *puella*: her look is full of erotic promise (2.2.83), her dress is delicate (2.2.36), her body defined by *forma* and *decens* (3.3.7-8).

To the attributes of a beauty, however, the pentameter verses 8 and 10 attach an incongruous limp. Accustomed to the physical characteristics usually allotted to the elegiac beloved, a reader would expect this *puella* to possess feet which were snowy-white or slight. A reminder arrives at *Amores* 3.3.7: *pes erat exiguus – pedis est artissima forma*. The Elegiac Woman's body has been awkwardly reshaped to serve poetic concerns. Now entitled Elegia and supplied with elegiac feet (matching the unevenness of elegiac verse), this comic representation of a female form has 'un caractère nettement fictif'.[23] In particular, the allocation to this woman of unequal feet demonstrates that here at least a female body has been shaped to suit an elegiac poetic programme, because physically they constitute a defect (*uitium*), stylistically an asset (*decor*).

In the pentameter verses *pes* signals ambiguously both human and metrical feet. But some critics have observed that such ambiguities are

---

[20] See Berman 1975, 15-16 and Morgan 1977, 17-18.
[21] Schrijvers 1976, 415.
[22] In the first poem of the *Monobiblos*, nothing is ascribed to the name *Cynthia* except a pair of eyes and the capacity to captivate.
[23] Schrijvers 1976, 416.

also generated by the language of the hexameter verses. So *forma* and *tenuissima* are recognised to be as applicable to a collection of words as they are to a woman. Guy Lee, for example, retains the ambiguity of these terms with translations such as 'she had style'.[24] The delicacy which *tenuissima* suggests is read as qualifying the clothing of a Callimachean discourse, since *tenuis* is a well-documented signifier of the writing-style which Callimachus had designated *lepton*.[25]

The vocabulary in which Elegia is formulated as flesh is thus allowed to point to her as being also a way of speaking, a mode of poetic composition. But, elsewhere, part of that vocabulary delineates the Elegiac Woman. So the question then arises whether other love elegies also present the female body in ambiguous terms. In the second poem of the *Monobiblos* for example, where Propertius first sets out the features of his Elegiac Woman, she too possesses clothing that is *tenuis*, and a body defined by *forma*. The Propertian *puella* is charged with an excessive use of ornament in a poem whose style is paradoxically ornate and whose central theme has been identified as artifice itself.[26] Since there is every reason to suppose that – as the subject of Propertian art – the female form is an appropriate site for the expression of artistic concerns, what theoretical justification is there for depriving Cynthia of literary-critical possibilities, when they are welcomed for Elegia?[27]

So in *Amores* 3.1, the flesh of the Elegiac Woman is reproduced and recalled in the hexameter verses 7 and 9. In the pentameters (vv.8 and 10), it is provided additionally with unequal feet. The comic incongruity reveals that here the beloved's body has been placed openly at the service of poetic concerns. Since the elegiac metre requires that the stylistic asset of foot-shortening be put into practice at the two moments when Elegia's physical defect is being pronounced, at least at this point in the elegiac corpus the body of a woman may be read uncontentiously as the anatomy of a text.

Tragoedia has now arrived in hot pursuit:

> uenit et ingenti uiolenta Tragoedia passu:
>   fronte comae torua, palla iacebat humi;
> laeua manus sceptrum late regale mouebat,
>   Lydius alta pedum uincla cothurnus erat. (3.1.11-14)

> (She came too in grand strides – impassioned Tragedy:
>   braids draping a darksome brow, her gown the earth,

---

[24] Lee 1968, 119.

[25] Bertini 1983, 227; Lee 1962, 169. On *tenuis* see also Quadlbauer 1968, 95-6; Fedeli 1985, 54 and 59.

[26] See for instance Curran 1975.

[27] Curran 1975, for example, distinguishes the 'real' woman of Prop. 1.2.1-8 from the artist's creation which he claims the remainder of the poem is advocating.

left hand wielding wide the princely sceptre,
a Lydian boot her foot's high prop.)

The second party to the *Stilkampf* is not the recipient of the favourable stylistic appraisal suggested earlier by *decens* and *tenuissima*. But once again the attributes of a writing-practice are fleshed out and a female figure constructed to suit a Callimachean polemic. As symbols of a Greco-Roman tragic tradition, *palla, sceptrum* and *cothurnus* have already made an appearance in *Amores* 2.18.15-16.[28] There they were associated with the narrator (as producer of tragic discourse). Here they are associated with a narrative practice personified. Thus *uiolenta* is suggestive of both human behaviour and dramatic technique.[29] In every way, Tragoedia is shaped to compare and contrast with Elegia. While Elegia's limp mimics the movement of elegiac couplets, Tragoedia's enormous stride embodies the grandeur of the tragic metres. Similarly her hairstyle, *fronte comae torua*, characterises the diction of a dignified writing-style.[30] Female flesh and its paraphernalia evidently operate here as a means of differentiating one poetic discourse from another. But if Tragoedia dramatises the *pachu*, then the body of the Elegiac Woman has entered the Ovidian narrative here because it is a manifestation of the *lepton*.

After Tragoedia has advocated her own production in terms which are both moralistic and appropriately passionate, the narrator next recalls her comportment and that of her rival for an author's attentions:[31]

hactenus, et mouit pictis innixa cothurnis
    densum caesarie terque quaterque caput.
altera, si memini, limis subrisit ocellis;
    fallor, an in dextra myrtea uirga fuit? (3.1.31-34)

(Thus far, and propped on her ornamented boots she bowed
    three times and four her thick-fleeced head.
The other (if I remember) stole a peek and giggled –
    am I wrong, or in her right hand was there a myrtle twig?)

Each woman is attired with an emblem of poetic practice (*cothurnis* and the *myrtea uirga*), and each behaves in a manner appropriate to her own literary production. Tragoedia nods majestically like an Homeric Zeus. Elegia flirts in the manner of the Elegiac Woman at the races in *Amores* 3.2.83: *risit et argutis quiddam promisit ocellis*. Diction matches behaviour as a means of differentiating levels of

[28] See Brandt 1963, ad loc. and cf. Reitzenstein 1935, 83.

[29] Cf. Brandt 1963, ad *Am*. 3.1.11.

[30] For the tragic tone of *torua* cf. Pacuvius Trag. 36 and 37, and Accius *Trag*. 223.

[31] Schrijvers 1976, 417-21 offers a detailed account of the speech as incorporating a parody of tragic diction.

discourse: *caesarie* is a highly poetic word, in Ovid's work found otherwise only in hexameter verse; *limis* does not usually belong in literary language.[32] Thus two opposed poetic traditions are demarcated by the two different ways in which these fictive females move.

So far in this reading of *Amores* 3.1, attention has been drawn to the poem as a narrative of conflicting literary interests in which female forms have been shaped to suit a poetic purpose. The body of the elegiac *puella* then enters such a discourse as a device to signify one particular practice of writing. A similar strategy is in operation when, in the course of her plea for production, Elegia mentions Corinna and the ease with which her pupil learned to slip through front doors (vv.43-52). For in the context of that speech (vv.35-60), Corinna functions demonstrably as a signifier of erotic (specifically Ovidian) discourse and therefore may be read as representative of elegiac fictions. First, the doors through which Corinna once stole have already been identified as the property of elegy's producers rather than as an obstacle facing Augustan lovers (vv.35-42), and secondly, the woman who taught Corinna is subsequently identified wholly as text (vv.53-58).

In the first part of her speech Elegia concedes:

non ego contulerim sublimia carmina nostris:
obruit exiguas regia uestra fores. (3.1.39-40)

(I would not set towering poetry beside my own;
your palace eclipses tiny doorways.)

The contrast between palace entrances and house doors is set within another opposition: Tragoedia is accused of being perpetually *grauis* (v.36), while Elegia boldly confesses that she is *leuis* (v.41). The signification of the *grauis/leuis* opposition is drawn away from the level of female dispositions and towards the level of writing-styles by frequent references in the course of the passage to poetic production – compare *carmina* here (v.39), with *uerbis* (v.35), *numeris* (v.37) and *uersibus* (v.38). Furthermore, the reader will recognise the *grauis/leuis* opposition within which the doorways are described as the terminology of a Callimachean polemic already so used in *Amores* 1.1. There weapons were to be narrated *graui numero* (v.1), but beloveds (either boy or girl) *numeris leuioribus* (v.19). Thus the doors are positioned in a literary-critical framework signalled in vv.39-40 by *sublimia* and *exiguas*.[33] The word *sublimia* is of particular interest. Its etymology is obscure but the possibility of its derivation from *sub limen* immediately connects it as a stylistic evaluation with the subsequent

---

[32] Brandt 1963, ad *Am*. 3.1.33; Reitzenstein 1935, 83-4; Schrijvers 1976, 421.
[33] For the array of literary-critical terms cf. Lee 1962, 169-70; Schrijvers 1976, 422.

discussion of doors. In such a context, *regia* and *fores* signify majestic and modest arenas of discourse respectively, as do allusions to streams of Helicon elsewhere.[34] So, since the royal palace constitutes the scenic backdrop for a tragic performance with no status independently of a tragic text, the house door becomes merely a property employed in elegy's production.

In the last part of her speech, Elegia offers three examples of how she has suffered for love (vv.53-58). The personification is continued through the use of active verbs such as *non uerita* (v.54) and *memini* (v.55), but the circumstances suffered – being pinned to a door, hidden in the folds of a dress, or submerged in water as an unwelcome birthday present – are appropriate for a tablet of wax, ludicrous for a woman. In each case, a comic mismatch between *puella* and love poem arises in which Elegy's status as text is paramount.[35] For the first of these examples identifies her clearly as a literary practice, a poetical scroll, because she is *legi* (v.54). Thus Elegia is first presented in *Amores* 3.1 as a living woman of flesh – although even that flesh is incongruously elegiac in its structure. But by the poem's close, the woman of flesh has been playfully reshaped into a work of elegiac art.

The centre-piece of Elegia's speech, vv.43-52, recalls both her own success as a *magistra amoris* and her prize pupil Corinna. But, as we have seen, this teacher is also a poetic text and her speech an avowal of a Callimachean poetics. So Corinna and the *custos* she has deceived constitute past samples of the writing-practice Elegia advocates and stand in opposition to the *facta uirorum* (v.25) for which Tragoedia has called. Both the elegiac beloved's demeanour and circumstances are fashioned in order to signal past poems of the elegiac corpus. First, memories of her *tunica uelata soluta* (v.51) recall Corinna's negligent appearance at *Amores* 1.5.9: *tunica uelata recincta*. Thus, in a poem which puts female flesh on the poetic genre Elegy, physical features ascribed elsewhere to the Elegiac Woman – most notably the first detailed depictions of both Cynthia *and* Corinna – are constantly recalled. Secondly, the elegiac beloved's past circumstances are so articulated as to survey the elegiacs of Tibullus. For Elegia claims to have provided Corinna with the sort of protection offered by Venus in Tibullus 1.2,[36] and sets the scene for that claim by reproducing terms which featured prominently in the first and last poems of that Tibullan poetry-book, namely *rusticus* from Tibullus 1.1.8 and *lasciuus Amor* from Tibullus 1.10.57. Similarly, Elegia's ability to render a *ianua laxa* (v.46) recalls poems by all three Augustan elegists. Centred on the beloved's closed door, these poems include Tibullus 1.2, Propertius

---

[34] See for instance Virgil, *Ecl.* 6 and Prop. 2.10.
[35] As Brandt 1963, ad *Am.* 3.1.57: 'hat nun das Mädchen weiter nichts als ein liebesgedicht bekommen'.
[36] As Reitzenstein 1935, 84.

1.16, Ovid *Amores* 1.6 and 2.19. Thus Corinna and her front door are constructed to recall an array of elegiac poems and function as signifiers of a poetic tradition opposed to the tragic narration of kings and palace entrances.

Finally, to conclude the narrative of *Amores* 3.1 and introduce a third book of love-elegies, the adoption of Elegia as a practice of writing is recounted (vv.61-70). Now her attractions are described solely in terms of poetic production and a Callimachean poetics. For she is said to grant *nostro uicturum nomen amori* (v.65). Elegiac composition is chosen not as the result of a pressing, romantic commitment to a *puella*, but out of a desire for lasting fame. In *Epigr*. 7(9) Pfeiffer, Callimachus had already suggested that since Theaetetus followed a clear poetic path towards the composition of epigrams rather than tragedies Greece would for ever sing his skill.

The theme of great glory arising paradoxically out of slight poetry features frequently in Latin literature descended from the Callimachean tradition.[37] Consequently, as a recipient of lasting acclaim, the Ovidian *amor* may be read as equivalent to a Callimachean *sophiê*: love is literary eroticism and its skilful composition. Thus by the close of *Amores* 3.1, the encounter between two female figures has been clearly identified as a contest between styles of writing, and love is understood to be a poetic activity. The only respect in which Ovid has veered from the clear path of Callimachus' poetics is in his suggestion that he has some interest in, and will shortly embark upon, tragic composition. The Elegiac Woman, as the embodiment of Callimachus' *lepton*, is only temporarily the poet's practice. For, at some point, Ovid does produce a tragedy – the now lost *Medea*.

Thus *Amores* 3.1 provides poetic genres with female flesh in order to dramatise a Callimachean opposition between poetic practices. But Corinna, along with her front door, enters the debate as an example of elegiac composition in the requisite Callimachean manner and, throughout the poem, the attributes and activities of the Elegiac Woman are recalled and subsumed under personified Elegy. The text sets up a series of witty mismatches between what is appropriate to the depiction of an elegiac *puella* and the description of an elegiac poem: supplied now with elegiac feet and subjected to a variety of indignities, the body of the Elegiac Woman has become a site for the humorous expression of Callimachean concerns.

Female flesh as politics

Amores 3.1 is not concerned exclusively, however, with issues of poetic practice and their articulation through representations of the female

[37] See for instance Quadlbauer 1968, 96-7 on Prop. 3.1.9.

form. The account it provides of the narrator's choice between the relative attractions of Elegia and Tragoedia travesties the structure of another famous choice between female forms – namely the allegorical presentation of Hercules' choice between Arete and Kakia first expounded by the sophist Prodicus and transmitted in Xenophon's *Memorabilia* 2.1.21-34. A few commentators have observed the correspondence,[38] but its implications for reading elegy's female forms as playful signifiers of a moral or political position have not been fully explored. Only P.H. Schrijvers noted briefly that moral arguments are employed in *Amores* 3.1 and that the allocation of victory to Elegia involves 'la réévaluation des valeurs'.[39] But the article in which these valuable points were made appeared as part of a *Festschrift* for J.C. Kamerbeek and was therefore concerned primarily with issues centring on the practice of tragedy.

The narrative strategy of positioning the conflict between Elegia and Tragoedia in a direct line of descent from that between Arete and Kakia discloses a structural function of female flesh as signifier of male political practices. For the recollection and comic debasement of the earlier moral allegory assigns the Ovidian narrator the role of a latter-day Roman Hercules deciding not just between writing-styles, but between life-styles, and it is through the shape, comportment and speech of the two female constructs that conflicting moral and political ideologies are articulated and appraised. Thus in their appearance, their attire and their pose, Elegia and Tragoedia are clearly differentiated as respectively *meretrix* and *matrona*. As matron, Tragoedia is clothed in the concealing garments of a respectable Roman wife, *palla iacebat humi* v.12, and adopts highly dignified gestures (vv.31-32).[40] As mistress, Elegia is provided with both a sexually provocative dress, *uestis tenuissima* v.9, and expression (v.9 and v.33). But the earlier, allegorical account of divergent modes of conduct had also been expressed in terms of a choice between *meretrix* and *matrona*.[41] For, according to Xenophon's account, Hercules had been faced with a choice between Arete as a woman wearing a modest look and the purity of white or Kakia as a woman wearing a brazen expression and a dress that revealed all.[42] So, in their features and in their dress, a counterpart for Elegia is to be found in Kakia, and for Tragoedia in Arete. By reproducing the features of female forms which are employed elsewhere to typify codes of conduct, the Ovidian text identifies its female figures also as such types: in *Amores* 3.1, Tragoedia functions as an Augustan embodiment of Virtue and Elegia

---

[38] Reitzenstein 1935, 81-2; Brandt 1963, ad *Am*. 3.1.11; Schrijvers 1976, esp. 407-13.
[39] Schrijvers 1976, 422.
[40] Ibid. 1976, 416-17 and see above, n.32.
[41] See for instance Gigon 1956, 64.
[42] Xen., *Mem*. 2.1.22.

as an embodiment of Vice. The victory of Elegia as Vice, the preference of a *meretrix* over a *matrona*, then constitutes a witty and provocative re-writing of the mythic parable in which Hercules chooses Virtue.

It is not just through female physiques that an ideologically provocative position is established for the narrator of *Amores* 3.1. Moral and political concerns are to the forefront of Tragoedia's plea for authorship. Before advocating herself as a practice of writing, Tragoedia condemns her opponent:

> nequitiam uinosa tuam conuiuia narrant,
> narrant in multas compita secta uias.
> saepe aliquis digito uatem designat euntem
> atque ait 'hic, hic est, quem ferus urit Amor.'
> fabula, nec sentis, tota iactaris in Vrbe,
> dum tua praeterito facta pudore refers. (3.1.17-22)

> (Your depravity tipsy parties tell,
> crossroads tell it – split into many streets.
> Often someone with his finger points out the passing bard
> and says 'That's him, that's the one cruel Love burns!'
> You're talk, you don't realise, spread round the whole city,
> while you report your own acts, shame abandoned.)

The context of this passage and its central reference to a *uatem* and *Amor*, rather than to a lover and his girl-friend, identify it as an assault on erotic elegy, although that assault is expressed in terms of an author's actions and is enclosed by the terminology of moral conduct – namely *nequitiam* (v.17) and *pudore* (v.22). As an Augustan matron and embodiment of Virtue, Tragoedia gives voice to the values of the establishment and interprets the production of elegy as vice. For matrons would be expected to regret the passing of *pudor* and to denigrate the sexual licence which *nequitia* suggests. The practitioner of poetic eroticism is portrayed as isolated from the rest of the community at Rome and labelled as morally corrupt. Tragoedia thus ascribes to Augustan elegy an unorthodoxy boldly proclaimed by its authors elsewhere: the poet was introduced at the beginning of a second book of *Amores* as *ille ego nequitiae Naso poeta meae* (2.1.2)[43] and in the Propertian poem 2.24, which *Amores* 3.1 here recalls, the scandal of *nequitia* is said to accrue to the creator of poems on Cynthia.[44] Once again, at this point in the corpus of Augustan elegy, its unorthodox nature is to be understood through the agency of a female form.

[43] Cf. Brandt 1963, ad *Am*. 3.1.17.
[44] The language of 3.1.17-22 recalls that of Prop. 2.24.1-8 where *urere, fabula, tota urbs* and *pudor* are also to be found.

Tragoedia continues her case by commanding her immediate production:

> tempus erat thyrso pulsum grauiore moueri;
>   cessatum satis est: incipe maius opus.
> materia premis ingenium; cane facta uirorum:
>   'haec animo' dices 'area digna meo est.'
> quod tenerae cantent lusit tua Musa puellae,
>   primaque per numeros acta iuuenta suos.
> nunc habeam per te Romana Tragoedia nomen:
>   implebit leges spiritus iste meas. (3.1.23-30)

> (Time, propelled by the weightier wand, to be moved –
>   there's been ample idleness. Undertake a greater task.
> Your material suppresses talent; celebrate the feats of heroes:
>   'this arena', you'll say, 'suits my spirit'.
> Ditties for delicate girls to sing your Muse has played,
>   first youth driven by its proper rhythms.
> Now, through you, let Roman Tragedy win fame;
>   your energy will satisfy my demands.)

Tragoedia offers not only the allurement of a grander writing-style but, following the mythic parable of Hercules, the attractions of work and social responsibility. According to Prodicus' tale, there are no thoughts of war or business in the pursuit of Kakia.[45] Similarly, in *Amores* 3.1, the rival of Elegia/Kakia describes elegy's pursuit as unemployment or an act of idleness; used of poetic eroticism *cessare* suggests that it involves the absence of any adequate political or social role for its author. Elegy is associated with girls, delicacy, adolescence and play; tragedy with men, deeds and dignity. Tragoedia concludes her speech by describing the result of her practice in the community: from elegy there arises gossip at Rome, but from tragedy glory. *Romana* marks the different positions tragedy and elegy hold in relation to the state. For drama may be read as a national genre – a state institution – while erotic elegy is often associated with the history of struggles against Roman militarism. Thus the *Amores* as a whole is rounded off by the location of its narrator within the Paelignian, rather than the Roman, race, and then that race is recorded as having fought against Roman oppression during the Social Wars, *cum timuit socias anxia Roma manus* (3.15.10). Propertius too had closed a collection of elegiac poems by linking its author's birthplace with civil war and a period *cum Romana suos egit discordia ciuis* (1.22.5).

While Tragoedia thus takes on the part of Arete in denying moral or social responsibility to the authorship of elegy, Elegia cleverly appropriates the vocabulary of Virtue to express a different ideological

---

[45] Xen., *Mem.* 2.1.24.

position for her narrator. In Prodicus' parable, Arete talks to Hercules about the necessity of suffering to achieve the good life awarded by the gods.[46] Elegia redefines what is to be thought of as the good achieved through *ponos* for the world of erotic discourses;[47] the end of some rather ludicrous ordeals becomes sexual access (vv.43-58).

In *Amores* 3.1, therefore, Arete and Kakia have been reproduced in the flesh and speech of Tragoedia and Elegia respectively. So the written women of this elegy are also to be read as signifiers of moral and political ideologies. However, in allowing his narrator to be won over by the attractions of the *meretrix*, rather than the *matrona*, Ovid has radically rewritten the mythic parable. Pursuit of Virtue is still depicted as a hard task – the Ovidian *labor aeternus* of writing tragedies (v.68) parallels the Prodican long, hard road to Arete.[48] But the glory which was once its reward is no longer Virtue's to bestow. According to Prodicus, the friends of Virtue are not forgotten and dishonoured, but remembered and celebrated.[49] In the morally perverse world of literary eroticism it is the awkward figure of limping Elegia/Vice who bestows on her poets everlasting fame: *nostro uicturum nomen amori* (v.65).

The female forms Elegia and Tragoedia have clearly been constructed to suit a playful Ovidian narrative of moral and political difference but the extent of the political unorthodoxy which the choice of Elegia articulates is best understood in the historical context of elegy's production as an ideological discourse. For the presentation of an Augustan 'Hercules' choosing Vice rather than Virtue, a *meretrix* rather than a *matrona*, actively conflicts with the contemporary, institutionalised role of Hercules as symbol of the Roman state and its *princeps*. In Roman culture, as Karl Galinsky has observed, Hercules had become idealised as the perfect embodiment of Stoic virtue and was so closely conjoined with Augustus as 'to be considered an Augustan symbol'.[50] Both through Augustus' own efforts, such as in timing his triple triumph of 29 BC to coincide with the official festival of Hercules on 13 August, and through such notable literary representations as those in Virgil's *Aeneid*,[51] Hercules became a symbol of political orthodoxy, of the hegemony of the Augustan state in the post-Actium period. Thus comic debasements of the Hercules mythology, such as the conversion of hero into clumsy suitor in Propertius 4.9 and in *Heroides* 9, are read as narrative strategies for the expression of anti-Augustan sentiment.[52] Here, in *Amores* 3.1, when faced with the same dilemma as Hercules in

---

[46] Xen., *Mem*. 2.1.28.
[47] Cf. Schrijvers 1976, 422.
[48] ibid., 424.
[49] Xen., *Mem* 2.1.33.
[50] Galinsky 1972, 153.
[51] ibid., 126-66.
[52] On Prop. 4.9 see Anderson 1964, 11, and Pillinger 1969, 189. And on *Heroides* 9 see Galinsky 1972, 153-60.

the shape of *meretrix* or *matrona*, the elegiac narrator rejects the expected response institutionalised in myth and opts for a female form openly dissociated from social and political responsibility.

Through the flippant association of Ovid's female forms Elegia and Tragoedia with the mythic parable of Kakia and Arete, *Amores* 3.1 signals that its written women articulate a political, as well as a poetic, heterodoxy for their narrator. Here women enter elegy's fictive world to formulate an amusing manifesto of both literary and political difference, and their bodies are clearly shaped to suit that manifesto. In particular, the asymmetric body with which Elegia is endowed functions as a signifier both of a Callimachean poetics (the advocacy of what is *lepton*) and an anti-Augustan politics (the advocacy of *nequitia*). But Elegia's body has already been identified, in all respects, except its unequal feet, with the body assigned elsewhere to the elegiac beloved. So the question immediately arises whether Elegia's narrative function in *Amores* 3.1 has any implications for the function of the Elegiac Woman elsewhere in the corpus of Augustan love-poetry.

III. The elegiac woman

It is not in fact possible to confine a reading of female flesh as political fiction to *Amores* 3.1 and thereby safeguard the identification of elegy's female subjects with specific individuals living in Augustan Rome. For, at the same time as *Amores* 3.1 incorporates many features of the elegiac *puella*, it encourages its readers to look both outwards to other modes of representing the female form and back at the role of the *puella* in articulating elegy's poetic and political concerns.

First, the narrative structure of *Amores* 3.1 locates its female figures firmly in a tradition for representing women which stretches back to Prodicus' parable and on beyond Ovidian elegy. Thus, although the story of *Hercules in Biuio* has been recounted in numerous and diverse ways, in the accounts of poets, Stoic philosophers and Greek rhetoricians the allocation of attributes to the female embodiments of man's moral or political choices falls into a set pattern: the features of Ovid's Elegia and the Elegiac Woman she comprises are thus also those commonly possessed by such figures as *Kakia, Hêdonê, Tyrannis, Pseudodoxia, Adulatio* or *Voluptas*.[53] When Silius Italicus presents P. Cornelius Scipio with a dilemma in his epic poem on the second Punic War, he structures his account to match the mythic dilemma of Hercules by depicting a contest between *Voluptas* and *Virtus* for the soldier's allegiance. The physiques of his goddesses closely resemble those of Elegia and Tragoedia:

[53] See the catalogue constructed by Alpers 1912, 51-8.

        alter Achaemenium spirabat uertice odorem,
        ambrosias diffusa comas et ueste refulgens,
        ostrum qua fuluo Tyrium suffuderat auro;
        fronte decor quaesitus acu, lasciuaque crebras
        ancipiti motu iaciebant lumina flammas.
        alterius dispar habitus: frons hirta nec umquam
        composita mutata coma; stans uultus, et ore
        incessuque uiro proprior laetique pudoris,
        celsa humeros niueae fulgebat stamine pallae. (*Punica* 15.23-31)

        (One from her crown breathed Persian scent,
        spilling her ambrosial curls, and brilliant in a dress
        Tyrian purple had traced with rosy gold;
        elegance on her brow acquired with a pin, her desirous eyes
        darted left and right repeated flames.
        Far different the other's look: a shaggy brow never
        by styled hair altered, a firm gaze,
        both face and pace nearer to a man's and joyfully modest;
        towering, her shoulders gleamed with thread of snowy robe.)

From Ovid's Elegia, *Voluptas* has inherited scented hair, expensive
clothes and a provocative look. From Tragoedia, *Virtus* has inherited a
mannish stride, dishevelled hair, a stern expression and matronly
gown.[54] The same grouping of physical features, the same
meretrix/matrona dichotomy for female flesh, is to be found in Silius'
hexameters as in Ovid's elegiacs because those features bring with
them a whole constellation of cultural values through which to
articulate the moral and political choices men face. The *meretrix* figure
again acts as a signifier of social irresponsibility and idleness, the
matrona of state duties and military pursuits. It is because everywhere
such female types may have ideological repercussions that Silius is
able to deploy the same *meretrix/matrona* dichotomy in order to
dramatise Scipio's Stoic pursuit of a command in Spain.[55]

        The employment of such archetypes for female flesh has not of course
been confined to variations on the theme of *Hercules in Biuio*. The
opposition between Innocent and Seductress has played a crucial role
in shaping the Christian Church's models for female behaviour – the
Virgin Mary and Eve –[56] while, for instance, 'the two most common
types of women in film noir are the exciting, childless whores, or the
boring, potentially childbearing sweethearts'.[57] For images of women
and the values attached to them arise out of both the social relations
between the sexes and concepts of gender in a given culture. In
patriarchal cultures, the central measurement of women, the way

[54] The list is that of Bruere 1959, 240-2.
[55] For Scipio as built in the image of the Stoic Hercules see Bassett 1966.
[56] See, for example, Warner 1976; Cameron, below.
[57] Harvey 1980, 25.

women enter cultural forms, is through sexuality. Patriarchy's familial ideology then associates the sexually unrestrained, childless woman with social disruption and locates her on the margins of society. Marriage and motherhood, being concerned with the ordering of female sexuality in terms which will be socially effective for patriarchy, restore women to a central position, while still withholding economic or political power.[58] In the case of the theme *Hercules in Biuio*, women enter discourse to define male moral and political choices and their physiques are shaped accordingly and appropriately labelled *meretrix* or *matrona*.

Thus the similarities between the *meretrix* figures of Prodicus' tale, Ovid's elegies and Silius' epic demonstrate that the flesh of the Elegiac Woman has a history beyond the physical features of any Augustan girl-friend and belongs rather to an archetypal dichotomy whore/ matron through which is expressed male political and moral conflicts. For it is the silks and scents, the coiffure and the provocative look borrowed from the elegiac beloved which link Elegia with symbols of pleasure and the absence of virtue. Silius' *Voluptas* owes more to the features of an elegiac *puella*, than to a personification of elegiac poetry since only the evident attributes of writing-styles have been carefully avoided in his version; elegy's limp, tragedy's boots.

Ovid's Elegia identifies her component parts as belonging to a pervasive tradition in which female flesh functions as a signifier of male ideological positions. In her flimsy dresses and adorned to lure lovers (Prop. 1.2, 1.15.1-8), the Elegiac Woman is differentiated from the *matrona* who wears the long gown of respectability (Tib. 1.6.67-8) and is said to have no place in elegiac discourse (*Ars Amat*. 1.31-2). Not the narrator's wife, she is a *meretrix* in the broadest sense of the word – a symbol of *nequitia* and the absence of *pudor* (Prop. 2.24.1-8). Thus by claiming to be entrapped by an unrestrained female sexuality, by the figure of 'une irrégulière',[59] the writers of elegiac discourse are able to portray themselves as abandoning traditional social responsibilities: not soldier, lawyer or politician, but poet of love (*Am*. 1.15).

There is a second, pressing reason why it is not possible to view the function of female flesh in *Amores* 3.1 as unique to this particular point in the corpus of Augustan love-poetry but necessary instead to view the poem as having important implications for reading the flesh of the Elegiac Woman elsewhere. For as a narrative which openly expresses poetic concerns – the rejection of a higher form of writing in favour of elegy – *Amores* 3.1 belongs to a group of Augustan elegies ultimately indebted to the rejection of epic which Callimachus had expressed in the elegiacs of the *Aetia*. Often to be found at the opening or close of

[58] See, for instance, Berger 1972; Lipshitz 1978; Kaplan 1980. For the prevalence of this mode of structuring femininity in antiquity see Lefkowitz 1981.

[59] Veyne 1983, 15.

132   *Maria Wyke*

poetry-books, these poems have been grouped together under various headings, such as the *recusatio* or the *apologetischen Form*.[60] 3.1. cannot easily be isolated from other such programmatic poems within the *Amores* since they have been read as offering a unifying movement to the collection, from an initial acceptance of elegy to its ultimate rejection.[61]

In particular, references within *Amores* 3.1 to a pressing demand for tragic composition bind it tightly to an earlier recusation:

> sceptra tamen sumpsi curaque tragoedia nostra
>   creuit, et huic operi quamlibet aptus eram:
> risit Amor pallamque meam pictosque cothurnos
>   sceptraque priuata tam cito sumpta manu;
> hinc quoque me dominae numen deduxit iniquae,
>   deque cothurnato uate triumphat Amor. (2.18.13-18)

> (Still, I seized sceptres and tragedy, thanks to my pains,
>   grew. But, however suited I was to this labour,
> Love laughed at my gown and ornamented boots
>   and the sceptres so quickly seized by a humble hand.
> From this also a cruel lady's sway fetched me back,
>   and over a booted bard triumphs Love.)

In this version of the *apologetischen Form*,[62] it is the narrator who plays Tragoedia's role as advocate of a grander writing-style. Here the symbols of tragic discourse – the sceptre, the gown and the painted boots – adorn the figure of a poet, not a personified genre.[63] The narrator is already equipped with the regalia Tragoedia offers him at *Amores* 3.1.63.

But if it is the narrator who plays Tragoedia's role, it is *Amor* and a *domina* who play Elegia's and orchestrate the retreat from the production of tragedy. It is also *Amor* and a *puella* who orchestrate a retreat from epic earlier in the poem, as *quoque* recalls:

> nos, Macer, ignaua Veneris cessamus in umbra,
>   et tener ausuros grandia frangit Amor.
> saepe meae 'tandem' dixi 'discede' puellae:
>   in gremio sedit protinus illa meo;
> saepe 'pudet' dixi: lacrimis uix illa retentis
>   'me miseram, iam te' dixit 'amare pudet?'
> implicuitque suos circum mea colla lacertos
>   et, quae me perdunt, oscula mille dedit.
> uincor, et ingenium sumptis reuocatur ab armis,
>   resque domi gestas et mea bella cano. (2.18.3-12)

[60] See esp. Wimmel 1960, *passim*.
[61] Du Quesnay 1973, 5-6.
[62] See Wimmel 1960, 305-6; Morgan 1977, 15-17; Fedeli 1980, 186.
[63] As Brandt 1963, ad *Am.* 2.18.15 and 3.1.11.

(I idle, Macer, in Venus' lazy shade
  and delicate Love shatters my grandiose ventures.
'At last', I've often said to my girl, 'leave':
  she's sat on my lap immediately.
'I'm ashamed', I've often said: with tears scarcely checked
  'poor me', she's said, 'are you ashamed to love already?'
She's wrapped her arms around my neck
  and kisses which kill me, she's given a thousand.
I'm beaten: my talent is recalled from the armour it seized,
  I celebrate domestic action and my personal battles.)

Just as Elegia lures the poet away from tragedy with a lover's look and
a provocative smile, so an Elegiac Woman lures him away from epic
with an erotic embrace.

But this *puella* is only as relevant to the real life of a love poet as
armour to an epic poet or painted boots and a sceptre to a tragedian.
For in *Amores* 2.18 weapons, stage properties *and* a girl function as
material symbols of poetic production in a *Stilkampf* where elegy
always gains ultimate ascendancy.[64] Thus elegy is humorously
identified as already incorporating elements of epic when military
metaphors are applied to erotic activity (vv.11-12):[65] overpowered by a
woman (*uincor*), a poet must summon his talent back from the front
(*reuocatur ab armis*) and write instead militant elegies on bedroom
battles (*resque domi gestas et mea bella*). Similarly the contrast
between *tener* and *grandia* with which the epic poet Macer is
confronted recalls the stylistic contrast between *lepton* and *pachu* set
out in the *Aetia*. But the elegiac *puella* is implicated in the victory of
delicacy since her physical prevention of epic composition (vv.5-12)
enacts and elaborates the destruction by delicate *Amor* of a poet's
ambitious schemes (v.4). So, in submitting to the attractions of an
Elegiac Woman, the narrator also embraces an embodiment of
Callimachus' *lepton*.

Positioned at the opening of a third book of erotic elegies, *Amores* 3.1
also invites comparison with the introduction to the second book of the
collection. Following the pattern for the *apologetischen Form*, *Amores*
2.1 rejects a higher form of poetic discourse in favour of elegiacs.[66] The
poet first declares that he had ventured on the production of a
Gigantomachy (2.1.11-16). As material symbols of such an exalted
practice, the Ovidian narrator is depicted playfully clutching clouds, a
thunderbolt and – most irreverently – Jupiter himself: *in manibus
nimbos et cum Ioue fulmen habebam* (v.15). The poet confesses that he
then dropped poor Jupiter and his thunderbolt to resume the

---

[64] For *arma* as a symbol of epic see Fedeli 1985, 57-58. For the actor's costume of gown
and boots as a symbol of tragedy see Brandt 1963, ad *Am.* 2.18.5.
[65] As Quadlbauer 1968, 94n.5.
[66] See Wimmel 1960, 303-5; Morgan 1977, 12-14; Giangrande 1981, 33-40.

production of elegiacs (2.1.17-22). Once again it is a Callimachean poetics which is expressed through such a bizarre evocation: Jupiter's thunderbolt marks the 'thundering' style which Callimachus had opposed to his own in *Aetia* fr. 120,[67] while production of elegies which are *leuis* (v.21) obeys the Callimachean call for *leptotês*.[68] But what instigates the retreat into Callimachean elegiacs? As in *Amores* 2.18, epic composition is disrupted by the Elegiac Woman who this time slams her front door – *clausit amica fores: ego cum Ioue fulmen omisi* (v.17). Just as Elegia institutes the third book of the *Amores*, so an elegiac *puella* institutes the second.

Thus, within the *Amores*, a succession of humorous programmatic poems deploys female forms to articulate a Callimachean apologetics. Elegia opens a third poetry-book playing the role already undertaken by the Elegiac Woman in the second, and the association between personification and realistically constructed *puella* is sustained by a reduplication of physical features. The ungainly figure of asymmetric Elegia then threatens romantic readings of the Elegiac Woman because it incorporates many of her attributes *and* replays her part in the elegiac narrative at the same time as it embodies ideological and poetic concerns. It is, moreover, the reproduction of the elegiac figure of the *meretrix* which enables Elegia to symbolise an anti-establishment politics, while in symbolising a Callimachean poetics Elegia plays with the beloved's function in earlier versions of the *apologetischen Form*. If *Amores* 3.1 encourages readings of elegy's female figures as political fictions, it correspondingly discourages the identification of the Ovidian *puella* with a specific Augustan girl-friend.

So the process of assimilating Corinna to a liberated lady living in Rome has been challenged on the grounds that the Ovidian *puella* appears to be as much a travesty of love elegy's conventions as the text in which she figures. The series of programmatic poems which culminate in *Amores* 3.1 contributes to that challenge by first ridiculing and then decoding the romantic convention that love poets begin to write because they are in love, that a frustrating passion for a woman who exists outside the confines of the text instigates its production. For comic circumstances surround the renewal of elegiac composition in *Amores* 2.1: a girl's door slams, the poet drops Jupiter in surprise. While in *Amores* 2.18 the poet is forced to abandon his ambitious schemes when pinned down by a girl in his lap. But as the last poem in the series to institute elegiacs through a female form, *Amores* 3.1 even abandons realism and, by providing its *puella* additionally with a limp and the title 'Elegy', reduces the romantic convention to an amusing conceit and finally exposes elegy's female subjects as political fiction.

[67] Cf. Innes 1979, 166-7.
[68] Giangrande 1981, 38.

IV. Liberated ladies revisited

Amores 3.1 recalls the earlier fictive practices of Tibullus and Propertius, belongs to a cycle of *Apologien* which extends beyond the Ovidian corpus and is even set in the landscape of Propertius' programmatic poetry. So the poetic text encourages its readers to locate it squarely within the corpus of Augustan elegy and to associate it with a particular pattern of narrative strategies deployed throughout the *Amores* to probe Propertian discourse. Does the poem's playful warning – that elegiac *puellae* are political fictions – then apply even to Cynthia?

The narrative of the *Amores* has been recognised as constructed within the framework of a general critical strategy variously described as a burlesque of elegiac conventions, a *reductio ad absurdum* of elegiac practices, a breaking of elegy's rules, a parody of Propertian poetry, a demystification of elegy's romanticism.[69] Ovid is seen to be decoding the romantic and realistic practice of writing associated most notably with the Propertian corpus. In this way, the strategy of recalling earlier Propertian poems has been called the most significant aspect of the *Amores* and the programmatic poems identified as important stages in its execution.[70]

As an example of this process, the first poem of *Amores* 1 reveals a rich seam of 'demystification'. There the first logical step is taken to construct a literary eroticism – the adoption of the elegiac metre; the poet was planning to write epic in solemn hexameters, when Cupid stole a foot from the second line and thus converted the poetry into elegiacs. At this point the narrator is not yet in love. He does not make the declaration of love for a specific woman which his audience would expect from a poet continuing the tradition established in Augustan elegy by Gallus, Tibullus and Propertius: *nec mihi materia est numeris leuioribus apta* (1.1.19). The role of poet is given priority over that of lover and the Ovidian narrator expresses his metrical, rather than emotional, concerns. The poem demands comparison with the beginning of the *Monobiblos* of Propertius.[71] There the narrator makes no such overt reference to poetic preferences. Cynthia is the cause of his being in love. The reader understands that the *Monobiblos* has been written in an autobiographical mode and that, at least on the narrative surface, the Cynthia of the text is to be read as if a 'real' woman. Ovid's poem, however, by drawing attention to the creative process, warns that realism is merely a property of the text. By describing the poet's mastery over his own material, Ovid exposes the conventions of elegiac romanticism and the fictionality of its female

---

[69] See, for example, Otis 1938; Du Quesnay 1973; Lyne 1980, 239-87; Davis 1981.
[70] Respectively Du Quesnay 1973, 6 and Morgan 1977, 7-26.
[71] See, for instance, Gross 1975-1976, 153-4.

subject. Similarly, the programmatic poems of Ovid's second book have been thought to imply a playful criticism of Propertian arguments in favour of elegiac production addressed to the epic poet Ponticus in poems 7 and 9 of the *Monobiblos*.[72]

But if *Amores* 3.1 is not commonly read as forming part of Ovid's general narrative strategy for exposing realism's conventions, it is precisely because here the realistic representation of female flesh undergoes demystification and exposure as a poetic convention. For the crooked contours of Elegia – the *puella* as a practice of writing – mark the culmination of a series of three programmatic poems (2.1, 2.18, 3.1) which first burlesque and then decipher the realistically constructed Propertian *puella* and her part in the expression of poetic and political concerns.

Moreover, the sequence of poems makes its own operations manifest by commencing with an account of how a beloved's antics thwarted the composition of a grand Gigantomachy (2.1.11-16). This isolated reference in the *Amores* to a failed Gigantomachy, its position in the first poem of a second book, its language and line structure, are all designed to recall another Gigantomachy rejected by Propertius in favour of elegiac composition in the introduction to *his* second poetry-book (2.1.17-20).[73] The first poem in Ovid's series thus indicates clearly that, on this occasion, the Propertian *puella* has been taken as starting-point for the process of demystification. For, among all the programmatic poems of the Propertian corpus, it is 2.1 which employs the body of the Elegiac Woman most openly and most extensively to trace its author's poetic and political heterodoxy:[74]

> siue illam Cois fulgentem incedere <cogis>,
>   hac totum e Coa ueste uolumen erit;
> seu uidi ad frontem sparsos errare capillos,
>   gaudet laudatis ire superba comis;
> siue lyrae carmen digitis percussit eburnis,
>   miramur, facilis ut premat arte manus;
> seu cum poscentis somnum declinat ocellos,
>   inuenio causas mille poeta nouas;
> seu nuda erepto mecum luctatur amictu,
>   tum uero longas condimus Iliadas;
> seu quidquid fecit siue est quodcumque locuta,
>   maxima de nihilo nascitur historia. (2.1.5-16)

> (If gleaming in Coan silks you make her go,
>   of that Coan dress the whole book will be composed;
> or if on her brow I have seen scattered curls stray,
>   she delights to walk with pride in praised hair;

---

[72] Morgan 1977, 12-17 and Du Quesnay 1973, 25-7.
[73] Cf. Morgan 1977, 16.
[74] Quotations from the Propertian corpus follow Barber 1960.

or if the lyre's song with ivory fingers she's struck,
  we wonder at the quick hands she presses with skill;
or when she lowers eyes that desire sleep,
  I discover causes, a thousand new ones for a poet;
or if naked she grapple with me, her robe extracted,
  surely then we construct lengthy *Iliads*;
or whatever she's done, or whatever she's said,
  from nothing the grandest history is born.)

The context makes it clear that this *puella*, who instigates a second book of love elegies, forms part of a serious polemic on literary and political choices. The first line of the poem introduces the Elegiac Woman as the answer to a literary question which concerns only the narrator and his readership: *quaeritis, unde mihi totiens scribantur amores* (2.1.1). After her appearance, Callimachus is called upon openly as a model for the production of alternatives to the epic writing-style (2.1.39-42) and the subject of Cynthia is presented as occupying the space of an unorthodox account of the birth of the Augustan state: the unwritten poem on Caesar's *bellaque resque* which a *puella* replaces locates Actium in a catalogue of bloody civil wars (2.1.25-34). Poetic and ideological concerns thus enclose and inform a serious and realistic depiction of the second book's heroine.[75]

Now the series of *Apologien* which culminates in *Amores* 3.1 has led its readers back to this earlier Propertian poem. With the playful warning offered by Elegia in mind, a re-reading of the Propertian *puella* here underscores some disturbing features of the text which jeopardise even the status of *Cynthia* as the pseudonym of a living Augustan woman. First, Cynthia's attributes and activities which are said to precede and excite elegiac production are already set in a tradition for erotic writing before they become the material of Propertian fiction. For a beloved's appearance and skills, her sleep and erotic battles are far more frequently the themes of Hellenistic erotic epigrams than the love elegies of the Propertian corpus.[76] Even Cynthia's clothing assists the identification of elegiac *puella* with elegiac practice, since *Cous* is used elsewhere in the Propertian corpus to signal the Hellenistic poet Philetas. Just as Elegia is adorned in a Callimachean delicacy, so Cynthia is decked in the poetic discourse of Philetas. Cynthia's attributes and activities are implicated further in a Callimachean apologetics. As inspirer of poetic *causas*, the Elegiac Woman becomes the key to a new version of Callimachus' *Aetia*, one which looks into the origins of a mistress's behaviour, rather than the workings of myth and ritual. This Propertian *Aetia* is then set against

---

[75] On the overt Callimachean polemic of vv.17-46 see Wimmel 1960, 13-43. For the unorthodox perspective on Roman history in vv.25-34 see Galinsky 1969, 81-2; Hubbard 1974, 100-2; Putnam 1976, 121-3; Nethercut 1983, 1839-40.

[76] Boucher 1965, 210-11.

the higher genres of epic and history through the agency of a female form. The erotic struggles of Propertius' *puella* match the battles of Homeric heroes and accounts of her every word and deed surpass all previous histories (vv.11-16).[77] Even as the Elegiac Woman is realistically presented as existing prior to elegiac discourse, a rejection of higher forms of writing in favour of a Callimachean practice takes place through her agency.

At one point, moreover, the vocabulary in which Cynthia is formulated as a creator of art also points to her as being an artistic creation. Momentarily Cynthia's physique is said to be manufactured out of ivory (v.9), suggesting a *puella* who is herself an artform rather than an instigator of art.[78] But since the epithet is transferred from a musical instrument to its player and is not incongruous with the features of a beauty, the attribution of ivory fingers is far less disturbing than the attribution of unequal feet.

Finally the entire depiction of elegy's female subject is enclosed by two terms which even further undermine Cynthia's superficial status as a woman who exists prior to the production of an elegiac text. Precisely because it does not give the beloved her expected independence, many commentators have queried the MS tradition's *cogis* (v.5, 'you make her').[79] While *de nihilo* (v.16, 'from nothing') suggests that the history of a beloved is being composed which has no firm basis in reality. Thus even the Propertian text itself argues against the attribution of an independent identity to its female subject and its reconsideration demonstrates that *Amores* 3.1 offers both amusing and useful clues to the operations of female representation elsewhere in the corpus of Augustan elegy.

To return again to our starting-point; to sustain a reading of the Elegiac Woman as a liberated lady living at Rome, critics have disengaged the textual characteristics of written women from their context in a poetry-book and reshaped them into portraits of Augustan girl-friends. The narrative strategies of *Amores* 3.1, however, have been shown to argue against such a practice because they expose female flesh as a signifier of its author's position in the literary and political tradition. But, although the account of female flesh provided by *Amores* 3.1 may be welcomed as relevant to readings of the Ovidian Corinna, nevertheless Romantic critics may resist its implications for the Propertian Cynthia – even though they acknowledge the role of the *Amores* as respondent to the Propertian corpus – simply because, in the history of classical scholarship, the Propertian corpus has been privileged in critical studies of Augustan poetry and readings of Cynthia have functioned as paradigms for the realist view of the

[77] King 1980, 63 and cf. Wiggers 1976-1977, 336.
[78] Cf. Wiggers 1976-1977, 335.
[79] See e.g. Camps 1967, 66 for the substitution of *uidi*.

Elegiac Woman. So it is appropriate at this point to conclude by offering a preliminary and selective examination of other textual characteristics assigned to Cynthia in the Propertian corpus in order to assess further the validity of employing *Amores* 3.1 as a key to their interpretation.

It is from the material of poems such as 2.2 that critics have built a living partner, an intelligent blonde, for its author Propertius, since 2.2 overtly describes the power of a look to restore its narrator to his occupation as lover. But the poem which immediately precedes presents elegiac poetry – and therefore the entire second book – as an alternative to epic, an erotic *Aetia*, when it calls openly on Callimachus as a model for Fine Poetry. So the same critics who have read the text of 2.2 transparently in order to construct a living mistress for Propertius have also disclosed the presence in the poem of literary concerns; thus the poem has been interpreted as 'a demonstration of the claim of Propertius in 2.1, to his Callimachean heritage', while a 'real' woman is retained to read her own conversion into a Callimachean literary practice. That poetic practice is observed at work in the physical shape of the poem (its epigrammatic brevity), its esoteric narrative style and its revision of epic motifs. Even the figurative presentation of Cynthia in 2.2.6-14 (her comparison with Juno, Pallas, Ischomache and Brimo, and her victory in a recast judgement of Paris) is read as a manifestation of a Callimachean writing-practice; the revision of epic material in slight poetry, the delineation of Cynthia in epic proportions.[80]

But not all of the poem can be thus decoded if the notion is still to be sustained that Cynthia is the pseudonym of an extra-textual addressee. After all, if Cynthia is to signify a woman of flesh she must be provided with some. So there occurs a noticeable silence, an absence of comment on the point in the poem where the Elegiac Woman is provided with physical properties:

> fulua coma est longaeque manus, et maxima toto
>   corpore. (2.2.5-6)

> (tawny hair and long hands, and vast entirely
>   in body)

What justification is there, however, for thus preserving by omission a referentiality for these lines? Can they be said to sketch the unique physical characteristics of one Augustan woman?

The documented popularity of the Junoesque blonde in classical literature suggests rather that Propertius has assembled here a selection from a repertoire of archetypal features for the female

[80] King 1981.

beauties of fiction. For example, the catalogue of feminine physical assets possessed and absent to be found in Catullus 86 and 43 respectively provides an obvious parallel for the features of this Propertian woman.[81] Moreover, since the Homeric poems, tall stature (*megethos*) had been a characteristic of literary representations of the ideal Woman and yellow hair (*xanthotês*) a set feature of the Beauty in the Greek novel.[82] A reading of the list of feminine qualities which occurs at 2.2.5-6 detached from the physique of any one Roman woman is aided by the syntax of the passage and the narrative mode adopted for the poem as a whole. A dative of the (human) possessor is provided neither for *fulua coma* nor *longaeque manus*, and *maxima* has no immediate noun to qualify. The whole may therefore be considered as loosely attached to the impersonal *facies* with which the poem opens and closes. The qualities of a body are allotted to an abstract Look, not to an individuated and realistically constructed beloved.

If the textual characteristics of Cynthia do not amount to the unique features of an Augustan girl-friend, could they have been chosen to suit the poetic context, the narration of a Callimachean literary practice, as a reading of *Amores* 3.1 has suggested? Interesting parallels for the delineation of Cynthia at 2.2.5-6 may be found outside the realms of erotic discourse, in the construction of the Warrior – the Epic Man. The adjective *fuluus* signals the area for comparison, for yellow hair is far more frequently identified by *flauus* in the discourses of Roman fictive eroticism. *Fuluus*, however, is employed in the *Aeneid* as an epithet of ferocious animals, such as the eagle or the lion, or of ferocious warriors. At *Aeneid* 10.562, for example, the bravery of Aeneas is matched by the resistance of his opponents; *fortemque Numam fuluumque Camertem*. The other physical properties with which the Elegiac Woman is provided evoke particularly the large-limbed Homeric Warrior. The more delicate build customarily devised for the Female Beauty would be suggested more readily by the application of *longus* to fingers rather than the whole hand. The transference allows a parallel to be drawn from an attribute of the Epic Man; the Homeric *cheiri pacheiêi*, the *manu magna* or *dextra ingenti* of the Virgilian *bellator*.[83] Similarly, the tall stature of the ideal Beloved is often signified by *longa* in erotic poetry. The wording here, however, compares with the description at *Aeneid* 11.690-1 of two opponents worthy of Camilla's military prowess: *Orsilochum et Buten, duo maxima Teucrum / corpora*.

It appears then that at 2.2.5-6 a selection has been made from among the standard features of the Female Beauty which produces a sketch of an Elegiac Woman in epic proportions. But in the previous poem, Propertius had illustrated his obedience to the Callimachean

---

[81] Quinn 1963, 66-73.
[82] Lilja 1978, 123-4 and 128-9.
[83] Virgil, *Aen*. 5.241 and 11.556.

call for *leptotês* by emphasising that his erotic *Aetia* would incorporate and thus subvert epic material: *Iliads* would be transformed into elegiac narratives of erotic battles (2.1.11-14). The second Propertian poetry-book takes as its project a paradoxical version of the Callimachean polemic: the revision of epic in elegy.[84] 2.2 then contributes to that project by presenting a woman of epic proportions in a short poem, incorporating into poetry which is *kata lepton* the *megalê gynê* opposed to it and rejected by Callimachus in the preface to the *Aetia* (fr.11-12).[85] Thus even the flesh of Cynthia is moulded to fit a poetic purpose. But a political as well as a poetic context is supplied for this project in 2.1. That poem contains not just one, but two tables of contents for the second book; one erotic (vv.5-16) and one political (vv.17-38), of which the first is formulated as substitute for the second, a sexual instead of a military *historia* (vv.13-16). Cynthia replaces Caesar as the subject of poetic discourse. One anti-epic speaks for another.

The flesh with which the Elegiac Woman is endowed in Propertius 2.2 is moulded to suit the politics and poetics of its author: Cynthia's body is built out of the bones buried at Perugia and yet signifies a style of writing which is *lepton*. A brief study of Cynthia's textual characteristics thus demonstrates again that useful lessons are to be learned from reading *Amores* 3.1. The awkward figure of Elegia operates in a direct line of descent from the massively proportioned Cynthia of Propertius' second book. Her title, her limp and her comic plight all contribute to a humorous demystification of female flesh and its exposure as a site for the expression of poetic and political concerns. Thus deprived of plausible portraits of Augustan girl-friends, critics may find it yet more difficult to treat elegy's female figures as a window onto the reality of women's lives at Rome.

I would like to thank Averil Cameron, John Henderson, Steve Hinds and E.J. Kenney for their comments on and criticisms of an earlier draft of this paper.

Bibliography

Allen, Archibald W. 1950a. 'Sincerity and the Roman Elegists', *CPh* 45, 145-60.
———— 1950b. 'Elegy and the Classical attitude toward Love: Propertius 1.1', *Yale Class. Stud.* 11, 253-77.
Alpers, J. 1912. *Hercules in Bivio, Dissertatio Inauguralis* (Göttingen).
Anderson, William S. 1964. 'Hercules Exclusus: Propertius IV.9', *Am. Journ. Philol.* 85, 1-12.
Balsdon, J.P.V.D. 1962. *Roman Women: their history and habits* (London).

[84] See King 1981.
[85] I am grateful to Professor Kenney for this suggestion.

Barber, E.A., ed. 1960². *Sexti Properti Carmina* (Oxford).

Barsby, John A. 1979. *Ovid Amores Book 1*. Bristol Reprint (Oxford 1973).

Bassett, Edward L. 1966. 'Hercules and the Hero of the *Punica*', in L. Wallach, ed., *The Classical Tradition: literary and historical studies in honor of Harry Caplan* (Cornell), 258-73.

Berger, John 1972. *Ways of Seeing* (London).

Berman, K.E. 1975. 'Ovid, Propertius and the Elegiac genre: some imitations in the *Amores*', *Rivista di Studi Classici* 23, 14-22.

Bertini, Ferruccio 1983. *Ovidio: Amori* (Milan).

Boucher, Jean-Paul 1965. *Etudes sur Properce: problèmes d'inspiration et d'art* (Paris).

Brandt, Paul 1963. *P. Ovidi Nasonis Amorum Libri Tres Text und Kommentar* (Hildesheim).

Bright, David F. 1978. *Haec mihi fingebam: Tibullus in his world*. Cincinnati Classical Studies NS 3 (Leiden).

Bruere, Richard T. 1959. 'Color Ovidianus in Silius *Punica* 8-17', *CPh* 54, 228-45.

Cameron, Alan 1968. 'The first edition of Ovid's *Amores*', *CQ* NS 18, 320-33.

Camps, W.A. 1967. *Propertius Elegies II* (Cambridge).

Curran, Leo C. 1975. 'Nature to advantage dressed: Propertius 1.2', *Ramus* 4.1, 1-16.

Davis, John T. 1981. 'Risit Amor: aspects of literary burlesque in Ovid's *Amores*, in H. Temporini, ed., *Aufstieg und Niedergang der römischen Welt*, II. 31.4, 2460-506.

Du Quesnay, I.M. Le M. 1973. 'The Amores', in J.W. Binns, ed., *Greek and Latin Studies, Classical Literature and its Influence: Ovid* (London), 1-48.

Fau, Guy 1978. *L'Emancipation féminine à Rome* (Paris).

Fedeli, Paolo 1980. *Sesto Properzio: Il Primo Libro delle Elegie* (Firenze).

——— 1985. *Properzio: Il Libro Terzo delle Elegie* (Bari).

Galinsky, G. Karl 1969. 'The triumph theme in the Augustan elegy', *Wiener Studien*, NF 3, 75-107.

——— 1972. *The Herakles Theme: the adaptation of the hero in literature from Homer to the twentieth century* (Oxford).

Giangrande, Giuseppe 1981. 'Hellenistic topoi in Ovid's *Amores*', *Museum Philol. Lond.* 4, 25-51.

Gigon, Olof 1956. *Kommentar zum zweiten Buch von Xenophons Memorabilien*, Schweizerische Beiträge zur Altertumswissenschaft, Heft 7 (Basel).

Green, Peter 1982. *Ovid. The Erotic Poems* (London).

Griffin, Jasper 1985. *Latin Poets and Roman Life* (London).

Grimal, Pierre 1963. *L'Amour à Rome* (Paris).

Gross, Nicolas P. 1975-6. 'Ovid, *Amores* 3.11A and B: a literary mélange', *Class. Journ.* 71, 152-60.

Harvey, Sylvia 1980. 'Woman's place: the absent family of film noir', in Kaplan 1980, 22-34.

Hubbard, Margaret, 1974. *Propertius* (London).

Innes, D.C. 1979. 'Gigantomachy and natural philosophy', *Class. Quart.* 29, 165-71.

Kaplan, E. Ann, ed. 1980. *Women in Film Noir* (London).

Kenney, E.J. 1961. *P. Ovidi Nasonis* (Oxford).

King, Joy 1980. 'Propertius 2.1-12: his Callimachean second libellus', *Würzburger Jahrbücher f. die Altertumswissenschaft*, NF 6b, 61-84.

———— 1981. 'Propertius 2.2: a Callimachean "multum in parvo"', *Wien. Stud.* NF 15, 169-84.

Lee, Guy 1962. 'Tenerorum Lusor Amorum', in J.P. Sullivan, ed., *Critical Essays on Roman Literature: Elegy and Lyric* (London), 149-79.

———— 1968. *Ovid's Amores* (London).

Lefkowitz, Mary R. 1981. *Heroines and Hysterics* (London).

Lilja, Saara 1978. *The Roman Elegists' Attitude to Women* (repr. New York; Helsinki 1965).

Lipshitz, Susan, ed. 1978. *Tearing the Veil: essays on femininity* (London).

Lyne, R.O.A.M. 1980. *The Latin Love Poets: from Catullus to Horace* (Oxford).

McKeown, J.C. 1987. *Ovid: Amores. vol. 1. Text and Prolegomena. Arca.* Classical and Medieval Texts, Papers and Monographs 20 (Liverpool).

Morgan, Kathleen 1977. *Ovid's Art of Imitation: Propertius in the Amores*, Mnemosyne Supp. 47 (Leiden).

Nethercut, William R. 1983. 'Recent scholarship on Propertius', in *ANRW* (see Davis 1981), II. 30.3, 1813-57.

Otis, Brooks 1938. 'Ovid and the Augustans', *Trans. Am. Philol. Ass.* 69, 188-229.

Pillinger, Hugh E. 1969. 'Some Callimachean influences on Propertius, Book 4', *HSCP* 73, 171-99.

Pomeroy, Sarah B. 1975. *Goddesses, Whores, Wives and Slaves* (New York).

Putnam, M.C.J. 1976. 'Propertius 1.22: a poet's self-definition', *Quaderni Urbinati di cultura classica* 23, 93-123.

Quadlbauer, Franz 1968. 'Properz 3.1', *Philologus* 112, 83-118.

———— 1970. 'Non humilem ... poetam: zur literaturgeschichtlichen Stellung von Prop. 1,7,21', *Hermes* 98, 331-9.

Quinn, Kenneth 1963. *Latin Explorations: critical studies in Roman literature* (London).

Reitzenstein, Erich 1935. 'Das neue Kunstwollen in den Amores Ovids', *Rhein. Mus.* 84, 62-88.

Schrijvers, P.H. 1976. 'O tragedia tu labor aeternus. Etudes sur l'élegie III, 1 des Amours d'Ovide', in J.M. Bremer, S.L. Radt and C.J. Ruijgh, eds., *Miscellanea tragica in honorem J.C. Kamerbeek* (Amsterdam), 405-24.

Stahl, Hans-Peter 1985. *Propertius: 'Love' and 'War'* (Berkeley and Los Angeles).

Sullivan, J.P. 1961. 'Two problems in Roman Love Elegy', *Trans. Am. Philol. Ass.* 92, 522-36.

———— 1976. *Propertius. A critical introduction* (Cambridge).

Syme, Ronald 1978. *History in Ovid* (Oxford).

Veyne, Paul 1983. *L'Élégie érotique romaine: l'amour, la poésie et l'occident* (Paris).

Warner, Marina 1976. *Alone of all her Sex.* (London).

Wiggers, Nancy 1976-1977. 'Reconsideration of Propertius II.1', *Class. Journ.* 72, 334-41.

Wimmel, Walter 1960. 'Kallimachos in Rom: Die Nachfolge seines apologetischen Dichtens in der Augusteerzeit', *Hermes Einzelschriften* 16 (Wiesbaden).

Wyke, Maria 1984. *The Elegiac Woman and her Male Creators: Propertius and the written Cynthia* (Diss. Cambridge).

———— 1987. 'Written women: Propertius' *scripta puella*', *JRS* 77, 47-61.

6

The Transformations of the Text: the reception of John's Revelation

The successive compositions and decompositions, elucidations and shadings, fragmentations and compactions, which the act of reading brings to a written text, are of such delicate multiplicity that we have no normative or verifiable account of them ... Rereading the identical passage or book, we are already other than we were.

George Steiner, *Antigones* (Oxford, 1984), 291.

The next three chapters all concern early Christianity. Does one any longer need to defend the inclusion, in a collection devoted to ancient history, of such subject matter? If we are interested in cultural history, then all of the religious history of the period in question is part of our subject, and one should rather be defending the exclusion of other topics, Judaism, for example, or the many forms of paganism. As it happens, though, early Christianity is peculiarly well suited to our theme, for its own striking dependence on texts, its formation of a sacred canon, its striving to express its teachings in verbal form, and to agree on a 'correct' formulation, and for its attention to communication and to interpretation. And besides the intrinsic interest for us of the development of Christianity as a text-based religion, there is also the spectacle of the efforts of modern historians and theologians to understand both it and the texts – to interpret the words.

The next three chapters are all, in their differing ways, concerned with this problem. For not only must historians use the texts in question to compose their picture of early Christianity as a historical development within the Roman empire; theologians, and indeed all Christians today, must also find a way of making them speak to themselves. They can neither, as Sr. Charles Murray shows, abandon the texts nor give up the sense that the texts must be true. Dimitris Kyrtatas shows how differently Revelation has been read over the centuries in order to keep that sense in the face of contradictory appearances; in other words, the meaning must be constantly adjusted to present circumstances, the texts reinterpreted to save them from themselves.

Feminist and liberation theology pose this issue in particularly acute form, and indeed some feminists explicitly defend their procedure as one of 'remembering', or, as a sceptic might see it, reading the desired present back into the early texts; but it is present for all Christian theologians and historians, however neutral their actual subject matter may seem to be. Thus the general issue of history and faith, on which a non-Christian might view Sr. Charles Murray as gallantly struggling to square the circle, is in fact a matter of great contemporary importance for writers such as Paul Ricoeur, for whom the interpretation of Biblical texts is a constant matter of engagement and interaction. Nor can this be marginalised by historians by leaving it all to the theologians, for at least some, and perhaps all, the texts are also historical documents from which the history of Christianity, within the wider history of Roman culture, must be written. We have here therefore something much more complex to deal with than the 'bias' of a given source; rather, a whole tradition which has itself developed in a self-conscious relation to its own texts, both shaping them and being shaped by them.

These chapters also raise the whole question of a canonical text or set of texts, texts which have a special kind of designated authority, and whose status must be retained at all costs. Many early Christian texts did not get into the canon; indeed, Dimitris Kyrtatas charts the fortunes of Revelation in this regard, and some of the texts which were excluded make an appearance in my own essay. The mechanisms which the Church evolved for this process of exclusion would themselves have made an interesting theme; this too, far from being finished and over with when the New Testament canon was settled around the end of the second century AD, continued in other ways for many centuries, and spilled over into the exclusion of individuals and doctrinal formulations from the corporate body of the Church. The Christian canon therefore has some relation to, though it is also different from, the notion of a literary classic, and we have only to think of the devaluation of the idea of a classic in modern literary theory[1] to see that a religious canon will pose peculiar difficulties for us today. It is not surprising that Christian writers find more congenial the hermeneutics of Gadamer and Ricoeur than the deconstructive turn of Derrida, for the former will allow a sympathetic and continuing engagement with the canonical texts rather than the total rejection of their canonical status. A theory of reception, like that of Jauss, whom Kyrtatas evokes in his study of Revelation, will allow both the reinterpretation of the canonical text and its retention. To return again to George Steiner (*Antigones*, p. 297):

The classic is a text whose initial, existential coming into being and realization may well be unrecapturable to us (this will always be true of

---

[1] See Frank Kermode, *The Classic* (London, 1975).

the literatures of antiquity). But the integral authority of the classic is such that it can absorb without loss of identity the millenial incursions upon it, the accretions to it, of commentary, of translations, of enacted variations. *Ulysses* reinforces Homer; Broch's *Death of Virgil* enriches the Aeneid. Sophocles' *Antigone* will not suffer from Lacan.

The Transformations of the Text: the reception of John's Revelation

Dimitris Kyrtatas

Historians usually examine texts from the point of view of their content: What can we learn about the history of the people mentioned in our written sources; What can we learn about the authors of these sources? Such are the questions asked most often by historians. But since texts in their transmission have their own history, they may also be used as sources for the history of those who read them, copied them down, preserved, interpreted them, or destroyed them. What I would like to discuss is, in short, the *history of reception of texts*.

Now and then, historians have made use of information provided by this history of reception. A small number of examples will suffice to illustrate the significance of this.

1. Collecting papyrological information, E.G. Turner has shed light upon the status of the owners of papyri. Reynolds and Wilson, drawing from similar sources, have written about scribes and scholars (Turner 1968; Reynolds and Wilson 1975).

2. Statistics on the manuscript tradition have led to arguments about the relative influence of texts. C.H. Roberts has claimed that the very small number of early Gnostic writings, as compared to orthodox writings of the same period in Egypt, is evidence of the pre-eminence of orthodoxy in early Christian Egypt (Roberts 1979).

3. The geographic distribution of documents is also used as evidence of the spread of particular ideas. Henry Chadwick believes that 'A papyrus find proves that Irenaeus' refutation of Gnosticism was being read at Oxyrhynchus within a very few years of its publication, which suggests much concern in Egypt for the maintenance of orthodoxy' (Chadwick 1967, 64).

4. According to B.M. Metzger a detailed examination of the manuscript tradition of the New Testament reveals that a number of variant readings were due to intentional changes, some of which were clearly made because of doctrinal considerations (Metzger 1968, 201ff.).

In these examples, texts have been of interest to historians not primarily because of their content, but because of their form, the number of surviving copies, their geographic distribution, their transmission, their reception in general. It is quite clear, I believe, even from these few examples, that evidence from the reception of texts has found its way into the writing of history. And yet, as far as I know, this field of research has been treated in a cursory and rather unsystematic way. What is lacking is a method, or perhaps a theory, which would allow for a long-term evaluation of the existing evidence. Broadly speaking, this theory would have to deal with a number of topics, and first of all with the reading proper of texts. How often was a text being read, who were its readers, what importance was attributed to the reading of texts, how did people react to what they read? Furthermore, our theory would have to deal with the various interpretations, criticisms, refutations or rejections of a text. In addition, the history of the imitations of a text and the history of the family of texts which spring out of the influence of an original work must also be considered. This family, or group of related texts, includes a course the so-called *pseudepigrapha* and *spuria*, which give a measure of the significance of the authentic works of an author.

All this may sound a bit strange to historians. What I have been saying derives primarily from recent considerations in the field of literary history. But history proper also has to profit by extending its horizon in this direction. It is surprising, for example, that C.H. Roberts, in his otherwise justly praised *Manuscript, Society and Belief in Early Christian Egypt*, based his argument on statistics of papyri finds, without considering the relative importance each Christian group attributed to texts during that period. We are in a position to know that the earliest Gnostics were far less keen on using written documents than their orthodox contemporaries. Doesn't this simple observation question the validity of Roberts' argument? If, on the other hand, one had kept in mind that the evidence from the reception of texts requires a more systematic treatment, such oversights would have been avoided. At the end of this chapter I shall come back to this problem. In the meantime I think it would be best to concentrate on just one example and try to illustrate some aspects of this theory of reception. Unfortunately, although I shall have to go into a rather lengthy discussion, my chapter may only serve as a very general introduction; I can in no way claim to exhaust the topic.

It will have certainly been noticed, perhaps not without some discomfort, that a number of my examples derive from Christian rather than pagan literature. And what is worse, from the New Testament and its related material, instead of the work of Christian historians. The text I have chosen to examine may seem even more surprising in a colletion meant to interest historians. For some years now I have been working on the Christianisation of the Roman world and I am obviously myself much more familiar with Christian documents. But there are also more important reasons which make the choice of Christian works appropriate for the needs of the present investigation. Homer's *Iliad*, by far the most popular pagan Greek text, is preserved in no more than several hundreds of papyri and manuscripts. The New Testament is preserved in several thousands of papyri and manuscripts. This simple comparison suffices, I believe, to remind us of the great importance attached to reading the New Testament. In the view of the orthodox churches, all Christians should, if possible, possess a copy. Reading, however, was not enough. Scripture had to be understood, and therefore explained. To put it crudely, the history of early Christian literature is the history of the interpretation and reinterpretation of its sacred texts. Commentaries and scholia on Scripture exceed by far anything similar concerning pagan literature. And, as it may be realised, commentaries are witnesses of the first order for our purpose, since they represent particular ways in which New Testament documents were read and understood. Finally, while 'the work of many an ancient author has been preserved only in manuscripts which date from the Middle Ages (sometimes the late Middle Ages), far removed from the time at which he lived and wrote', as Metzger has pointed out, 'several papyrus manuscripts of portions of the New Testament are extant which were copied within a century or so after the composition of the original documents' (Metzger 1968, 34f.).

From this family of New Testament documents, I have chosen to consider the most peculiar and perplexing text – today as in ancient times: the Revelation of John. I shall make use of the perplexity this text has caused, as further evidence of the way it was received, i.e. read, interpreted, accepted and rejected. The more a certain text has provoked discussion, the more our reflections on its reception find material to work on.

The Revelation of John has given rise to endless discussions. Very little however of the contemporary literature is of use for our present purpose. Norman Cohn's very interesting and important book *The Pursuit of the Millennium* comes in a way much closer to a history of the reception of ideas propagated in Revelation than anything similar that has been written on the topic. As far as general introductions to the apocalyptic literature of early Christianity are concerned, I have found P. Vielhauer's chapters in E. Hennecke's *New Testament Apocrypha* extremely useful and informative (Hennecke-Schneemelcher II, 1965). A few more works are mentioned in the bibliography. I shall commence by giving an account of the evidence concerning the reception of the book of Revelation in the centuries which followed its composition.

John's Revelation, as most scholars agree today, was composed (incorporating perhaps older material) in the last years of the first century, during the persecutions of the age of Domitian. This dating of Revelation had already been proposed in the late second century by Irenaeus. An alternative dating of the text to the reign of Nero is by comparison unlikely, since persecutions in Asia Minor at such an early age are not attested, and Jewish Christian relations had not yet come to such a low state as our text presupposes (as is known, they were particularly aggravated after the Jewish War of 66-70). Early Christian persecutions, as had happened with the persecutions of Jews in the Hellenistic age, gave rise to eschatological expectations. At the time Revelation was written, the faithful and their martyrs were still expecting to be avenged – in one way or another – upon earth. Under these circumstances, the author of Revelation was influenced by the Jewish prophetic style and in particular the apocalyptic style of the Book of Daniel.

We have to wait for about 30 years for the first direct information about the impression this work made on the Christians who first read it. But we can form an idea of a possible first reception of the book judging from its author's expectations. In his short preface, John presented his work as a revelation and a prophecy: 'Happy is the man who reads, and happy those who listen to the words of this prophecy and heed what is written in it. For the hour of fulfilment is near.' (1:3) This preface is followed, however, by a second preface which introduces a collection of seven letters, and the reader has to go through several pages before coming to what was promised in the opening words. The book ends with closing greetings as it was customary with letters. There seems to be a contradiction (reflected in the double preface) between a pseudoepistolary form and an apocalyptic or prophetic content. The readers of Revelation were predisposed to expect a collection of letters, to which a visionary prophecy was being affixed. As is well known, the common medium by which early Christians communicated their ideas was the letter, and though they must have been familiar with the Jewish literature, they did not themselves pursue the literary forms of the Hebrew Bible. Thus, a rather unfamiliar apocalyptic style was presented under the thin disguise of a familiar epistolary form.

At the end of Revelation a warning was given to all who listened to the words of the prophecy. 'Should anyone add to them', the author wrote, 'God will add to him the plagues described in this book; should anyone take away from the words in this book of prophecy, God will take away from him his share in the tree of life and the Holy City, described in this book' (22:18f.). Early Christian texts, circulating from church to church, almost inevitably fell victims to additions and omissions; there was no way of protecting them, and John appealed to

God to safeguard his own work. John was aware of his authority, but no authority in those days could produce works that would not fear corruption. How much our own Revelation corresponds to the original, we have no means of saying, but it is clear that interpolations would almost certainly find their way into the most successful and influential works, and John anticipated that his document belonged to this category.

One final remark: At the time of the composition of the text, most symbols and symbolic expressions used in it were well known – or easily understood – such as Babylon for Rome, Lamb for Christ. But some cryptograms, such as the number/name of the Beast, were left to be deciphered by the 'intelligent'. 'Here is the key; and anyone who has intelligence may work out the number of the beast. The number represents a man's name, and the numerical value of its letters is six hundred and sixty-six' (13:18). It is believed today that the number stands for Nero and refers to one of his successors, probably Domitian, who was known as Nero *redivivus*. As we shall see in a moment, there is evidence that this cryptogram was in fact understood by at least some of the very first readers of Revelation, but that soon, for reasons that can be understood, the original meaning of the number was lost.

Our first direct witness of the reception of Revelation is Papias, bishop of Hierapolis in Phrygia, who died about 130. According to Irenaeus, he was 'the hearer of John', but, as Eusebius noted, judging from his own words Papias 'makes plain that he had in no way been a hearer and eyewitness of the sacred Apostles' (*HE* 3.39.1f.). He seems, nevertheless, to have been formed as a Christian in the circle of the author of Revelation. According to early tradition, Papias had written five volumes under the general title *The Sayings of the Lord Explained*. This is the earliest recorded commentary on the dominical sayings of the Gospels and oral tradition.

From what very little of Papias' work has survived, it seems that it could have been also titled *The Sayings of the Lord Expanded*. In Revelation we are told that in the kingdom of God there would be a river flowing from his throne. 'On either side of the river stood a tree of life, which yields twelve crops of fruit, one for each month of the year …' (22:2). According to Papias, 'The days will come, in which vines shall grow, each having ten thousand branches, and in each branch ten thousand twigs, and in each true twig ten thousand shoots, and in each one of the shoots ten thousand clusters, and on everyone of the clusters ten thousand grapes, and every grape when pressed will give five and twenty metretes of wine' (Irenaeus, *AH* 5.33). Eusebius, giving his own summary, reported that Papias 'adduces other accounts, as though they came to him from unwritten tradition, and some strange parables and teachings of the Saviour, and some other more mythical accounts.

Among them he says that there will be a millennium after the resurrection of the dead, when the kingdom of Christ will be set up in material form on this earth' (*HE* 3.39.11f.). On Jerome's testimony, Papias is supposed to have written a further work under the title *Second Coming of Our Lord or Millennium*. The authenticity of such a work is doubtful, but it indicates how preoccupied, according to later tradition, Papias was believed to have been with the subject of the millennium and the kingdom of God (Jerome, *De viris illustr.* 18).

The idea of the thousand-year reign of Christ upon earth derived of course from John's Revelation, about the inspiration of which Papias is reported to have given 'satisfactory testimony'. Once again, our Revelation is very epigrammatic on the subject: 'Those who had been beheaded for the sake of God's word ... came to life again and reigned with Christ for a thousand years, though the rest of the dead did not come to life until the thousand years were over' (20:4f.). How much Papias had to say about this, we cannot tell. What seems certain is that not more than a generation after its composition, Revelation was being taken seriously in some quarters in Asia Minor, and that emphasis was laid on its very last sections where the thousand-year reign and the kingdom of God were described. Not a word is reported referring to the letters to the seven churches of Asia. Those were the years of the Jewish revolt of AD 133-5 (although we cannot say whether it was before or after its suppression by Hadrian) and, as we shall see later on, it was during this period that the Christian apocalyptic literature flourished. As for the pseudoepistolary form, it seems to have served its purpose; it was not needed any longer.

Our next witness is Justin Martyr, who was converted to Christianity somewhere in the East about 130. In a work he wrote soon after his conversion, the *Dialogue with Trypho*, Justin claimed that 'There was a certain man with us, whose name was John, one of the apostles of Christ, who *prophesied*, by a *revelation* that was made to him, that those who believed in our Christ would dwell a thousand years in Jerusalem; and that thereafter the general, and, in short, the eternal resurrection and judgement of all men would likewise take place' (*DT* 81). Justin was one of the first authors to attribute Revelation to John the apostle (Papias may have attributed it to another John known as John the elder or presbyter). Like Papias he was interested in the very last sections of this work which he clearly read as a revelation, not as a collection of letters. It appears, however, that Justin was aware of other, not 'right-minded', i.e. orthodox, Christians, who did not share his reading of Revelation (*DT* 80).

Not long after Justin, another Asian bishop, Melito of Sardis, who flourished in the mid-second century, wrote a whole book on the Revelation of John. Nothing is known of the view he took, but the titles of some other works of his, such as *On the Lord's Day* and *On the Devil*, suggest that he too was preoccupied with the topics of the last sections of Revelation (Jerome, *De viris illustr.* 24).

About 156, according to Epiphanius, or 172, according to Eusebius (our sources are not consistent), a certain Montanus is reported to have inspired and led a Christian sect with strong millenarian beliefs. In Phrygia, where it originated, and all over Asia, this new movement found numerous supporters. Some scholars, such as Harnack, have understood Montanism as an attempt to revert to primitive Christianity. At any rate most Christian leaders reacted against Montanism and attacked it bitterly. A number of these orthodox leaders are known, but very little about their works. Judging from scattered evidence, however, it seems that Montanism and anti-Montanism were inevitably involved in a discussion of Revelation and its last millenarian sections. As a rule, in the third century, pro-Montanist authors, such as Tertullian, were fervent supporters of Revelation while anti-Montanists, such as Gaius, its fervent opponents.

Before the end of the second century, however, we have the extremely important testimony of Irenaeus, who stands out as the first great orthodox theologian and an eminent advocate of millenarian Christianity. The last chapters of his work *Against Heresies* are more or less concerned with the Revelation of John. Very briefly I shall make a number of points which are related to our topic.

1. Irenaeus understood Revelation in accordance with Old Testament prophecies and in particular in accordance with the Book of Daniel. He seems to have been one of the first to have noticed the resemblance of the two works.

2. According to Irenaeus, in his days not all orthodox Christians shared his own literal reading of Revelation. As far as the earthly kingdom of Christ was concerned, he argued, certain Christians derived their views from heretical discourses. Despite Papias, some attempted to interpret the traditional expectations in an allegorical manner.

3. The name of anti-Christ could not easily be deciphered any longer. Irenaeus recorded a number of (improbable) possibilities, but could not include Nero nor Domitian (Nero *redivivus*), both dead for more than a century, while still expecting the prophecy to be fulfilled in the future. Writing about the number/name of the beast, Irenaeus gave very useful information. He said that this number was found in all the most approved and ancient copies of Revelation, thus making it clear that the autograph had already perished. 'I do not know', he went on, 'how it is that some have erred ... and have vitiated the middle number

in the name, deducting the amount of fifty from it, so that instead of six decades they will have it that there is but one' (*AH* 5.30). That is, instead of 666, some manuscripts read 616. The first number could stand for the Greek 'Neron Kaisar', while the second for the Latin form of the same name, 'Nero Caesar' – in the Hebrew Talmud the name appears in both forms. (The idea is that by transferring the Greek spelling of Neron Kaisar into Hebrew characters and then giving them numerical values we get the following series: n = 50, r = 200, o = 6, n = 50, k = 100, s = 60, r =200. By adding these numbers we get 666. Transferring the Latin spelling Nero Caesar into Hebrew characters and giving them once more numerical values, the last n in Neron disappears, and thus, by adding the numbers, we get 666–50 = 616.) If this decipherment, first proposed in the mid-nineteenth century, is correct, it proves that the earliest readers of Revelation were able to understand the meaning of the cryptogram, as some of them corrected it into what they believed to be its more appropriate form. In the late second century, however, as Irenaeus reports, many were venturing to seek out the name using either number with little success.

4. One last point. Through his own interpretation of Scripture Irenaeus calculated that the End of the World would come six thousand years after Creation. This means that according to the chronology of the apologists the world had still about three hundred years to go before its final destruction. This new calculation was necessary since more than a century had passed without the imminent expectation being realised. Thus the promise given in Revelation, 'I am coming soon', now called for a new meaning which, whether Irenaeus liked it or not, favoured an allegorical interpretation of the text.

Other important second-century witnesses, such as Tertullian, Clement of Alexandria and the Muratori Canon, confirm that John's Revelation enjoyed the status of Holy Scripture, but very little can be said about the particular ways in which it was read and understood.

In the early third century, however, Revelation was brought to the centre of bitter conflicts among Christians. Thus, an Egyptian congregation led by a bishop called Nepos defended with vehemence its millenarian beliefs. Basing his opinions on the Revelation of John, Nepos, in a work entitled *Refutation of the Allegorists*, attacked his opponents (who had already made their appearance in the days of Irenaeus) arguing 'that the promises which had been made to the saints in the divine Scriptures should be interpreted after a more Jewish fashion' (i.e. literally), and 'that there will be a kind of millennium on this earth devoted to bodily indulgence' (Eusebius, *HE* 7.24). On the other side some Christians found that allegorisation was not enough; Revelation had to be totally rejected. To substantiate his point Gaius, a fervent anti-Montanist Roman presbyter, argued that

Revelation was not the work of John (either the apostle or the elder), but of the heretic Cerinthus – a personal enemy of the apostle. Thus, a work until then considered to have been inspired by God was now altogether impugned, examined chapter by chapter and found to be illogical and with a false title. It could not be an apocalypse, an unveiling, since it was veiled by its own heavy, thick curtain of unintelligibility. Gaius strongly objected to the idea of a kingdom of Christ upon earth after the resurrection and in particular to the thousand-year reign. In the polemic of the period the doctrines of Revelation (now attributed to Cerinthus) were presented as if caused by carnal desires and indulgence of the flesh (Eusebius, *HE* 3.28, 7.25). By scrutinising Revelation, its critics could not fail to examine the epistolary sections as well. Although appearing to be more rational in character, the letters to the seven churches were found to be even more absurd. How could a letter be addressed to Thyatira, the critics asked, if there was no church at all there? (Epiphanius, *Haer.* 51.33). The geographic map of early Christianity had obviously changed within a century, but this fact was not taken into account.

By the first half of the third century, tempers regarding Revelation were high. There were those like the Montanists and the followers of Nepos who attempted to read it literally; there were those who accepted it as Scripture, but allegorised its content either mildly, as was the case of Hippolytus of Rome, or completely, as was the case of Origen (Hippolytus' *Commentary on Revelation* has not survived, but his views are reflected in his *Commentary on Daniel*; the work discovered by Dioubouniotis and Harnack and presented as Origen's *Commentary on Revelation* is actually a compilation of shorter notes by Clement of Alexandria, Irenaeus and Origen); finally there were those like Gaius who vulgarised its literal sense and rejected it altogether.

In the second half of the third century the great bishop of Alexandria and renowned disciple of Origen, Dionysius, intervened in the disputes over John's Revelation. Dionysius was urged to deal with the subject because conflicts between millenarians and allegorists were now causing schisms and defections of whole churches. Unlike his predecessors, this church father sought reconciliation and the union of the Christian congregations without, however, abandoning his own views. Intellectually, Dionysius belonged to the Alexandrian school and was, therefore, an allegorist, but in his intervention he advanced instead arguments of a different order. He called his treatise *On Promises* and in the sections of it which have been preserved, three main propositions were put forward:

1. Concerning the author of Revelation, he argued that many early Christians must have had the name John, just as Paul and Peter are

favourite names for the children of believers. It was also said that at Ephesus two tombs were reputed to be John's. The author of Revelation was thus not necessarily the apostle – in any case he himself did not claim to be the apostle, but simply John.

2. Comparing the ideas and notions advanced in the Johannine Corpus he noticed that 'it is obvious that those who observe their character throughout will see at a glance that the Gospel and Epistle have one and the same complexion. But the Apocalypse is utterly different from, and foreign to, these writings.'

3. Finally, according to Dionysius, one can also estimate the difference between the Gospel and Epistle on the one hand and the Apocalypse on the other, by means of the style. The former were written in faultless Greek while the latter employed barbarous idioms, in some places committing downright solecisms.

Developing these propositions and substantiating them with numerous and carefully chosen examples, Dionysius meant to reject the apostolic authorship of Revelation, without declaring it a forgery or twisting its content. On the contrary, supporters of this work could still hold it in esteem and regard it as an inspired prophecy. But at an age when apostolic authorship of a text was the primary criterion for its inclusion in the New Testament Canon, Dionysius' arguments would necessarily have led to the exclusion of Revelation. The Alexandrian father knew only too well that being excluded from the Canon, Revelation would have in effect the same fate as being attributed to Cerinthus, the only difference being that in this way opposition would be milder (Eusebius, *HE* 7.25).

After Dionysius, apart from a few, such as Athanasius, the majority of Christian leaders in the East excluded Revelation from the holy Canon (among them the Cappadocian fathers, Cyril of Jerusalem, John Chrysostom, Theodore of Mopsuestia and in the fifth century Theodoret). According to Amphilochius, a late fourth-century bishop of Iconium, Revelation was considered spurious by most fathers of his day. The *Canons of Laodicea* and the *Apostolic Canons* did not include Revelation in the canonical books. The early (third century) Syriac and the (fifth century) Armenian versions of the New Testament omitted Revelation. The ninth-century *Stichometry of Nicephorus* rejected it and an even later Catalogue, reflecting the attitude of the Greek Church, did not include it among the canonical books (Hennecke-Schneemelcher I, 1963, 51).

During this whole period only three Greek commentaries on Revelation are known – two in the sixth century by Oecumenius and Andrew of Caesarea and one in the tenth by Arethas. All three interpreted Revelation allegorically and in one way or another rejected its millenarian connotations.

It was different in the West. There, despite Gaius and his friends, no attempt to question the canonicity of Revelation was successful. A number of Christians are known to have favoured a millenarian interpretation. Such was Victorinus of Pettau in Pannonia, the earliest Latin exegete, who died in 304. His *Commentary on the Revelation*, which draws upon Papias, Irenaeus, Hippolytus and Origen, is still extant. Such was Lactantius, who was active a few years later. In the late fifth century Gennadius, a presbyter of Marseilles, wrote a *Commentary on the Revelation* and a treatise, *On the Millennium*, which indicates that such ideas were still influential. The millenarian poet Commodian also bears witness to this. In a sixth-century catalogue of apocryphal books (the so-called *Decretum Gelasianum*), a book ascribed to Nepos and the works of Victorinus, Lactantius, Montanus and Commodian were among those enumerated, which could mean that these works were being still read, though the Church was attempting to distinguish them from Scripture.

But on the whole, the attitude of the Western Church was in line with Augustine's extreme allegorisation of the text. I have no space here to go into Augustine's reading of Revelation, but those who are interested may easily find it in the 20th book of his *City of God*. I need only say that having reduced Revelation to a number of points, he interpreted them in his own way, regarding the millennium as having already been realised upon earth: it had been realised in the Church 'as it now is'.

It is quite clear that as we leave behind the date of its composition, increasing difficulties in the understanding of Revelation made interpretation necessary, whether literal or allegorical. All the more so, as Christianity was becoming a religion of the Book, and everything that was religiously important, moral conduct, doctrine, beliefs, church organisation, etc., had to be justified in Scripture. In fact, as the age was expressing itself increasingly in religious terms, not only religious matters, but social aspirations and even political positions were being discussed in the light of the sacred texts. Much of what I have already said remains to a large extent within the limits of dogmatic history. A history of the reception of texts should also take into account the general developments and tendencies, which form the background of dogmatic history. I shall therefore now turn my attention to these factors. But as I do not have enough space to cover the whole field, I shall concentrate upon a particular area which is concerned with the so-called horizon of expectations.

'A literary work', to put it in the words of the German literary historian Hans Robert Jauss, 'even when it appears to be new, does not present itself as something absolutely new in an informational vacuum, but predisposes its audience to a very specific kind of reception by announcements, overt and convert signals, familiar characteristics, or implicit allusions. It awakens memories of that which was already read, brings the reader to a specific emotional attitude, and with its beginning arouses expectations for the "middle and end", which can then be maintained intact or altered, reoriented, or even fulfilled ironically in the course of the reading according to specific rules of the genre or type of text' (Jauss 1982, 23).

In short, a literary work, or any text in general, is produced and understood within a frame of reference determined by a convention of genre, style, or form. The Revelation of John, to come back to our example, has some of the external characteristics of a catholic epistle (i.e. of a treatise addressed to the community as a whole), while much of its content depends on, and perhaps Christianises, Jewish prophetic literature, with apocalyptic elements, to which it owes its dualism, determinism and pessimism. On the other hand, strictly speaking, when it appeared it did not belong to any known genre in particular. It was more of a hybrid, unless we presuppose the existence of a pre-Christian Jewish apocalyptic genre, which has perished. To its first readers it must have appeared as at once familiar and strange. It presented itself as an epistle (or collection of epistles), the established type of early Christian communication, yet its content was prophetic and visionary rather than hortatory. It imitated in content some of the Old Testament books, yet instead of a review of history (as found for example in the Book of Daniel), it provided a description and critique of the present situation of the Church. In fact, unlike its Jewish prototypes, the author of Revelation emphatically stressed his contemporaneity with his readers: 'I, John, your brother, who share with you in the suffering and the sovereignty, and the endurance which is ours in Jesus – I was in the island called Patmos ...' (1:9) (Vielhauer, in Hennecke-Schneemelcher II, 1965, 623).

It thus becomes clear that Revelation presented itself within a given horizon of expectations (conditioned by the epistolary genre), without, however, fulfilling these expectations. In fact, it gave rise to new expectations, as it appended to its critique of the present situation of the Church a vision of what was to soon come. With the popularity it gained and the influence it exercised, this initially strange hybrid became a classic text in the sense that it induced a change in the horizon of expectations. Revelation, however, remained a prototype for not more than a generation or so. In the early second century, as the testimony of Papias bears witness to, the situation had changed. The Lord was still being expected, but not imminently, while persecutions by Jews (under Bar Cochba) and pagans continued. The church was still being troubled by divisions and sects, but those heretics mentioned in particular in Revelation were already forgotten. The

Revelation of John had different things to say to this new age from what it had to say to the previous one. Interest shifted from the struggle and triumph of the Redeemer, who was no longer seen to be coming, to the after-life. Thus, the greater part of Revelation lost its significance; what was emphasised was the brief description of the End-events, in its last sections. But what is more important, the Revelation of John created within a generation or so, a new and distinct literary genre.

The second century witnessed the rise and flourishing of a new type in Christian literature – apocalyptic. Christian and Jewish-Christian Apocalypses appeared in numbers. These works were to a large extent products of the influence and failure of the Revelation of John. For John had touched upon the topic of after-life, but had said extremely little about it. After-life was not of prime importance in the first century. Christians in the second century, on the other hand, asked for more information. It was given to them in the Apocalypses, which now emerged like mushrooms. One of the earliest examples of this new genre was the *Apocalypse* of Peter, written in about 135. This work was almost exclusively concerned with the description of different classes of sinners, the punishment of evil and the salvation of the righteous. Strictly speaking, the Revelation of John did not belong to this new genre. But as this new genre gradually developed further the new horizon of expectations, John's Revelation was now read in a new context as if it had belonged to this genre. The late second-century Muratori Canon was the last witness to be perplexed at whether to classify it with the epistles or the apocalypses. All later witnesses classified it with the latter. The change in the horizon of expectations imposed a new reading on Revelation.

Am I pressing the evidence too far? I shall try to support what I have said by giving two examples. In book 1.6 of the *Apostolic Constitutions* which originated in the early third century, it is written: 'Abstain from all the heathen books ... For if thou hast a mind to read history, thou hast the books of the Kings; if books of wisdom or poetry, thou hast those of the Prophets, of Job, and the Proverbs ... if laws and statutes, thou hast the glorious law of the Lord God ... When thou readest the law, think not thyself bound to observe the additional precepts; though not all of them, yet some of them. Read those barely for the sake of history ...' This passage illustrates, I believe, how instructions were given to read into the Old Testament what was written in the New Testament. It is not often that we have such explicit remarks about the transformation of older texts in the light of new ones.

My second example is from Augustine. In the 20th book of his *City of God* he wrote: 'Now in this book called the Apocalypse (of John) there are, to be sure, many obscure statements, designed to exercise the mind of the reader; and there are few statements there whose clarity enables us to track down the meaning of the rest, at the price of some effort. This is principally because our author repeats the same things in many ways, so that he appears to be speaking of different matters, though in fact he is found on examination to be treating of the same subjects in different terms.' To modern readers this is not so at all. The Revelation of John, read historically, has a great many different things to say. But as the apocalyptic literary genre developed, from the second century onwards, its themes were limited to very few. Actually, we hardly find much more than visions concerning the after-world, descriptions of heaven and hell. Read in this new literary context, our Revelation may indeed appear limited in its themes as well. And it was actually read in this way; not only because some fathers like Augustine said so, but also because second-century and later readers were expecting to find in it the ideas developed in the apocalyptic genre to which they had become accustomed.

From the third century onwards, orthodox Christianity was becoming more and more hostile to millenarianism. The organised Church increasingly regarded itself as of this world and behaved as if it was there to stay for a long time. In its effort to establish itself it fought a number of battles, among which rejection of the apocalyptic literature was not the least important. The New Testament Canon, the symbol of the orthodox Church's victory over a number of heresies, excluded permanently all apocalyptic literature. The case of the Revelation of John was more complex, since belief in its apostolic authorship was widely spread. In the West, the Church accepted the apostolic authorship of Revelation and consequently followed Augustine's extreme allegorisations. In the East the Church struggled for many centuries to question its authorship (in one way or another), and to exclude it from the Canon; none the less its inspiration was often accepted by important personalities such as Andreas of Caesarea.

From the third and fourth century onwards, Christianity was much too influential and popular to be effectively controlled by the organised Church alone. Numerous simple believers continued their own practices and clung to their own ideas despite the efforts of their bishops and the decrees of Councils. Among many of these believers, millenarianism prevailed. Thus, the orthodox Church in the East could not rely only on its successful exclusion of Revelation from the Canon. It had to adopt the allegorical methods of the West as well. The three commentaries which survive were the product of this attempt. But from the point of view of the history of reception, these commentaries and these attempts to exclude Revelation from the sacred texts are evidence of the wide reception of this work in the exactly opposite way. Numerous Christians did not read it allegorically and continued to accept it as apostolic. Only when the Church after Arethas felt sufficiently strong with its allegorisations was Revelation once more accepted in the Canon.

Having been accepted in the Canon Revelation was once more left on its own. At a different level the apocryphal apocalypses continued to exercise their influence. It is known that the ideas of the *Apocalypse* of Peter lived on in numerous later texts 'right up to the full tide of description in Dante's *Divina Commedia*' (Maurer, in Hennecke-Schneemelcher II, 1965, 667). But as part of the Bible the Revelation of John was left alone as the *only* officially recognised apocalyptic book. Read within the horizon of expectations framed by the rest of the Bible, it was once again transformed into a peculiar and perplexing text. As a New Testament book, it became unintelligible. It passed through long vicissitudes which I cannot record here. But I can add perhaps that in the sixteenth century, and while peasants in Germany were in revolt, once more taking Revelation's millenarianism seriously, Luther felt compelled to write: 'About this book of the Revelation of John, I leave everyone free to hold his own ideas, and would bind no man to my opinion or judgement: I say what I feel. I miss more than one thing in this book, and this makes me hold it to be neither apostolic nor prophetic ... There is one sufficient reason for me not to think highly of it, – Christ is not taught or known in it ... Therefore I stick to the books which give me Christ, clearly and purely' (Kümmel 1973, 25f.).

I have already exceeded by far my chronological limitations, but I cannot resist giving one final piece of information, which will not be found in any history of Christian dogma. Writing in the late nineteenth century, Frederick Engels in an article about the Book of Revelation claimed that 'instead of being the darkest and most mysterious', this text 'is the simplest and clearest book of the whole New Testament'. 'Here we have Christianity in the crudest form in which it has been preserved to us. There is only one dominant dogmatic point: that the faithful have been saved by the sacrifice of Christ. ... Of original sin, not a trace. Nothing of the trinity. Jesus is "the lamb", but subordinated to God ... The murdered saints cry to God for revenge ... a sentiment which has, later on, been carefully struck out from the theoretical code of morals of Christianity ...' As a critic of the Bible Engels was a pupil of the German protestant scholars, but in his general outlook he was the pupil of the German revolutionary peasants of the sixteenth century. The socialist movement of the nineteenth century brought Revelation to the foreground and Engels recorded Ernest Renan's words with approval: 'When you want to get a distinct idea of what the first Christian communities were, do not compare them to the parish congregations of our day; they were rather like local sections of the International Working Men's Association' (Engels 1957, 183ff.).

In the late twentieth century, while New Testament scholars are still struggling to distinguish the particular phases of the material which forms Revelation, numerous laymen are reading it as poetry (to speak of Greece, two Nobel prize winners, G. Seferis and O. Elytis, produced good poetry by translating Revelation into modern Greek). Still, there are some who continue to try to decipher the number/name of the beast, and although they are admittedly few, on the eve of a nuclear holocaust they will certainly increase. This constant ability of Revelation to change content and meaning is due to a large extent to its 'hybrid' nature; it is neither here nor there, always giving rise to expectations which it never actually fulfils. In this sense Revelation has always remained a classic, i.e. it has always something different to say whenever read in a new context. To historians, on the other hand, as I have tried to argue, it has also much to say about the successive generations of Christians who read and interpreted it. The transformations of texts are revealing signs of historical development.

This paper was written while pursuing research financed by the A.S. Onassis Public Benefit Foundation. I wish to express my sincere thanks to the Foundation for this valuable help.

Bibliography

Ancient works

Andreas, *Commentary on Revelation*, ed. J.P. Migne, *Patrologia Graeca* (Paris, 1863), 106, cols. 216-457.
Apostolic Constitutions, trans. in *Ante-Nicene Fathers* 7 (New York, 1896-97, repr. Grand Rapids, 1971).
Arethas, *Commentary on Revelation*, in Migne, *PG* 106, cols. 493-785.
Augustine, *City of God*, Penguin trans., Harmondsworth, 1972.
Eusebius, *Ecclesiastical History*, Loeb ed., 2 vols., 1926, 1932.
Irenaeus, *Against Heresies*, trans. in *Ante-Nicene Fathers* 1.
Jerome, *Lives of Illustrious Men (De Viris Illustribus)*, trans. in *Nicene and Post-Nicene Fathers* 3 (Oxford and New York, 1892).
Justin Martyr, *Dialogue with Trypho*, trans. in *Ante-Nicene Fathers* 1.
Oecumenius, *The Complete Commentary on the Apocalypse*, ed. H.C. Hoskier, Ann Arbor, 1928.
Victorinus, *Commentary on the Apocalypse of John*, trans. in *Ante-Nicene Fathers* 7.
Revelation is cited from the *New English Bible* (Oxford, 1970).

Modern works

Chadwick, H. 1967. *The Early Church* (Harmondsworth).
Cohn, N. 1970. *The Pursuit of the Millennium* (Oxford).
Engels, F. 1957. 'The Book of Revelation', in K. Marx and F. Engels, *On Religion*, Eng. trans. (Moscow).

Hennecke-Schneemelcher 1963, 1965. E. Hennecke, *New Testament Apocrypha*, ed. W. Schneemelcher, 2 vols., Eng. trans. (London).
Jauss, H.R. 1982. *Towards an Aesthetic of Reception*, Eng. trans. (Minneapolis).
Kümmel, W.G. 1973. *The New Testament*, Eng. trans. (London).
Maurer, Ch. 1965. 'Apocalypse of Peter', in Hennecke-Schneemelcher II.
Metzger, B.M. 1968. *The Text of the New Testament* (Oxford).
Reynolds, L.D. and Wilson, N.G. 1975. *Scribes and Scholars* (Oxford).
Roberts, C.H. 1979. *Manuscript, Society and Belief in Early Christian Egypt* (Oxford).
Turner, E.G. 1968. *Greek Papyri* (Oxford).

Further reading

Argyriou, A. 1982. *Les Exégèses grecques de l'Apocalypse à l'époque Turque (1453-1821)* (Thessaloniki).
Bauckham, R. 1978. *Tudor Apocalypse* (Oxford).
Collins, R.F. 1983. *Introduction to the New Testament* (London).
Jauss, H.R. 1982. *Aesthetic Experience and Literary Hermeneutics*, Eng. trans. (Minneapolis).
Ramsay, W.M. 1904. *The Letters to the Seven Churches of Asia and their place in the plan of the Apocalypse* (London).

7

History and Faith

Up to the end of the sixteenth century AD, Europe remained trapped
within a nostalgia for what it dreamed of as the language of Adam. Given
directly by God (and persisting, perhaps, in the queer spatial figurations
of written Hebrew), primordial language was a transparent duplication
of the Universe. ... Even with the arrival of the Renaissance, Christian
Europe continued to give the Word – religious revelation – precedence
over both reason and the evidence of the senses as final index of the Real.

James Harkness, intro. to M. Foucault, *This is not a Pipe*
(Eng. trans., Berkeley and Los Angeles, 1982), 6-7.

Sr. Charles Murray's chapter raises two fundamental questions: what
is the relation between theology and history, and how does a
theologian today – or indeed a Christian historian – reconcile the fact
that Christianity sees itself as a revealed religion enshrined in words,
indeed, in the Word of God, with the present-day loss of confidence in
words as signs of the Real or the True? If there is a crisis in history
today, there is also a crisis in New Testament scholarship, as scholars
struggle to find a mode of interpretation which will allow them to
retain their sense of revelation and 'truth' while still responding to
wider intellectual trends. As Sr. Charles Murray shows, the problem
had presented itself, in different forms, long before the impact of
modern literary theory; indeed, this century has seen a series of heroic
efforts to 'save the texts'; whether for a traditional kind of historical
interpretation or, casting that aside, in terms of 'proclamation'. The
result of all this effort does not however seem to be great, either in
consensus or in general confidence in handling the documentary
material. Perhaps an index of that is the present tendency among the
public at large to set the texts aside, and with them the equally painful
and difficult struggle to agree on their interpretation during the first
centuries of the Church's existence, and instead to equate Christianity
with a general ethical code; even the debate about women priests is as
often conducted in terms of the changed role of women in modern
society, or by appeal to a 'feminine principle', as by serious discussion
of the biblical texts. Nor is the level of biblical criticism among
Christian congregations always high; it seems generally not to be

thought wise to expose them in sermons or elsewhere to the actual levels of scepticism which have prevailed and still do so among many academic theologians, especially under the influence of Form Criticism. An interesting contrast with the situation in the early Church: bishops then were often highly conscious of their need to preach intelligibly to the uneducated as well as to the elite, but were adept at combining direct simplicity with highly intellectual argument in the same composition.

From the second century AD onwards in early Christianity (nor was it a new technique then), a whole interpretative technique had evolved for the reading of the Word when its surface meaning seemed inconveniently at odds with what the reader would have expected. Allegorical interpretation, applied most naturally to the Old Testament, was a way of saving the entire body of the Scriptures; while it could lead to absurdities, it was in fact the ancestor of modern critical approaches to the Bible, and so highly developed a technique that it seems odd to have to say as Sr. Charles does that our own Scriptural criticism began only in the nineteenth century. What happened, in fact, was that modern criticism did not comprise the discovery of a new method or methods, but the rediscovery of old problems. For while it may be true that the Fathers did not in general read the Scriptures historically, they were certainly highly aware of the difficulties they presented to the critical interpreter.

To claim an allegorical meaning for a text not easily intelligible or acceptable in literal terms is, after all, to follow the same path as many modern critics when they assert that the Scriptures do not speak literally but in religious terms, whether as 'proclamation', according to the school of Bultmann, or in non-propositional or performative language.[1] Like St. Augustine, more alive than anyone to the problem of meaning in religious language, modern theologians are sure that it must mean *something*; where they differ from him is not in the what but in the how. And literary critics add a further dimension to the problem by reading the language of Christian texts as essentially secretive and hidden,[2] needing to have their meaning teased out by the skilled interpreter. Very naturally, parable, the characteristic mode of the Gospels, and the least open to 'rational', let alone empiricist exposition, has become a particular focus of attention.[3] In much wider

---

[1] See e.g. J. Macquarie, *God-Talk* (London, 1967); I.T. Ramsay, *Religious Language* (London, 1957).

[2] Frank Kermode, *The Genesis of Secrecy* (Cambridge, Mass., 1979); cf. chapter 5 'What precisely are the facts?', describing the Gospels as not history, but 'history-like'.

[3] See e.g. Dan O. Via Jr., *The Parables* (Philadelphia, 1967); Daniel Patte, ed., *Semiology and Parables* (Pittsburgh, 1976).

terms, we also find it argued that the very essence of the Christian texts lies in their use of symbolic language, their tendency to speak in terms very different from the 'rational' discourse commonly preferred today[4] – in Kermode's language, in a mixture of fact and *figura*.

All of this makes the task of a theologian attempting to follow good historical methods in the traditional sense an extremely difficult one, as his very material shifts and eludes him. It is difficult in another way too (and this is the other problem raised in this chapter), for he is by definition guilty of a traditional crime of historical method, that is, he is necessarily engaged with his subject, and therefore liable to be subjective in his judgements. As we shall see, one way round this problem is to face it head on and make a virtue out of it, even to argue that the writer *must* be engaged. A far more difficult solution is to continue the struggle for objectivity within an overall commitment; to save the writer himself *and* his texts.[5] Nor is it a defence to point to the well-known general problem of subjectivity in historical work and argue that the present case is not really different; historians in general may be more subjective than they care to admit in their judgements, but they are not often, and certainly not always, committed in the same way to belief in the truth of certain propositions as theologians must be to the basic beliefs of Christianity. Indeed, the very word 'faith', used in the present title, signifies a very special, and even an unreasoning kind of belief.

Finally, Sr. Charles's chapter makes frequent mention of truth. In the present intellectual climate both 'truth' and 'objectivity' have become such heavily loaded terms that many deny altogether that their aims are so high, and take refuge in a sceptical disparagement of the value of their own results, or else adopt a functional rather than an absolute definition. The theologian can do neither in relation to historians, philosophers and literary critics, that, above all, is his dilemma.

History and Faith
Sister Charles Murray

The problem of the relation between history and faith, which has always preoccupied Christian theological scholarship, has become a central issue again recently as part of the wider intellectual debate concerning historical studies in general, particularly with regard to the

---

[4] E.g. Paul Ricoeur, *Essays on Biblical Interpretation*, ed. L.S. Mudge (Philadelphia, 1980).

[5] See the argument in Paul Ricoeur, *History and Truth*, Eng. trans. (Evanston, Ill., 1965).

much discussed question of the interpretation of texts. It arises specifically because of the claim of Christianity to be a historical religion, not simply a religion with a history, or itself constituting an active force in history, but whose very essence lies in something accomplished by its founder in historical time. To express this theologically, Christians believe that in a series of events God revealed himself in action for the salvation of mankind. Since therefore Christianity is peculiarly dependent on historical events, it is essential both for Christians and others to know if those events really took place or not.[1]

The nature of the problem for the Christian theologian can be quite simply laid out: if what is recounted did not happen there is no salvation and faith is in vain. The Christian faith therefore contains within its belief-structure elements which present serious and difficult historical problems. The difficulty is further complicated in that while the revelation is believed to lie in events extrinsic to it, it is witnessed in a written text, or set of texts, the Bible. Thus a text, in particular the New Testament, becomes the locus of difficulty for the problem of history and faith. The problem then lies first in the nature of Christianity as a Scriptural religion and then in the relationship of its texts to 'facts'. We may define it further in terms of two related issues: (a) the relation of faith to historical judgements about the New Testament, and (b) the problem of interpreting the Scriptures.

The first was identified and analysed in the nineteenth century when critical studies of the text were shown to have practical consequences for the assessment of the Scriptures as historical narration, and so on judgements about the knowledge obtainable concerning the actual events narrated.[2] The well-known problem of the historicity of the Gospels is seen in its most acute form in the doctrine of the Resurrection, which may be briefly be illustrated here as an example. According to the New Testament, the story of the resurrection of Jesus contains two basic elements: his tomb was discovered empty on Easter morning and he appeared to various people as risen from the dead. Every part of the New Testament carries the proclamation of the Resurrection: it is found in all four Gospels, Acts, most Epistles and Revelation. The earliest evidence, based on apostolic testimony, is that of Paul at 1 Cor. 15.3-8, giving a list of appearances and claiming to have seen Jesus himself. Mark, usually regarded as the earliest of the Gospels, adds the report of the empty

---

[1] For general discussion see Harvey 1967 and Roberts 1960.

[2] The classic statement is to be found in various works by E. Troeltsch (1865-1929), influenced by Dilthey, who argued that as a result of the rise of the historical method Christian origins were no longer to be seen in terms of unique divine acts in history, but as historical occurrences to be taken in the context of their own times. In the present day, D. Nineham's approach to the historical interpretation of the New Testament closely mirrors Troeltsch's views; see Nineham 1976.

tomb, vouched for by the allegedly eye-witness account of the women
who visited it. The Resurrection event itself is nowhere directly
narrated but must be inferred from the appearances and the
corroborative story of the empty tomb. Even then, the inconsistencies
between the differing accounts are so obvious as to make them appear
unbelievable; attempts to harmonise them have proved useless. Are
the New Testament texts therefore untrustworthy, and is the doctrine
of the Resurrection historically untrue? For the believer, the problem
is apparently insoluble. It is certainly in principle a matter open to
historical investigation that someone who died was raised to life with a
transformed body; in that sense the Resurrection may be called a
historical event. But it is not historical in the sense that it was
witnessed; and as an affair between God and Christ it is a matter of
faith, not a subject of historical research. 'Evidence' for the
Resurrection then reduces itself to evaluation first of the accuracy of
the reports of the appearances, however they may be interpreted, and
then, to a lesser extent, of the story of the empty tomb.[3] This chapter
however will be concerned in the main not with the question of the
historical reliability of the Gospels, but with the second of the two
issues raised earlier – that of the methodology involved in trying to use
them as a source of historical information.

It is striking that in contemporary theological and biblical study,
discussion concentrates increasingly on the problem of interpretation.
Thus the attempt to find a method suitable to the nature of the
material has raised basic questions of hermeneutics.[4] Other questions
necessarily arise of more general philosophical concern, such as the
nature of knowledge, the use of language and the scientific and
ontological presuppositions present in the mind of the reader. Modern
literary theory also influences this discussion with its emphasis on
texts in themselves, aside from the intention of their authors, and the
view that a literary work must be understood on its own conditions and
in the form in which it exists, author, original audience and authorial
intention being regarded as irrelevant.

All historians share in the dilemma created for their subject by these
ideas, for they challenge the foundation of traditional historical study
based on texts. Since history, unlike literary criticism, seeks to
understand processes of development, its organising principle is of
necessity the search for change. Yet in the case of the study of the
documents of Christianity, synchronic analysis can prove illuminating
as well as interesting. The prospect of reading the texts non-
historically should not be *prima facie* alarming, since for long periods

[3] For an analysis representing the current scholarly consensus see Fuller 1972, and for
a more pessimistic view, Evans 1970; for a survey, cf. Harris 1983.
[4] On the relation between theology and hermeneutics see Thiselton 1980, with much
influence from the work of H.-G. Gadamer, e.g. Gadamer 1975.

in the history of the Church they were indeed so read. We have only to remember that in the patristic period, the most creative period in the history of doctrine, the usual method of reading the texts drew on all available current knowledge whether scientific, philosophical or linguistic. It was an intellectual rather than a specifically historical method, for the Fathers were not conscious of a distance between the historical events and the texts, or between the texts and themselves; in a sense they saw themselves as contemporaneous with them. Quite recently one church historian has advocated a return to this sort of approach.[5] That such a call can be made at all is due to the nature of theology as a discipline, neither history nor philosophy but straddling a frontier between them.

Now the nature of theology clearly affects the study of the problem of history and faith, so before proceeding to examine the relation between theology and texts it will be helpful to glance at the kind of discipline theology actually is.[6]

The nature of theology

If by a 'discipline' we understand methodical reflection along lines appropriate to the subject matter, then the discipline of theology consists of a critical reflection on faith. Its aim is to establish the truth about the faith and the self-understanding of the Christian community. But since the faith of the Church is linked to a history dependent on Scripture and traditional formulations such as creeds, theology must be both a historical and a literary enterprise. And since the faith belongs to a community and therefore to an institutional society, whose past is partly responsible for its present, theology also considers the social nature and relevance of the faith. As such it is subject to both intellectual and experiential pressures.

But because its goal is to seek the truth, theology must also be influenced by the other truth-seeking disciplines. Critical theology has always used the tools of historical-literary analysis and logic, but now that anthropology, which regards itself as independent of philosophy, has become important for human self-understanding it too has come to play an important role. The anthropology of religion in particular, as the methodical reflection on the phenomenon of culture in its religious form, makes an increasing contribution.[7] Yet this character of theology as a pluralism rather than a single discipline, which is demanded by the needs of the Christian community, means that the relation of

5 Louth 1983.

6 See Chadwick 1981.

7 For an example see Davies 1984. Anthropology seems to be moving now in the direction of becoming a philosophy of man; cf. Needham 1985. For a criticism of the sometimes inept use of anthropology by theologians see Leach and Aycock 1983.

theology to the texts cannot be straightforward.

In particular, theology differs from secular history in that the latter proceeds on the assumption that study of the past is only possible if all notion of the supernatural is removed. From history's point of view, the documents of faith are a legitimate field for the complete and free exercise of historical investigation. But for theology a completely unfettered study on this model is an impossibility, for theology cannot exclude the transcendent element which is the a priori of faith, and which determines the evaluation of the documents. It is for example a historical task to discover whether Jesus was actually crucified. The historian would identify and weigh the evidence and might go further and provide an interpretation, for instance that Jesus was crucified because the Romans perceived him to be a threat to imperial security. But the judgement of the Christian faith is that this crucifixion was uniquely significant and that Jesus was crucified as part of God's plan. Clearly this proposition is not verifiable on historical grounds; it claims that there is a special relation between the event of the crucifixion of Jesus and God, and while there is indeed a plainly historical element in the claim that Jesus was crucified because God willed it, the historical claim is interpenetrated by the religious one.[8] Similarly, Christians view the Bible not simply as a book but as a book about the activity of God. In both cases it is the a priori of faith which allows the Christian view. Thus a completely neutral study of Christian origins cannot be possible for a Christian and has never actually been undertaken within Christian thought.

Even so, theology is not absolved from the moral obligation of a vigorous application to the texts of historical criticism and its techniques for evaluating evidence.[9] The question 'Is the Gospel true?' must be first answered at the historical level, even if historical criticism is of its nature useless to evaluate the religious affirmation of the faith.

This combination of event and belief, which may roughly be termed revelation, represents the problem of religious truth.[10] How then can analysis work? Relevance may help. The meaning of Scripture can often be understood when its material is organised in a particular way, or when the Scriptures themselves are perceived to have been organised in a certain way. Theologies also can themselves be seen as organising principles, giving higher emphasis to some elements and lower to others, or, for instance, accepting some accounts as literal and others as figural.[11] Thus theology draws on other disciplines for a means by which to identify differing structures and organisations within Scripture.[12]

[8] See further Roberts 1960, ch. 3 and 169f.
[9] Harvey 1967.
[10] See Farrer 1976, prologue on 'Credulity'.
[11] See Barr 1983, 38.
[12] Barr 1983, 116ff.

Yet while relevance is often a starting point for theology, its ultimate criterion is truth. Thus for example it accepts the perceptions of sociology with regard to the social formations underlying texts,[13] but will wish to know not merely whether a particular model such as Jesus as revolutionary or Jesus as charismatic wonderworker is useful, but also whether it is true.[14] It will then go further and ask why it is true, or in what way. In the case of the Virgin Birth, for instance, the doctor may inform the theologian that the fact is physically improbable, and the historian may add that the literary testimony is weak and indecisive. When literary criticism observes that the texts betray further accretions to the simple narrative, that they appeal to Davidic or messianic passages in the Old Testament for their intelligibility, then we are truly in the realm of an interplay between history and faith. In contrast to that of the Resurrection, the doctrine of the Virgin Birth has a very limited attestation in Scripture. Only Matthew and Luke seem to know it as historical, and they are interested in it for its theological importance as an indicator of the unique relation of Jesus to God the Father; their accounts are embedded in infancy narratives generally agreed to be of a figurative and non-historical type. For the two evangelists the Virgin Birth represents divine election and expresses the belief that Jesus was God's Son or the Davidic Messiah from the moment of conception. There is a further contrast with the case of the Resurrection. There, it could be argued, the meaning of the texts was not in doubt, since they purport to record a real event; here, the question is more obviously one of interpretation – do the texts disclose historical events, or are the evangelists rather using the imagery of virgin birth in order to answer a different question, who Jesus was? The texts in themselves can neither guarantee nor fail to guarantee the historicity of the event.[15] Thus, a Christian theologian would argue, criticism of these texts requires a particularly sensitive approach to the interplay between history and faith.

It is just the interrelation between the character of Scripture as revelation and the nature of the text as historical that accounts for the interpretative approaches utilised in New Testament scholarship since the nineteenth century. On the other hand, academic theological study cannot be separated from wider trends within the discipline of history itself, and has always in practice followed general developments in the philosophy of history; this is why theology is now taking an engaged interest in the current crisis in historical studies. We can move on,

[13] For surveys of sociological approaches within theology see Scroggs 1980; Tidball 1983.

[14] For the first, which has been with us since Reimarus in the seventeenth century, see e.g. Carmichael 1963, and for the latter, Tiede 1973.

[15] See in general Brown 1973, 1978.

therefore, to discuss briefly the interpretative procedures adopted so far.

Methods of New Testament interpretation to date

In the search for an understanding of the historical status of the Scriptures, and in particular of the Gospel narrative, we may say that this century has witnessed three dominant trends, which in turn show the importance for theologians of changes in the conception of historical method. All have achieved lasting results.

The beginnings of critical study came particularly in Germany in the nineteenth century, with the assumption that the Gospels were written as historical documents; they were then analysed to yield the historical basis on which a portrait of the historical Jesus could be established.[16] *Leben Jesu Forschung*, as it came to be known, in fact proved to be an elusive and ultimately barren quest,[17] but it bequeathed to the twentieth century an effort to establish the exact nature of the New Testament sources in the hope that something positive could be said on their basis about the life of Jesus. The historical issues were thus directly addressed.

Building on this foundation, the first dominant trend in the twentieth century was the method usually known to theologians as Source Criticism. Based on a positivistic idea of history as telling 'what really happened', it is best represented in English by the work of Streeter, who gathered up all the known results of Gospel study in a systematic and comprehensive way.[18] When applied to the Gospels, Source Criticism attempted to discover for instance whether the existing Gospels were compiled from earlier documents no longer extant, and, by critical examination, especially of the Gospel of Mark, to disentangle the 'bare facts' about Jesus and his movement from the theological interpretation already present in the Gospels themselves. Of necessity its methods were those of literary criticism, based on the analysis of documents in relation to each other. Thus it worked almost entirely on internal evidence.

Source Criticism's greatest triumph was its proposed solution of the notorious 'synoptic problem',[19] with the resulting hypothesis, still accepted, of the chronological priority of Mark over Matthew and Luke and the hypothesis of a lost document 'Q' (from the German *Quelle* –

[16] See the pioneering work of D.F. Strauss (Strauss 1846).

[17] Cf. the celebrated book of A. Schweitzer, *The Quest for the Historical Jesus* (Schweitzer 1926), which concluded that 'historical research' had merely eliminated those components of the life of Jesus which did not accord with nineteenth-century liberalism.

[18] Streeter 1926; cf. p.543 'history is the effort to find out what actually happened'.

[19] i.e. that of the relation between the synoptic Gospels (Matthew, Mark, Luke), which share a large amount of common material and even similar language.

'source'), which was the source of the common, non-Markan material in Matthew and Luke. Thus the two-document hypothesis, that is, the use of Mark and Q by Matthew and Luke as the primary literary sources of their Gospels, is still regarded as one of the firm achievements of the source-critical method of Gospel study. However, Source Criticism also succeeded in profoundly shaking the supposition that the earliest documents carry us back directly to the earthly Jesus.

It was however soon considered to have outlived its usefulness, and attention was directed to the development of the Gospel material in its pre-literary stage, during the period between the crucifixion, *c.* AD 27-32, and the first extant written documents, Mark and Q, *c.* AD 60-70. The pressing question was now the form or forms in which this material reached the first Gospel writer. Hence the second method of approach, known as Form Criticism,[20] which rests on three fundamental assumptions: first, that the preservation and development of the material in the pre-literary period occurred through oral tradition, consisting basically of individual sayings and narratives joined together later by the Gospel editors; second, that the shaping of the material was decisively influenced by the specific needs and interests of the communities concerned; third, that the material can be classified according to literary forms which will enable the student to reconstruct the history of the tradition. The form critics appealed in addition to the idea of a *Sitz im Leben* ('situation in life'), in accordance with which they analysed the changes in the forms during the period of oral transmission, emphasising the apologetic and dogmatic interests of the early Christian communities.

For these critics, earlier attempts to reconstruct the life of Jesus had to be abandoned, not merely as historically impossible, but more importantly, as illegitimate in themselves. For the form critics, the texts were not so much histories as religious documents speaking from one context of faith to another. Accordingly Rudolf Bultmann, the most celebrated exponent of Form Criticism and the most influential New Testament critic of this century, went so far as to adopt a position of fundamental scepticism in relation to the problem of history and faith.[21] All that could be recovered from the past, he argued, was the life and ministry of Jesus not as it actually was but as the early Church saw fit to portray it. He thus distinguished between the Jesus of history and Christ as an object of faith, and made an almost complete separation between history and faith, leaving only the single fact of Christ crucified as necessary for Christian belief. His later work extended this scepticism into a wholesale programme of 'demythologising' the New Testament. He considered that not merely did certain

[20] See McKnight 1970.
[21] Most clearly seen in Bultmann 1963.

specific narratives or incidents such as the Virgin Birth or the Resurrection give expression to mythological elements, but that the entire structure of the Gospel message implied an antiquated universe of belief which could not now be accepted in its surface meaning, and should be interpreted in the language of existentialist philosophy if it was to be made meaningful for modern man. The salvation proclaimed in the New Testament was not a matter of supposed acts of God in history but a personal decision in favour of authentic human existence; the Gospel, he believed, taught us how to be truly human.[22] Interestingly, Bultmann turned for philosophical support for his views on the ultimate impossibility of justifying the historical claims of Christianity to Collingwood's arguments on the nature of history as essentially interpretative.[23]

Impressed by the paucity and apparent historical unreliability of the available data, the form critics thus diverted theology from the search for historical explanation and subverted existing ideas of what was historically trustworthy. Form Criticism also resulted in a renewed interest in dogma and in the Gospels as a source of doctrine. Taken together with Source Criticism it created a revolution in attitudes to the source of the Christian faith by increasing knowledge of the circumstances which shaped it.

A reaction from within the movement on the part of those who felt that historical questions still needed to be answered if the christological claims of Christianity were to be upheld nevertheless occurred in 1953 when Bultmann's pupil Käsemann delivered his lecture on 'The problem of the historical Jesus', in which he sought to refute the view that questions about the historical Jesus were impermissible. Far from separating the earthly Jesus from the Christ of faith, he argued that the texts as they stood showed that the early Christians took seriously the identity between the two, and raised again the question of the criteria to be used in analysing the material.[24] The kinds of information present in the New Testament texts were now painstakingly differentiated, with the result that scholars now, while remaining certain that a complete biography of Jesus can never be written, are no longer totally sceptical about the possibility of at least some historical study of the earthly Jesus.

The third dominant trend, Redaction Criticism, is a self-conscious method of inquiry[25] which grew out of Form Criticism and logically extends and intensifies certain of its procedures. It is interested in the formation of the Gospels as finished products, and in the interaction

---

[22] See his *Jesus Christ and Mythology* (Bultmann 1960).
[23] See his *History and Eschatology* (Bultmann 1957); on his appeal to Collingwood see Thiselton 1980, 240f.
[24] See Barbour 1972.
[25] The name derives from W. Marxsen and others; see Perrin 1971.

between the inherited tradition and the later interpretative procedures of the evangelists. Its goal is to understand and elucidate the editorial process expressed in and through the final composition, a task which is again both theological and historical in import.

From the foregoing brief and necessarily over-simplified sketch the constant change within New Testament scholarship can be clearly seen. In fact the three methods are commonly now used together, and collectively labelled Traditio-Historical Criticism.

Until comparatively recently, nevertheless, there was little explicit methodological discussion among New Testament scholars, but that situation too has now changed,[26] under the challenge of the traditio-historical method, which seemed increasingly to have called dangerously into question the historical reliability of the Gospel tradition. In the face of this sceptical attack, it was soon argued that it was not so much the texts that were unreliable as the method of analysis. Several criticisms can indeed be made of the traditional method, among which one of the most serious is its lack of adequate criteria for judging what is or is not reliable historical information. It divided material about Jesus into two over-rigid categories – the authentic and original and the inauthentic and secondary. Clearly there is an intermediate category, now being taken very seriously by many scholars. There are for instance pieces of material so embedded in the tradition that disentangling their origin is well nigh impossible. An outstanding example is provided by the title 'Son of Man', which Jesus attributes to himself in the Gospels, but which some scholars consider to be entirely a formulation of the early Christian community.

Precisely because most of the material was inherited from an earlier time, it had a kind of inertia which made it resistant to change even when important shifts in attitude took place. According to Barr, much of it was resistant to interpretative adjustments, and was left unabsorbed, remaining as authentic early material.[27] Form Criticism, in its roots a literary enterprise, also tends to distort the historical picture by taking units of material out of their context in the whole. Not surprisingly, therefore, the most recent trend is a movement away from the approaches represented by traditio-historical criticism to a newer, though less homogeneous, form of interpretation under the influence of structuralism, particularly to be seen in the work of scholars such as B.S. Childs and F. Belo.

Childs is the chief exponent of a movement known as 'Canonical Criticism'. For him, the final text of a biblical book or passage as found in the canon of Scripture is definitive, and the shape and structure of the canon the ruling norm for exegesis. As a departure from an

[26] See Barbour 1972.
[27] Barr 1983, 95.

approach showing more interest in putative sources than in the interpretation of the extant text this emphasis was certainly overdue, although both the theory and its practice have been heavily criticised.[28] Childs's approach has an affinity with the notion of the 'world of the text', with its own autonomous power to generate communication. In contrast with traditional biblical criticism which valued the idea of the original, canonical criticism has reacted against the conception that the original is necessarily better or more desirable than the 'final', which, he now argues, is to be preferred as the important category for the theological interpretation of Scripture. So canonical criticism rests on a dual foundation, theological conviction and response to a current and more general cultural and literary emphasis on the text in itself. In turn, the wider contemporary trend has naturally provided a background for its favourable reception in many quarters, and given support to the view that the Bible should be read in the same way as other texts.

Nevertheless, as the history of exegesis outlined above shows, it has to be recognised that it was also a serious concern with the final and surface shape of the text which led the source critics originally to raise their critical and historical questions. Yet for theology, the 'original' meaning, in the sense of the historical events concerning Jesus, can never be entirely overlooked. Because of its link with the category of the 'true', that of the 'original' can never be omitted from explorations of the problem of history and faith. The search for truth makes it ultimately impossible not to adopt a historical approach.

Another type of exegetical development relating theology and the interpretation of the New Testament texts to the contemporary intellectual situation comes from the side of sociology.[29] Here again authorial intention is rejected as the superior interpretative instrument, while the general setting of the story is considered of essential importance. History is often called upon, moreover, to validate present practice. To take two examples, feminist theology and Latin American liberation theology share certain clear modes of biblical interpretation which show prime concern for the social world of the biblical authors. Not that this is a new pursuit; social history has always been a recognised part of the approach to the New Testament: what is new is rather that in much of the recent scholarship the tools of sociology and anthropology are overtly utilised. We have begun therefore to acquire sociologies of early Christianity in which interpretative models derived from social anthropology are explicitly applied to Scriptural material.[30] Naturally many of the conclusions and techniques of the traditio-historical

[28] The major statement is to be found in Childs 1979, severely criticised by Barr 1983, ch. 4 'Further adventures of the canon: "canon" as the final shape of the text', and App. II 'Further thoughts on canonical criticism'.
[29] See Rowland 1985.
[30] Gager 1975; Meeks 1983; Schussler Fiorenza 1983 etc.

method are adopted by scholars working in this vein, whose exegesis often follows traditional patterns; the concerns, however, are different. Besides throwing light on neglected features of the texts, the proponents of this mode would argue that their approach has revealed how far mainstream biblical exegesis has failed to show the real character of Christianity as an ethical religion; certainly its outcome, while posing considerable problems of engagement, especially in the case of feminist theology, has been to strengthen the already increasing tendency to move away from the dogmatic theology of the biblical writers to a preoccupation with their social world and practice.[31]

A clear example of this approach is the explicitly Marxist interpretation of early Christian literature provided by the liberation theologian F. Belo in his book on Mark.[32] Belo works with an eclectic assembly of tools drawn from prevailing European exegetical method, but with the addition of some distinctive emphases deriving from the case of Latin America. His study is concerned to elucidate both the ideology expressed in Mark's Gospel and the economic base on which it rests. For Belo, Mark's Gospel is the result of the social formation of its time and must be examined from that point of view. Unlike the traditional critics, he has no concern in going behind the text to see what really happened in the activity and ministry of Jesus, or even in the life of Mark's community. His method is rather to examine the Gospel as a story which takes place in a specific historical context, and for whose understanding knowledge of this wider context is important; it is this wider context, rather than the historicity of the recorded events themselves, that is emphasised. Belo joins to this concern with the social setting a form of structuralist exposition of the text which deemphasises, without however completely disregarding, the role and interests of the author and his readership, the church.

As Rowland observes, Belo shows that concern for the historical context need not be completely abandoned in a structuralist analysis, but there is an obvious difficulty in the severe lack of external information about the social setting in which individual early Christian texts were composed.[33] It is thus difficult even in principle to write a fully satisfactory social and economic history of the early Christian community, even if we accept Belo's premise that economic struggles affected the development of religious ideology and not vice versa, as some would now want to argue.

Perhaps we may now draw together some concluding remarks about the use and interpretation of Christian texts in relation to the problem of history and faith.

[31] Rowland 1985.
[32] Belo 1981, on which see Rowland 1985, 159f.
[33] Rowland 1985, 171; 166-7.

Conclusions

We have seen that the profoundly religious aspect of Christianity, based on faith, influences and continuously interpenetrates any examination of its historical claims. For Christians this is the fundamental dilemma in the interpretation of the documentary evidence. Yet although in terms of religion the two aspects of history and faith cannot be separated, nevertheless, in the investigation of written documents they have to be disentangled. For theologians the problem of faith and history is a real one. It is essential for them that the Christ of history should have been what the Church believes him to have been. The history has to be true. W. Pannenberg has been at the centre of attempts to reconcile these competing demands of historicity and faith, in part by moving away from a conventionally positivistic understanding of history as constituted by 'facts' or objectively knowable events. Instead, he denies the absolute distinction between event and interpretation, and argues that meaning is inherent in the events themselves. The advantage of such an approach is that it can provide a respectable way of escape from the excessive scepticism about the historical origins of Christianity. It is still possible, in other words, to retain a historical understanding of the life and teaching of Jesus if we shift our view of the degree of certainty that is actually possible in historical enquiry, of whatever kind. For if the expectation of absolute truth in historical investigation proves to be unfounded, the disjunction between history and faith to some extent closes up.[34]

The student of Christian origins is therefore in a peculiar position. What kind of general conclusions might he or she wish to draw for their own discipline from the present general intellectual ferment with regard to the study of the past?

First, it seems important (and this is a traditional Christian attitude) to welcome approaches to texts from whatever side they may come. If modern literary theory is right in claiming that the form and content of literature have a timeless autonomy and that in this lies their ability to speak to all generations, this must also be a potentially fruitful angle from which to explore the documents of a community of faith, in which the concept of continuity, tradition, is of major significance. It may also be a helpful corrective to an overemphasis on the diachronic study of change. The canonical critics may after all be right in seeing the synchronic study of the documents as logically preceding rather than following the diachronic. If this timeless significance of the texts is what makes them 'inspired', there may well be illumination to be gained here in relation to the Christian concept of the inspiration of Scripture in the sense in which the texts are, besides being human narratives, also the word of God.

[34] See e.g. Pannenberg 1969; Galloway 1973; Tupper 1974; Placher 1975.

Nevertheless, this line of inquiry can never be undertaken at the cost of anti-historical bias. A purely literary reading of the texts breaks down as soon as detailed questions are put. Moreover, there is in the context of Christianity a much more fundamental objection to a completely ahistorical reading, namely that the texts are seen to be much more than just literature. For the Church, they have an external referent in the incarnation of God, which is both the datum of faith and an event in history. Thus the literary synchronic reading and the historical diachronic one cannot be regarded as alternatives but must always be combined.

This is a critical conjunction for theology to make. For if the principle of interpretation is simply understood as the present-day appropriation of the material, then the texts quickly become marginalised and reduced to the level of the utilitarian. Theology cannot afford to lose all sense of the authors and their original intentions.

The same kind of reasoning applies to the last approaches which we have examined, where the interpretative criterion is not relevance but faith. These interpretations do not marginalise the text; on the contrary, because of their concern with history they make it central, but what is sought is identification with it in order to legitimise the 'praxis', analysis and living being regarded as simultaneous operations. This inevitably raises the question of 'eisegesis', the reading *into* the text of the particular concerns of the interpreter. For liberation theology, for example, the Bible is read as the literary expression of the poor, while the feminist hermeneutic of Schussler Fiorenza and others is passionately concerned with the legitimation of female participation in the activities of the church.

Whether the presuppositions in such theologies are those of western philosophy such as Bultmann's existentialism, or third-world concerns, they can offer exciting new perspectives by widening the scope of inquiry into the texts. Sometimes, by focussing on for example 'unintentional data', pieces of evidence not directly related to the author's main intention in writing, they may reveal authentic and hitherto underemphasised levels of concern in the texts. Nevertheless, the risk is that they will be too limited. It does not follow that their conclusions are wholly true; indeed, in some exegesis like that of liberation theology, and much modern religious literature, there appears to be an increasing blurring between the two traditional categories of the spiritual, a reading based primarily on religious concern, which has always allowed for a freer interpretation of biblical material, and the theological, intended as a considered judgement on the material it uses. This blurring may be to some extent regarded as a 'post-academic' way of conceiving the problem of history and faith. But the problem of eisegesis remains, and any view will tend to founder on the evidence when only one approach is claimed as the right one.

Perhaps I may be allowed a final reflection on the nature of theology in the context of the changing thought-forms of the late twentieth century. One might interpret the present cultural confusion in two ways. On the one hand it represents at bottom a challenge to the concept of the 'academic' community and the primacy of the idea of 'research' over experience; this fear may have contributed to a crisis of confidence within the discipline of history. On the other, however, the present uncertainty can be read rather as a development in the intellectual understanding of how we approach the past; as such it is not a matter for alarm, but an opportunity for learning and enrichment, the fruit of the recognition that history is necessarily an imprecise science because of the nature of its subject matter. The latter seems to be the most promising attitude for theology to take. For although theology may indeed seem to be an elaborate academic enterprise for the marshalling of the basic material of the Christian faith, it has no strict methodology of its own and must take what it can from elsewhere. Yet in spite – or because – of this situation, it is perhaps also one of the few disciplines which openly admits its own sense of methodological inadequacy and seeks consistently to find a conceptual understanding of itself.

Bibliography

Barbour, R.S. 1972. *Traditio-Historical Criticism of the Gospels* (London).
Barr, J. 1983. *Holy Scripture* (Oxford).
Belo, F. 1981. *A Materialist Reading of the Gospel of Mark* (New York).
Brooten, B.J. 1985. 'Early Christian women and their cultural context: issues of method in historical reconstruction', in A. Yarbro Collins, ed., *Feminist Perspectives on Biblical Scholarship* (Chico, Ca.), 65-91.
Brown, R.E. 1973. *The Virginal Conception and the Bodily Resurrection of Jesus* (London).
——— 1978. *The Birth of the Messiah: a commentary on the Infancy Narratives* (London).
Bultmann, R. 1957. *History and Eschatology* (Edinburgh).
——— 1960. *Jesus Christ and Mythology* (London).
——— 1963. *History of the Synoptic Tradition* (Oxford).
Carmichael, J. 1963. *The Death of Jesus* (London).
Chadwick, H. 1981. *The Frontiers of Theology* (Cambridge).
Childs, B.S. 1979. *Introduction to the Old Testament as Scripture* (London).
Davies, D.J. 1984. *Meaning and Salvation in Religious Studies* (Leiden).
Evans, C.F. 1970. *Resurrection and the New Testament* (London).
Farrer, A. 1976. *Interpretation and Belief* (London).
Fuller, R.H. 1972. *The Formation of the Resurrection Narratives* (London).
Gadamer, H.-G. 1975. *Truth and Method* (London).
Gager, J. 1975. *Kingdom and Community. The Social World of Early Christianity* (Englewood Cliffs, New Jersey).
Galloway, A.D. 1973. *Wolfhart Pannenberg* (London).
Harris, M.J. 1983. *Raised Immortal* (London).

Harvey, Y.A. 1967. *The Historian and the Believer* (London).

Käsemann, E. 1964 (1953). 'The problem of the historical Jesus', in E. Käsemann, *Essays on New Testament Themes* (Eng. trans., London, 1964), 15-47.

Leach, E. and Aycock, D.A. 1983. *Structuralist Interpretations of Biblical Myth* (Cambridge).

Louth, A. 1983. *Discerning the Mystery* (Oxford).

McKnight, E.V. 1970. *What is Form Criticism?* (Philadelphia).

Meeks, W.A. 1983. *The First Urban Christians* (New Haven).

Needham, R. 1985. *Exemplars* (Berkeley).

Nineham, D. 1976. *The Use and Abuse of the Bible* (London).

Pannenberg, W. 1969. *Revelation as History* (Eng. trans., London).

Perrin, N. 1970. *What is Redaction Criticism?* (London).

Placher, W.C. 1975. *History and Faith in the Theology of Wolfhart Pannenberg* (PhD dissertation, Yale).

Roberts, T.A. 1960. *History and Christian Apologetic* (London).

Rowland, C. 1985. 'Theology of liberation and its gift to exegesis', *New Blackfriars*, 157-82.

Schussler Fiorenza, E. 1983. *In Memory of Her* (London).

Schweitzer, A. 1926. *The Quest for the Historical Jesus*, 2nd ed. (London, repr. 1948).

Scroggs, R.C. 1980. 'The sociological interpretation of the New Testament: the present state of research', *New Testament Studies* 26, 164-79.

Strauss, D.F. 1846. *The Life of Jesus Critically Examined*, 4th ed. (London).

Streeter, B.H. 1926. *The Four Gospels* (London).

Thiselton, A. 1980. *The Two Horizons* (Exeter).

Tidball, D. 1983. *An Introduction to the Sociology of the New Testament* (Exeter).

Tiede, R.L. 1973. *The Charismatic Figure as Miracle Worker* (Missoula).

Tupper, F.E. 1974. *The Theology of Wolfhart Pannenberg* (London).

8

Virginity as Metaphor: women and the rhetoric of early Christianity

Where the virgins are soft as the roses they twine,
And all, save the spirit of man, is divine.

Byron, *Childe Harold's Pilgrimage*

There is currently a great deal of writing about the position of women in the early church, both as part of the general interest in women's studies and now in particular in association with the various movements towards the ordination of women. Certainly an ambivalence in early Christian attitudes to women has long been recognised: on the one hand, women have traditionally been seen as prominent among the first converts, while on the other the extreme misogyny of some early Christian texts has not failed to strike modern readers. There is therefore a double problematic. For early Christianity itself women seem to have been an object of attention in a way which calls for explanation, while clearly any feminist in our day, or indeed anyone interested in the history of women, is going to find that understanding their role in Christianity presents a particularly acute methodological problem.

What is not so standard, however, is the development of critical interest in early Christian texts in terms of the contemporary concern with rhetoric, for which those writings which focus on virginity present a special and interesting case. Insofar as this is in practical terms a literature directed at women, even though the call to virginity was often expressed as applying to both sexes, it is clearly relevant for the historical question of the role of women in the real world of early Christianity. But, as in the case of Latin love elegy (above, Chapter 5), many of the texts themselves are first in need of closer criticism for their rhetorical features; moreover, before drawing on them like raw material for a historical reconstruction, we need to consider their place within the whole edifice of Christian textuality as it was evolving in the early period. In most cases, an interpretation that is actually going to be useful for historians will involve a literary analysis as well as the theological one which the texts have usually had in the past.

One result of such an analysis will be to reveal close connections between Christian writings on women, sex and virginity and classical and other texts dealing with the same themes, or using the same metaphorical language. Christian writers were not after all detached completely from their surrounding culture; thus there will inevitably be common ground.[1] The virgin choir in Methodius' *Symposium* (p. 000 below) had its ancestors not only in Philo's Therapeutae but also in the virgins of Greek ritual and myth.[2] The overall suspicion of women, moreover, together with many of the categories in which it was expressed, had nothing essentially Christian about it; it is not surprising, then, if in a discourse centreing on female sexuality many of the standard *topoi* make their appearance.

But that is not to say that there is no difference between the classical and the Christian presentation, or that the one necessarily derived from the other. In the light of Christianity's character as a religion based on a physical divine incarnation, by definition miraculous, and its desire, especially after Constantine, to set an orthodoxy by defining its doctrines ever more precisely, the mechanics of conception and birth necessarily acquired a special place in the articulation of the faith. Whatever social reasons may have contributed to the growth of asceticism as a Christian practice in the early Christian period,[3] the development of a whole Christian rhetoric, and a set of metaphors, relating to celibacy and virginity was completely natural in terms of the central doctrines of Christianity, merely a step further from that conspicuous insistence on the metaphor of the body which is already built into the New Testament. It was natural, too, that the developed articulation of Christian discourse on celibacy and virginity should have reached its height (though the ideas had been present long before) together with the fourth and fifth-century preoccupation with Christology. Its culmination, in a logical sense, came with the Council of Ephesus in AD 431 which recognised the status of Jesus' mother, Mary, as the mother of God, that is, which settled the orthodox doctrine of the Incarnation, for which Mary's virginal status and

---

[1] For discussion see Aline Rousselle, *Porneia* (Paris, 1983).

[2] In general, see the very interesting paper by Giulia Sissa, 'Une virginité sans hymen: le corps féminin en Grèce ancienne', *Annales E.S.C.* 39 (1984), 1119-39, pointed out to me by Ann Bergren. The classical/pagan background has here been more influential than the Jewish.

[3] See Peter Brown, *The Body and Society: men, women and sexual renunciation in the early Church* (New York, 1988).

miraculous delivery were prerequisites.[4] It was also entirely predictable that it was exactly now – not earlier – that the Virgin Mary began to acquire the beginnings of a cult in her own right.

Thus the theme of virginity, with all its implications for the role of women in real life, is not a separable element in Christian texts which can be disregarded once we have recognised its prevalence. It is built in, in a very integral way, to the articulation of Christian doctrine. Naturally there was a transference to the realm of practice: generations of Christian men and women actually practised sexual renunciation, and based their own lives on the precepts enunciated in these highly rhetorical texts. But what has interested me here is not so much the relation of theory and practice, complicated and fascinating though that can be, but the way in which the theoretical expression has itself developed.

As I argued above (p. 144), it is the extraordinarily high premium placed by early Christianity on the articulation of its own beliefs into an all-embracing system that makes it particularly interesting for the subject of these chapters. It might be difficult to argue convincingly that in the early stages that articulation had much effect on the spread of the faith; indeed, it is a commonplace that few pagans bothered to get through the barrier presented, in their view, by the relatively low cultural level of Christian writings – though that should not be exaggerated.[5] But by the later fourth century Christianity had evolved a religious and political discourse as comprehensive and highly sophisticated as anything in pagan culture and which became one of the means by which it could indeed convert itself into a universal faith.[6]

The theme of virginity in Christian writing, far from having to do only with 'the position of women in early Christianity' (which is after all a convenient way of marginalising it), is part of this much wider and more complex development. It deserves to be understood in that context.

[4] See Mary Douglas, *Natural Symbols* (Harmondsworth, 1970), 196, for an explanation in similar terms of the necessary condemnation of Arianism, in which the human in Christ was too far separated from the divine.

[5] It applied mainly to the Scriptures themselves; there were certainly Christian writers of the second century and after who were as well educated as any pagans, and let it show in their writing.

[6] See now Michael Mann, *The Sources of Social Power* I (Cambridge, 1986).

Virginity as Metaphor:
women and the rhetoric of early Christianity

Averil Cameron

The rhetoric of the early church was a male rhetoric,[1] and it is only recently that readings of it have not also been male readings. Thus the entire debate about the 'position of women in the early church' has taken place, and still must take place, within a framework of male textuality. That debate has, as we know, been a traditicnal topic of attention. It was so already for ancient critics of Christianity, and it has become so agaiin recently for specific contemporary reasons. Not only Celsus, but also modern histories of the early church, commonly say, for instance, that the Christian faith spread first among outsiders to Roman society – slaves, the lower classes and women;[2] this was a view which suited early Christian writers themselves – they could claim that it was one of Christianity's great advantages that it was made for everyone, even the uneducated, and most women in the ancient world fell by definition into that category.[3] And now it is seductive again for different reasons: feminist theologians can use it to claim that whatever the Christian texts themselves might imply, there was once a golden age of early Christianity in which women played a role they were scarcely to enjoy again until the rise of the feminist movement.[4] The saying of Paul to the Galatians: 'There is neither male nor female, neither bond nor free; for ye are all one in Christ Jesus' (Gal. 3:28) has become a rallying cry for all parties.[5]

We have therefore a seemingly strange situation – one in which a debate about the 'position' of women is carried on on the basis of texts that are in the main highly misogynistic, and yet in which it has also been thought possible to argue for a kind of early Christian feminism.[6] My purpose here is to show how the misogynistic rhetoric of the early Christian texts became established; I would also want to argue that at least some of the statements made in pagan and Christian sources alike about the attraction of Christianity for women are simply the product of an easy rhetorical convenience, like the claim often made by

---

[1] Despite valiant efforts to rehabilitate early Christian writing as women's writing, cf. e.g. Wilson-Kastner 1981. Davies 1980 argues that the apocryphal acts of the late second and third centuries originated in a female context and were actually written by women. For a balanced view of the whole subject see the works of Elizabeth A. Clark, especially Clark 1986a, 23-60.

[2] Celsus, ap. Origen, *c. Cels.* III.55; Harnack 1908, II.64ff.

[3] Like 88 per cent of Saudi women today, and like most slaves in Roman society.

[4] See for example, Schussler Fiorenza 1983; Ruether 1979, 30-70.

[5] See Cameron 1980, with Betz 1974. There is a large modern literature devoted to the question of whether Paul was 'conservative' or 'liberal'.

[6] See e.g. Swidler 1971, 1979; more seriously, Ruether 1979, 30-70; Fiorenza 1983.

even the most sophisticated of the Fathers that they were able to speak directly to the 'simple'.[7] The question of how women really fared in the early Christian world is a second-order question, to be approached only after we have first examined the rhetoric of the texts, and it is with the latter that this collection is concerned.

In any case, scholars are no longer so sure that Christianity flourished first among the lower classes. Rather, it is increasingly argued that from a very early stage indeed Christian groups depended on what can better be described as the relatively prosperous urban middle class, or at any rate, people of substance with households of their own and with a vested interest in maintaining the social system.[8] Indeed, the millennial and marginal characteristics of Christianity in its earliest stages soon survived only at the cost of being labelled heterodox in the face of a powerful impulse towards unity and social respectability.[9]

The rhetoric of contemporary critics of Christianity, as of the many modern scholars until quite recently who pointed to its supposedly particular attraction for women, begins to look somewhat suspect. And yet it is true that a striking number of those named in the Acts of the Apostles, like the members of the Christian community at Rome named in the Epistle to the Romans, are indeed women. We might argue that women feature in the anti-Christianity polemic of pagan writers like Celsus, and thus necesarily also in Christian answers to it, because they represent (as so often) the outsider, the unconsidered other, not worthy of serious consideration and therefore the ready target for abuse.[10] But how does that leave these first Christian women, not merely Phoebe and Dorcas and Prisca, but also the women in the Gospels, the women 'whom Jesus loved', who were the first witnesses to the Resurrection as Mary had been to the coming of Christ into the world?[11] Why, when Jesus (if such statements are possible about Jesus as a historical figure) seems to have gone out of his way to encourage a following among women, did early Christianity develop a rhetoric of out and out misogyny, and in laying such emphasis as it soon did on virginity, do so in the context of a denigration of marriage, the normal and indeed the only expectation in life for the vast majority of all women in the ancient world?[12] Why,

[7] The notion of Christian literature, for example, as by definition 'lowly' in style (see Auerbach 1965) could be turned to advantage as well as disadvantage.

[8] See e.g. Judge 1960; 1982; Theissen 1978, 1982. De Ste. Croix 1975 vividly shows the early transformation of Christianity from a religion of the *chora* to one of cultured urbanism; Paul himself was one of the most important agents in this process.

[9] Well argued in Pagels 1979.

[10] Padel 1983.

[11] For the former, Ruether 1979, 32ff.; in general, Schussler Fiorenza 1983, part II; Brooten 1985, 65ff.

[12] Despite exhortations to virginity and attested examples, it would be hard to demonstrate that the lives of the majority changed in practice; see Patlagean 1977, 128ff., discussing the Greek Fathers; useful collection of passages in Clark 1983, 27-76, 115-55. Shaw 1987 sees no distinction in marriage practice between Christian and pagan

finally, did it exalt Mary the mother of Jesus to near-divine status, in the paradoxical role of perpetual virgin?

The question here, therefore, is not so much whether women were indeed prominent among early Christian converts, or whether they were particularly instrumental in spreading the faith, but rather why they became such objects of attention in early Christian discourse.

Current feminist inquiry is interested in both sorts of question. Much work is done, for instance, to collect references to the participation of women in early Christianity, usually, it must be said, with a view to showing that there is both Scriptural and historical precedent for a significant female role in the Church.[13] At the same time, feminist writers are at pains to expose the extent of actual hostility to women in the early Christian texts, whether in the New Testament itself or in the works of the early Fathers.[14] It is easy (and common) to point to Tertullian, calling woman 'the doorway of the devil', or Jerome, advocating total abstinence from feminine adornment, to the point of never washing and dressing only in sackcloth,[15] or to the desert fathers, who, like the monks of Athos today, allowed nothing female to come near them. John of Lycopolis, for instance, had not seen a woman for forty years.[16] Moreover, it is easy to show that for many Christian writers of the period, women were inextricably bound up in the imagination with the idea of human sinfulness: it was Eve who tempted Adam, and so it had to be Eve who had brought about the fall of man.[17] It was agreed that sexuality and reproduction must be intimately connected with man's fall; thus man's salvation could be brought about only by a reversal of the circumstances of the fall, that is, by an absence of sexuality, and specifically by the virginity of Jesus and Mary.[18] At certain moments the question of whether there had been sexual relations before the fall assumed an importance matched only by the parallel problem of whether men and women would be sexual beings in Paradise; Jerome

---

women. Yet Jerome can compare a woman remarrying to a dog returning to its own vomit (*Ep.* 54).

[13] Brooten 1985 provides a thoughtful discussion of feminist aims and methods in this field; see also Murray above.

[14] E.g. Ruether 1974.

[15] Tert., *De cultu feminarum* I. 1.2; the elder Melania claimed never to have washed any part of her body except for the tips of her fingers in all her sixty years: Pallad., *Laus. Hist.* 55.

[16] *Hist. Mon.* 1.4; contrast however Palladius, *Lausiac History*, where women play a much more prominent role in relation to the desert fathers.

[17] E.g. Irenaeus, *Adv. Haer.* III.22.4 (late second century). For the various attempts of later writers to work out the consequences, and sometimes to defend women from perpetual slur, see the collection of passages in Clark 1983, 27-76.

[18] The connection is already there in Irenaeus, though he lays his emphasis on the obedience of Mary as much as on her virginity. Later writers (e.g. Jerome, *Ep.* 22.21) make Mary's virginity paramount. On the connection, e.g. Koch 1937; Giannarelli 1980, 32f.

was in no doubt – marriage arose for Adam and Eve only after the Fall, when it was intended to 'replenish the earth', while virginity replenished Paradise.[19] Marriage on the other hand could receive negative praise in that it might produce more virgins.[20] Women themselves did not write about such matters, of course, though in a sense they were the target of those who did: the debate was conducted instead by men about women and in the context of unquestioned assumptions about the nature of woman.[21] Inevitably, though, women who embraced the Christian life, and especially the notable women of the later fourth century who followed the teaching of the great contemporary Christian leaders – Jerome, John Chrysostom, Augustine, Ambrose – framed their own lives and their understanding within the same rhetorical context. Indeed, when we read the sharp and authoritarian remarks which some of their male patrons felt free to direct towards them, it is obvious that they had little alternative.[22]

How then to get beyond the texts? Feminist writers wishing to recapture a positive role for early Christian women must proceed by reinterpreting the texts which provide their main evidence. Elizabeth Schussler Fiorenza is quite open about this, advocating first a 'hermeneutics of suspicion' (exposing the misogynistic rhetoric) and then a 'hermeneutics of remembrance'.[23] To the objection that such a process is illicit, in that it renounces historical objectivity, the reply is given that on the contrary it is a fallacy to suppose that any historian is not himself somehow engaged, and further, that the prevailing doubts about historical certainty and the status of historical evidence in fact support the respectability of such an approach.[24] Yet it is a legitimate question to ask whether the 'hermeneutics of remembrance' is not itself also a way of constructing reality, no more valid than the negative image of women constructed by the early Fathers. The procedure is the more striking in that feminist writers on early Christianity are bound to and constrained by a fixed canon of texts, which they cannot escape, but only manipulate, that is, lead to yield a

[19] E.g. Jerome, *Adv. Iov.* I.16, 35; excellent general discussion in Clark 1986a, 353-85; 1986b. For the contribution of the recently discovered new letters of Augustine to this question see Brown 1983; Clark 1986b.

[20] Jerome, *Ep.* 22.

[21] The female speakers who extol virginity in Methodius' *Symposium* (see below) are of course the literary creations of a man.

[22] In fact Augustine, *Ep.* 262, upbraids Ecdicia for an excess of ascetic zeal. The tone of some contemporary male objectors to women's ordination is no less offensive to women, and their premises too are often accepted by some women themselves; if there is more tendency to reject their case now than in the fourth century, it is not because the case has changed, but because of the pluralistic nature of our own society, even within modern Christianity.

[23] Fiorenza 1983, 1985 (in clear continuation of earlier hermeneutic theory – see Murray above).

[24] Cf. Brooten 1985, 66f.

more acceptable meaning by re-interpretation.[25] Moreover, even within the range of material which must be used, there are major variations; thus it may be theoretically possible to recapture, or rather to postulate an unpolluted source in the Gospels, but a more sympathetic reading of, say, Jerome, is hardly on the cards. Finally, the feminist writer in general, and even more so the feminist theologian, is by definition engaged, and must therefore in some sense be aiming at the revelation of truth – not the history of rhetoric but the thing itself.

Nevertheless, the example of feminist theology forcibly reminds us that history is itself indeed a matter of interpretation. Certainly the texts of early Christianity require a great deal of interpretation before they can be made to yield anything like usable historical data.[26] Here historians have in my view yet to learn from their colleagues in other disciplines. In New Testament studies, for instance, there seems to be a noticeable emphasis at the moment on literary-critical approaches to the texts, that is, to their analysis as the literary and cultural products of a given society.[27] Similarly, historians of early Christianity in the Roman empire who are not themselves engaged as feminist or specifically Christian writers need to question what the texts say and how they say it just as much, the more so since one of Christianity's chief distinguishing characteristics is precisely the amount of attention it gives to the articulation of its belief system. The fact that women receive so much prominence within this articulation of ideas is not therefore merely a matter for feminists or feminist theologians. It must also affect any judgements made about the historical position of these women.

Not surprisingly, perhaps, it is French scholarship that has been most sympathetic to the textual aspects of this question. Paul Veyne, for example, moved to the subject of the construction of women in Roman elegy[28] from a more general consideration of the relations between the sexes in the early empire and the contribution of Christianity to them, to which he has now returned[29] – a theme, of course, which became a major preoccupation of M. Foucault's unfinished *History of Sexuality*,[30] in terms both of narratives and

[25] Brooten 1985, 84ff., indeed, sees that a writer of 'women's history' must in fact go outside the canon in order to make any progress at all, yet for the theologian (in any sense) any appeal to materials outside the canon inevitably raises the awkward question of their relation to what is within it.

[26] The writings of Paul Ricoeur represent one of the most serious attempts to confront these issues: see Ricoeur 1965, 1977, 1980.

[27] Cf. e.g. Via Jr. 1967; Crossan 1975; Perrin 1969. Also in more traditional ways: Votaw 1970; Wuellner 1979.

[28] Veyne 1978; 1983. See Wyke, Chapter 4 above.

[29] Veyne 1987.

[30] Foucault 1983; also in Ariès and Béjin 1986. On the similarities between Plutarch's writings on marriage and passages in the New Testament, see Wicker 1975, 1978.

practice (an interest already developed in Aline Rousselle's *Porneia*).[31]
On the whole, however, the focus has been either on the actual relations
between the sexes, or on the topic of Christian misogyny itself, rather
than on the development of its mode of expression.

As has been remarked before, while celibacy was enjoined on men and
women alike, it was women who were above all the object of this
repressive discourse. Their perceived role as temptresses of men was an
obvious reason. In today's argument the exclusion of women from the
priesthood is a way of containing the danger which their assumed
sexuality is felt to represent; but in addition in the early Christian
period a whole series of treatises appeared which on the whole we are
now spared, regulating their dress, makeup and demeanour, underlin-
ing both this perceived role and their metaphorical status as representative of the hidden 'other', and thus indicative of deceit, trickery and
deception.[32] It was not just sexual relations that were to be restricted, or
better, avoided, but every aspect of female life that had to be regulated,
down to the most minute detail, in particular those concerning their
appearance, which thus might conceal their 'true' natures. Living as a
total celibate is one end of a spectrum of rules which begin with veiling
the head and proceed upwards on the scale through not talking in
church and other like injunctions. The peculiar position of women in
relation to the story of the Creation provided a ready justification:
woman was not made in the image of God but only in that of man,
therefore while man can go about uncovered, she should veil herself.[33]
And if the Gospels offer 'peculiar opportunities' for study of the
processes of interpretation, the uncovering of the hidden meaning,[34]
then women, who cover themselves in makeup, or the disguise of fine
clothes, can come to stand, in the real world, for a different, and
dangerous, kind of secrecy.

It is not difficult to see, in particular, how women came to stand for the
sexuality which many male Christian writers condemned. For just as it
had been read back into the story of the Creation, it was implicit also in
that of the Incarnation of Christ. The latter implied both his birth from a
woman and his freedom from the taint of the fall. He must therefore be a
virgin himself, so as to lead Adam, the first man, out of Hell, and his
mother – for he can have no wife – must be equally free of all possibility
of sexual impurity, that is, must be a perpetual virgin:

---

[31] Rousselle 1983, esp. 170ff.
[32] Danger: Girard 1977, 139f. See in general Hayes 1964; Bloch 1987; the same set of
assumptions underlies medieval texts about women; the parallelism with witch hunts is
obvious.
[33] Clark 1983, 34f.
[34] Kermode 1979, ix; cf. Matth. 13.35 'I will utter things which have been kept secret
from the foundation of the world'; Girard 1978. Make-up and dress in general:
Lichtenstein 1987.

Just as in the case of Mary the Mother of God, 'death had ruled from
Adam' to her (Rom. 5:14), ... when it also approached her, it was crushed
by striking against the fruit of her virginity as against a rock:[35]

Virginity stood for the paradoxes at the heart of Christianity. It is
this very paradoxical quality – the notion that only through virginity,
that is, by denying nature, can true virtue be attained – that gave the
theme a centrality over and above mere misogyny. Some of the most
extreme statements are to be found in Syriac sources, for instance the
answer given by Isaac of Antioch, albeit in a male context, to the plea
'Would that someone would pull me down and rebuild me and make me
a virgin again' – 'this request of yours is possible with Jesus'.[36] But
Mary was the prime example. The virginity of Mary, already a theme
at the end of the second century AD for Tertullian (one of the foremost
of Christian misogynist writers), and the subject of narratives
supplementary to the laconic statements about her in the Gospels,
became in the late fourth and early fifth centuries, when
preoccupations with Christology and with the theme of virginity in
general were both at their height, one of the central topics in the
rhetoric of the Church; it was then drawn specifically into its
discourses about sexuality.[37] The Virgin of late antiquity was neither
the *mater dolorosa* nor the domesticated maternal figure of more
recent times[38] but rather a rhetorical construction formed from the
need to weave together contemporary attitudes to women and
sexuality and the logical implications of the doctrine of the
incarnation. In this process, we should note, there is no attempt to
rehabilitate Eve in the same way as Adam, who is led out of Hell by
Christ after the Crucifixion; rather, she is left as the example of the
evil inherent in woman, to be neutralised only by the advocacy or saved
by the opposing example of Mary, the perfect woman, who is yet by
definition an impossibility.[39] The establishment of a developed

[35] Gregory of Nyssa, *De virginitate* 14.1. Jesus himself, being similarly virginal, could
put an end to the 'constant succession of corruption and death', everlasting so long as
marriage continued (ibid.). Whether Mary's virginity was impaired or not by the birth of
Jesus was a hotly debated issue on which Jerome came to change his mind, from an early
defence of a natural birth to a later acceptance of a miraculous one (*In Helvidium* 18; cf.
Contra Pelag. 2.4). For the controversy, see Graef 1985, 78ff; Clark 1986b.

[36] Cited by S. Brock, in Garsoian, Mathews, Thomson 1983, 27-8. For misogyny as a
theme in Syriac sources – largely a fourth-century development – see Harvey in
Cameron and Kuhrt 1983, 288-98. I necessarily here confine myself to Greek and Latin
texts, but no doubt a similar argument could be constructed about Syriac ones.

[37] Brown et al., 1978; Graef 1985, 66ff.

[38] Warner 1978 gives a fascinating demonstration of the flexibility of the image of the
Virgin over many centuries and in many cultures; see Alexiou 1974 for the more
personalised Virgin of later Byzantine times, and now also Carroll 1985.

[39] Mary's advocacy of Eve: Irenaeus, *Adv. Haer.* 3.22; 5.19. Ephraem the Syrian makes
Christ visit Eve in Sheol – see Graef 1985, 61. But by a capacious double interpretation
Eve is also the mother of all mankind.

discourse about the Virgin in the later fourth century, the logical consequence of current Christian doctrinal debate, therefore confirmed contemporary attitudes to women within the limitations of current male rhetoric. As for practice, the model it offered was one which women could emulate only by denying the natures which men believed them to have.

Woman as metaphor was not only readily available, but also peculiarly well suited to a Christian rhetoric, whose very essence was hiddenness, its message needing to be uncovered from layers of symbol, allegory and metaphor.[40] The Gospels emphasise the paradoxes of faith, the inability of the disciples to penetrate them, the covering of truth by symbol, its perception 'through a glass darkly'.[41] As Christian literature developed, its continued use of the Old Testament, like its own inner message, could only be justified by the further elaboration of modes of reading based on complex hermeneutics; at a certain stage, allegory became a key to Christian understanding equal only to paradox and analogy as techniques for expressing Christian truth. It was not to be expected that Christian writers remained unconscious of what they were doing; rather, they exploited the full ambiguities of their position, claiming a 'simplicity' in the face of their own rhetorical skills[42] which allowed them to appropriate both apparent directness and realism and sophisticated techniques of allusion. In such a context of art versus 'simplicity', the theme of women presented an ideal vehicle for rhetorical display. For if the truth was clothed in words requiring interpretation, then equally falsehood came in seductive disguises. The truth about women was that of their capacity for deception; their fine clothes represented falsehood; only if they wore cheap clothes and neglected their appearance could they avoid misleading with false impressions,[43] for clothes, after all, were necessary only because of Eve's disobedience. Thus Genesis 2:25 'they were both naked' (i.e. Adam and Eve before the Fall) 'and were not ashamed' and 3:21 'unto Adam also and to his wife' (after the Fall) 'did the Lord God make coats of skins, and clothed them' became proof texts; clothes stood for the deceitful covering of woman's true nature, or even for marriage, that is sexuality.[44] For

---

[40] See e.g. Kermode 1979; Palmer 1981; Ricoeur 1977; Crossan 1976; Matt. 13:34-5 'without a parable spake he not unto them, that it might be fulfilled which was spoken by the prophet saying "I will open my mouth in parables" '.

[41] I Cor. 13:12.

[42] Auerbach 1965 on *sermo humilis*.

[43] Tert., *De cultu fem.* 1.1.1.

[44] Greg. Nyss., *De virginitate* 12 'They hid themselves in leaves and shadows and after that they covered themselves with skins. And in this way they came as colonists to this place which is full of disease and toil, where marriage was contrived as a consolation for death.' Exegesis of Gen. 1-3 proliferated in the late fourth and early fifth centuries, e.g. John Chrysostom's *Discourse on Genesis*, Augustine's *Literal Commentary on Genesis*; see Clark 1986a, 353-86; 1986b; Pagels 1985, 1988.

Christian women themselves an acute contradiction presented itself
between the opportunities that were genuinely present for them now
and which they had not enjoyed before and the paradox that in order to
realise them they must deny their sex – a situation reflected in
literature, especially in written saints' lives, by the recurring theme of
the female ascetic who is said to be 'like a man', or who is even
represented as dressing in men's clothes.[45] While for male ascetics
asceticism itself was enough, for women who aspired to the ascetic life,
the 'life of angels', far more was involved: it was also a matter of
denying their gender.

How such women felt about it all is an interesting question, but one
for which they do not provide us with an answer. But there was little
choice: they were trapped within the same rhetoric. How women
regarded the development of the cult of the Virgin in its early stages is
also an interesting question, on which there is little if any direct
evidence. Later, quite naturally, she might appear particularly suited
to female devotion,[46] though here too we enter the realm of
speculation. While the sixth-century poet Corippus represents a
prayer to the Virgin as especially suited for an empress, while her
husband addresses God the Father,[47] it is worth remembering that all
the many treatises on the Virgin were nevertheless as far as we know
written by men. The well-known icons of Virgin and Child in Byzantine
art are not from this period; indeed, she was depicted in one of the
earliest representations, in the fifth-century mosaics in S. Maria
Maggiore in Rome, not as a tender mother but as a majestic empress.
More recent developments in Marian cult too tend to be associated
with authoritarian political or ideological positions;[48] in just the same
way there is a sharp division between textual presentations of the
Virgin in the late fourth and fifth centuries and our knowledge of the
religious attachments of real women.

Having said that, it remains the case that Christian writings of the
period, even when not directly on the subject of virginity, do show an
emphasis on women that would have been unusual in pagan texts, and
that not all of them are as hostile as I have been suggesting. Yet it will
usually be found that the relation between 'realistic' and textual
elements in any individual case is not simple. The early fourth-century
Symposium of Methodius, for example, is a work patterned on Plato's
dialogue of the same name.[49] All the participants are female; the

---

[45] On the latter topic see Patlagean 1976; Davis 1976; Warner 1981, 139ff. The 'manly'
woman, a weaker version of the same idea, is a stock theme in early Christian writing
about women.

[46] Herrin 1983a and b; but cf. Cameron 1978.

[47] *Iust.* II.11-42; 52-69. Sophia's prayer is shorter than her husband's and is placed
after it.

[48] See the discussion by Pope 1985.

[49] Ed. H. Musurillo (Paris, 1963).

subject of the dialogue is not love, as it was for Plato, but (female) virginity. The winner of the prize for the best speech on the subject is named Thecla (see below), and she leads her girl companions at the end in a hymn to virginity. Obviously such a work is not only literary in the formal sense but also far from being realistic in any degree. Nevertheless, that a Christian philosophical dialogue could be written at all with such a *mise-en-scène* is remarkable. The name Thecla, given to the main character, opens up another realm of Christian attention to women, for the late second-century *Acts of Paul and Thecla* had presented in Thecla a female character in fact far more popular and influential in early Christianity than the Virgin Mary.[50] Her popularity can be seen from the minor arts; although a totally legendary character, she rapidly acquired both a cult and a saintly status. Not only does Methodius choose the name for his heroine; Gregory of Nyssa makes great play with the model offered by Thecla in his life of his sister Macrina.[51] In a sense, Thecla offered a more positive model for Christian women. Yet her story, as told in the apocryphal *Acts*, is not simply filled with motifs of celibacy and asceticism (Thecla too, for instance, dresses as a man)[52], but also belongs somewhere within the still mysterious literary world of second and third-century Greek fiction.[53] To argue therefore, as has been done, that this and similar texts emanate from women's communities, or even that they are written by women,[54] is premature. Certainly we should be asking why this group of apocryphal writings lays emphasis on women;[55] but it still has to be proven that one can argue so directly from text to 'reality'. Certainly there are many features in the *Acts of Paul and Thecla* that suggest caution, not least for example the striking emphasis on rhetoric and the erotic undertone to the relationship between Thecla and the apostle.[56] Thecla's mother

[50] The later cult and popularity of Thecla are very well discussed by Dagron 1978.

[51] *Life of Macrina*, 2, *PG* 46.961: Thecla is the secret name of his sister given to her by her mother as the result of a vision seen before her birth, in contrast to Macrina, after her grandmother, who had suffered during the persecutions.

[52] See above, n.45.

[53] See e.g. Hägg 1983, 162f.; audience, 88ff.; Söder 1932.

[54] Davies 1980.

[55] Macdonald 1983 suggests that the Pastoral Epistles were in fact an answer to this dangerously heterodox tendency; but this too is to assume that the apocryphal writings are a direct index of real situations.

[56] cc. 9-10. Especially, for the former, in the context of the silence to which women have been assigned in the history of female representation (Kappeler 1986, 65f.). Paradoxically (for it was suspect for Tertullian precisely because it displayed a woman in an active preaching role), this text also perfectly illustrates Kappeler's point about how women are represented as reflected by men; Thecla is constantly listening for Paul, and has a separate existence only in relation to him. On the other hand, others of the apocryphal Acts, as well as the ps. Clementines, share this stress on the power of the word, and the contrast between rhetoric and 'simplicity', so that in the early Christian context, the silence of women belongs in a wider context of Christian articulation.

complains 'my daughter ... is like a spider at the window, bound by his [Paul's] words', and asks her 'My child, why are you sitting like this, eyes cast down, making no response but behaving like a mad person?'

An equally famous early Christian text much used by feminist writers also seems to present women in a more favourable light, namely the account of the matryrdom of Perpetua in Carthage in the time of Tertullian (an interesting juxtaposition), allegedly in part written by Perpetua herself.[57] She was a well-to-do young married woman in Carthage at the turn of the second and third centuries. She was evidently able to cross social boundaries in her religious life, for her father and most of her family remained pagan, indeed, her father came to remonstrate with her in prison and his intervention at her trial led to the removal of her baby, which up to then she had been allowed to keep with her. The group arrested with her included males to whom she was not related as well as her own slave Felicitas who was to die with her. Yet though Perpetua is altogether more 'real' than Thecla, she too is presented to us within a certain rhetorical nexus. On the night before she is due to go into the arena, for instance, she dreams of going to her death as a man[58] (though in her dream the devil is not deceived), and when she actually does meet the beasts on the next day her chief concern is reported to be the preservation of her modesty in dress. Even in this text, often seen, with Auerbach, as realistic and unadorned,[59] the writer consciously draws on contemporary expectations about gender. Perpetua, like Thecla, is an honorary man. As the Virgin Mary was to be called the 'glory of mothers' for having eluded both the necessary preliminaries and the physical consequences of motherhood, so Perpetua's glory as represented here was that she transcended the supposed limits of her sex while at the same time continuing to observe the boundaries placed on female behaviour by men.

We do not in fact know many Christian women of the early period in any detail. It is only in the late fourth century, when sexuality and renunciation had become a major focus of attention on which virtually all the leading churchmen of the day had written, that women come seriously to the fore. Often this has most to do with their social class: they are members of the upper classes, both in the east and the west, most conspicuously from the Roman senatorial class in Italy, now

[57] See e.g. Barnes 1971, 71-80, 263ff.; Rossi 1984 (overstated); Lefkowitz 1986, 103-5, cf. 105 'Perpetua does not go to her death so much because she is a woman, as in order not to be a woman'.

[58] The Freudian associations of this dream attracted the attention of E.R. Dodds (Dodds 1968, 47-53), but the text still needs analysis in terms of its rhetoric of gender. Perpetua as 'male': Giannarelli 1980, 24, and generally, Clark 1986a, 43-6.

[59] Auerbach 1965, 60ff.

increasingly penetrated by Christianity,[60] thus they bring with them the habits and expectations which that entails. It is true that the lives which at least some of them lived were necessarily shaped by the prevailing ethos in their circles of ascetic renunciation. On the other hand, we may read between the lines of Jerome's strictures to conclude that those women who took his exhortations to asceticism completely seriously were only a small minority. He complains of others among the Christian ladies of Rome who continued to like clothes and makeup, who read frivolous authors (Horace, for example), or made going to church into an occasion for social display. Of course, Jerome too is a rhetorician, and his tirades are the tirades of a satirist; yet the very urgency of his persuasion towards asceticism shows perhaps that it was not really very common, while the extremes, not to say the grotesqueries, to which he took his own teaching in relation to those with whom his persuasion had been successful caused such a scandal that he was forced to leave Rome.[61] Even Roman society at the end of the fourth century, about whose asceticism we know most, was probably less ascetic and more 'normal' than we sometimes tend to think. Yet we can allow some measure of freedom and influence to some of these Christian ladies, who, ascetic or not, nevertheless started a long tradition of Christian female patrons – the elder Melania, for instance, whose long life of Christian travel and works was emulated by her granddaughter.[62] They were followed by a long line of Christian empresses who were very active in political as well as monastic life, and often pilgrims and donors to sites in the Holy Land.[63] Reading Palladius' *Lausiac History* certainly gives the impression that Christian women were being given as much attention as Christian men in written accounts, though usually, it must be stressed, for their chastity, either (preferably) as lifelong virgins, or as having turned to the celibate life after fulfilling their minimum duties of procreation. Candida, for instance,

> having instructed her own daughter for the condition of virginity ... brought her to Christ as a gift of her own body, afterwards following her own daughter in temperance and chastity and the distribution of her goods (ch. 57).

[60] Brown 1961 is still fundamental; see also Yarbrough 1976, Clark 1986a, 23-60; Ruether 1979, 72-98.

[61] Kelly 1975, 108ff.; cf. especially the scandal caused by the death of the young Blesilla in AD 384 (*Ep*. 39.6). Ten years later, however, he was to return to the theme in the blistering attack on Jovinian, a monk who actually praised marriage and argued against Jerome's kind of extreme asceticism (Kelly, 182ff.).

[62] Clark 1984.

[63] Holum 1983. A precedent had been set between AD 326 and 328 by Constantine's mother Helena, who was constantly cited thereafter as a model for the later imperial ladies, but virtually nothing is known of Helena herself from contemporary sources, and Eusebius, writing nearest to the events, puts most of the emphasis on Constantine himself (VC III. 41ff.). See Consolino 1984.

In the case of the upper-class women at least, then, limited though it might have been, the advance of Christianity offered a prominence and a set of possibilities in their own right to some women which would not have been present before. Virginity – the denial of female weakness and the potential threat women presented to men – conferred power.[64] On a practical level, it even became possible for these desexed women to adopt a role as patrons of letters, commissioning translations and editions of suitable texts and themselves becoming learned in the Scriptures and Christian literature.[65] They listened to Jerome and the like, as Thecla did to St. Paul in the *Acts*, but they also did what they wanted to do themselves.

The effects of such an emphasis on virginity on real women were therefore deeply ambiguous. It was now too that Greek Christian literature began to take women seriously, even while maintaining its misogynistic tone overall. Gregory of Nyssa is a particularly notable example. His life of his sister Macrina, already mentioned, is remarkable both for its female subject and its treatment.[66] Gregory had certain problems in tackling this project, not least that Macrina had not been educated like her many brothers in classical rhetoric, but had stayed at home and led a pious but dull life. He endeavours therefore to suggest that hers, not theirs, was the true philosophy; Basil, the greatest of the family and a prize student in his days at Athens, was, we are told, converted by Macrina to real wisdom – that is, ascetic piety in contrast with the wisdom of the world.[67] Gregory deals with the uneventfulness of Macrina's life by presenting her in the guise of the female philosopher Diotima from Plato's *Symposium* – the same text used by Methodius – and by dwelling on a protracted death-bed scene. Macrina also appears as a speaker in a philosophical dialogue by Gregory on the soul reminiscent of Plato's *Phaedo* and inspired by the death of Basil. The *Life* is very far from being a simple account of Gregory's sister; on the contrary, matters of gender feature largely in its presentation of Macrina and in the text as a whole.[68] On the other hand, it is certainly remarkable that he should have written it at all, in the context of earlier, classical biography. A contemporary

[64] Atkinson et al., 1985.

[65] Consolino 1986, 292ff.; cf. *Laus. Hist.* 55: 'being very learned and loving literature she turned night into day by perusing every writing of the ancient commentators, including 3,000,000 lines of Origen and 2,500,000 lines of Gregory, Stephen, Pierius, Basil and other standard writers. Nor did she read them once only and casually, but she laboriously went through each book seven or eight times. Wherefore also she was enabled to be freed from knowledge falsely so called and to fly on wings, thanks to the grace of these books; elevated by kindly hopes she made herself a spiritual bird and journeyed to Christ.'

[66] See recently Momigliano 1985.

[67] Ch. 6. The theme (see also n.65) goes back to the Pauline rhetoric of the New Testament (e.g. I Cor. 2).

[68] Giannarelli 1980, 43f.

and friend, Gregory of Nazianzus, also chose to write about women – his mother, Nonna, subject of a large number of verses, and his sister, Gorgonia, for whom he composed a funeral oration.[69] Unlike Macrina, Gorgonia was married and a mother. Yet she too is praised for leading a life of such chastity and restraint that she virtually overcame the taint of the married state; Gregory cites the Book of Proverbs on a virtuous woman: 'in contrast to the woman who wanders abroad, who is uncontrolled and dishonourable, who hunts precious souls with wanton ways and words he [sc. Solomon] praises her who is engaged honourably at home, who performs her womanly duties with manly courage [sic], her hands constantly holding the spindle as she prepares double cloaks for her husband, who buys a field in season and carefully provides food for her servants and receives her friends at a bountiful table, and who exhibits all other qualities for which he extols in song the modest and industrious woman'.[70] Better still, says Gregory, his sister did not wear makeup or jewellery or see-through dresses: 'the only red that pleased her was the blush of modesty and the only pallor that which comes from abstinence'.[71] Predictably, in this litany of negative praise, we are told that Gorgonia has transcended the limits of her sex: 'O female nature overcoming the male in the common struggle for salvation, and showing that male and female are physical differences only, not differences in the soul!'[72]

It turns out, then, that these works in praise of women use the same categories as the more critical rhetoric that is actually more common. And before drawing any conclusions from them about 'real' women, we must also remember that they were written also in the context of a highly literary development, the writing of lives of saints and ascetics of all kinds and the utilisation of the techniques of the classical encomium for Christian subjects; the contemporary oration on Basil by Gregory of Nazianzus, for instance, has been called 'the most perfect example of Greek rhetoric since Demosthenes'.[73] Again, too, we hear from men, not from the women themselves. It is still possible dimly to recapture an awareness of strong and active Christian women, like the mother of Gregory of Nyssa, Basil and Macrina, for instance, who was left a widow with estates to run, and with a large family, at least four of whom embraced the religious life. Yet the same Gregory of Nyssa, himself married, also wrote a treatise on virginity of which a major portion is devoted to the denigration of marriage:

[69] I am grateful here to Franca Ela Consolino.
[70] *Gorg.* 9.
[71] Ibid., 10.
[72] Ibid., 14.
[73] Kennedy 1983, 237; for Gregory of Nazianzus as a rhetor see Ruether 1969. There is no space here to deal with the writing of *Lives* and the influences exerted on it by classical rhetoric, but for an introduction see Cox 1983.

we [married men] are only spectators of the virtue of others, and witnesses of their blessedness ... like servants at the banquets of the rich, who do not taste what has been prepared.[74]

Likewise, Gregory of Nazianzus' praise of his sister Gorgonia is most enthusiastic when it imposes the norms of female regulation most successfully: 'Who spoke less?' he asks, extolling his sister's silence, that proper mode for women;[75] men, by contrast, have set before them as the true object of the Christian paideia still largely denied to women the expression of the word of God.[76]

Feminist theologians would do well to consider again the question why the cult of the Virgin became prominent just at the time when the strong Christian women whose memory they have successfully rehabilitated were at their most active. For the figure who is depicted in the S. Maria Maggiore mosaics and described in the paradoxes of Christology[77] was also a ready reinforcement for a convenient picture of female docility and submission. Later, and in more popular texts already, she acquired the touching and sympathetic traits of the little girl brought up in the Temple, the weeping but patient mother, or the venerable lady carried off to heaven by angels.[78] But now, and in these circles, she belonged firmly within the rhetoric of female obedience and female renunciation that her virginity vividly symbolised. Some of the real women of the period were able to find a more balanced way, but for others, like Paula's daughters, the price was too high.[79] Perhaps only in a few extreme cases was the struggle posed at this time (as it was in later periods) in terms of food and abstinence from it,[80] or in the morbid asceticism thrust upon his female followers by Jerome; but the possibility of such a struggle, now objectivised in the cult figure of the Virgin, was embedded in the prevailing religious rhetoric. It may still be that women actually were a significant element in the early stages of Christian development, both as converts and in the spread of the faith (just as we know that in the high aristocratic families of the later fourth century it was often the women who were converted first). There might be many good reasons for that in the context of the restricted

---

[74] *De virginitate* 3; all the absurdities in life result from marriage (c.4). Nevertheless, Gregory claims not to be condemning it (c.8).

[75] Tsirpanlis 1985 offers a warm defence of Gregory.

[76] Rousselle 1983b.

[77] Reaching their culmination in this period in the homily of the patriarch Proclus of Constantinople, AD 428 (PG 65. 680c-92B).

[78] For an account of the developing views of Mary from the second century onwards see Graef 1985, 35ff.

[79] Blesilla and Eustochium: Kelly 1975, 93ff. Jerome was blamed by many for Blesilla's death, hastened by self-mortification, but he himself attacked her mother for what he thought misplaced grief.

[80] See Bynum 1987.

social opportunities available for Roman women.[81] But from as early as the first and second centuries the Christian texts already show a desire to control and discipline female participation; later, Christianity was to differ profoundly from pagan cults in the far-reaching discourse with which it was to justify this control, and one of the chief components of that discourse was its recommendation of sexual renunciation. To quote Peter Brown, 'sexual renunciation rapidly became a badge of specifically male leadership in the Christian communities of the second and third centuries'.[82] This is not the place for another consideration of the reasons for this advocacy of sexual renunciation, which was not of course confined to women as object, but one thing can perhaps be said: the early Church's first task, in which it spectacularly succeeded, as can be seen from its survival through persecution and its emergence as a fully-fledged major institution once persecution was lifted, was to establish itself as a strong body with clear identity and strong boundaries.[83] Deviant groups, like those Gnostic communities in which women seem to have played a quite different role,[84] were among the obvious sufferers, and women, already seen as potentially dangerous if not strictly controlled,[85] would not for long be allowed to continue in an active role, if indeed they ever truly enjoyed it. The development of the rhetoric of their confinement is part of that early process whereby the church lost its early millennialism and took on the garb of social respectability.[86] The particular form which it took was not new – neither hostility to women nor advocacy of virginity were Christian discoveries[87] – but it was the more powerfully articulated in that it was able to draw justification from the two poles of Christian mythology – creation and salvation. Thus Christian misogyny was not simply that; it was part of a far bigger and more powerful systematisation in the face of which women could have no answer to give.

At the same time the rhetorical themes of 'woman' and of virginity served as metaphors for the paradoxes of faith. In them both the tensions and assumptions of contemporary society and the remarkable effort made by Christian theological discourse to express the inexpressible found a congenial conjuncture. When one strand in theological language arrived at the logical position of being unable to say anything at all about God,[88] metaphor and paradox, and especially the metaphor of female virginity, offered one of the most powerful ways out of the impasse.

[81] Cf. Veyne 1986, 70 on slave participation in pagan cults.
[82] Brown 1987, 266.
[83] Meeks 1983 is particularly good on the earliest stages of this process.
[84] Pagels 1979.
[85] King 1983; Padel 1983; above, n.32.
[86] Theissen 1978, 1982.
[87] Foucault 1983; Rousselle 1983 for the pagan background.
[88] Mortley 1986.

So when men like the two Gregorys in the later fourth century choose to write about women in the way in which they do, it is not for simple reasons. For just as real women were denied an answer to the rhetoric of their portrayal, so a male author ostensibly writing about women was writing about authority and control, and about the resolution of irreconcilable polarities. Like the other major writers of the period whom we have encountered, each of them also wrote on Christological themes and on the theory and practice of virginity. For Jerome, the perpetual virginity of Mary was a topic of intense current dispute,[89] for Augustine, the question of sexual relations in Eden and the value to be placed on human marriage represented issues equally crucial – if he eventually resolved them in a less extreme way, it was only after prolonged and difficult effort.[90] It was hardly possible therefore for the Fathers of these generations, when they tried to write about women, to do so without a consciousness of the wider issues, or for them not to be affected by them in their own relations with real women. Nor was it possible for them to write except within the rhetorical frame which they had inherited.

The matter could not stand still. The rhetorical frame invited ever more refinements: mere physical abstinence from sexual relations was not enough – there must also be a total absence of desire. For a virgin to be looked on by a man could be held to besmirch her. It is not enough to point, for instance, to the personal psychology of Jerome as a causative factor in the development of such excesses;[91] rather, they were built into the rhetoric itself and an inevitable product of it. Women had come to stand for a tension both theological and rhetorical. There was no simple way in which the Fathers of the fourth century could write about women, and there is no simple way in which the real women can be recaptured.

Finally, this discourse of control and denial implied the coexistence of a complementary and different language. It is just because of this density of ideas and associations which the topic of women by now held that it was possible to write of the relation of the female ascetic with Christ in openly erotic language, which we, in more squeamish days, find questionable to say the least. The notion of the 'bride of Christ' did not begin in the fourth century, when Jerome applies it to his young protegées. It was built in, in a sense, to the earlier ways of looking at women, and especially to the denigration of human marriage. But it opened the way for the use of some extremely erotic language in describing the relation of female ascetics to Christ. Should we be

---

[89] Above, n.35.

[90] Brown 1983; Clark 1986a, 291ff; 353ff.; and especially 1986b.

[91] E.g. Kelly 1975, 51-2 (the standard biographical explanation). Jerome is admittedly a difficult case from which to argue, but though more extreme, the ideas he expressed were sufficiently widely held to counter the objection that he was exceptional.

looking for a psychoanalytic explanation for this language, as one might be tempted to do? It is after all the complement to the ascetic 'madness' whose origin Dodds found in just such a direction.[92] Or is it rather that the rhetoric has taken on a polarity which in asserting the negative also licenses the positive? It is not the suspect Jerome but Gregory of Nazianzus, the most accomplished classical rhetorician among the Greek Fathers,[93] and one of those who argued *against* the denigration of women as the weaker sex,[94] who can write of Gorgonia, a respectably married lady, that as she felt her death approaching,

> no one of the amorous and unlicensed so loves the body as she, having flung away these fetters and surmounted this slime with which we live, desired to be purely joined with her Fair One and embrace her Beloved completely, and, I will even add, her Lover.[95]

Bibliography

Alexiou, M. 1974. *The Ritual Lament in Greek Tradition* (Cambridge).

Ariès, P. and Béjin, A. 1986. *Western Sexuality* (Eng. trans., Oxford).

Ariès, P. and Duby, G., eds. 1987. *A History of Private Life* I (Eng. trans., Cambridge, Mass.).

Atkinson, Clarissa, Buchanan, Constance H. and Miles, Margaret R. 1985. *Immaculate and Powerful. The Female in Sacred Image and Social Reality* (Boston, Mass.).

Auerbach, E. 1965. *Literary Language and its Public in Late Latin Antiquity and in the Middle Ages*, (Eng. trans., London).

Barnes, T.D. 1971. *Tertullian. A Historical and Literary Study* (Oxford).

Betz, H.D. 1974. 'Spirit, freedom and law: Paul's message to the Galatian churches', *Svensk. Exeg. Arsbok* 39, 145-60.

―――― 1978. *Plutarch's Theological Writings and Early Christian Literature.* Studia ad Corpus Hellenisticum Novi Testamenti IV (Leiden).

Bloch, R. Howard 1987. 'Medieval misogny. Woman as riot', *Representations* 20, 1-24.

Brooten, Bernadette J., 1985. 'Early Christian women and their cultural context: issues of method in historical reconstruction', in Collins 1985, 65-91.

Brown, Peter 1961. 'Aspects of the Christianization of the Roman aristocracy', *JRS* 51 (1961), 1-11.

―――― . 'Sexuality and society in the fifth century AD: Augustine and Julian of Eclanum', in Gabba 1983, 49-70.

―――― 1987. 'Late antiquity', in Ariès and Duby 1987, 235-312.

―――― 1988. *The Body and Society. Men, Women and Sexual Renunciation in the Early Church* (New York)

Brown, Raymond E. et al., 1978. *Mary in the New Testament* (London).

[92] Dodds 1965.
[93] Above, n.72.
[94] Tsirpanlis 1985, 34-5.
[95] *Gorg.* 19.

Bynum, Caroline 1987. *Holy Feast, Holy Fast* (Berkeley and Los Angeles).

Cameron, Averil 1980. 'Neither male nor female', *Greece and Rome* 27, 60-5.

────── 1983. (ed. with Kuhrt, Amélie) *Images of Women in Antiquity* (London).

────── 1986. 'Redrawing the map: Christian territory after Foucault', *JRS* 76, 266-71.

Carroll, Michael 1985. *The Cult of the Virgin Mary. Psychological Origins* (Princeton).

Clark, Elizabeth A., 1983. *Women in the Early Church* (Wilmington, Delaware).

────── 1984. *The Life of Melania the Younger. Studies in Women and Religion* 14 (New York and Toronto).

────── 1986a. *Ascetic Piety and Women's Faith. Studies in Women and Religion* 20 (Lewiston, N.Y. and Queenston, Ont.).

────── 1986b. ' "Adam's only companion": Augustine and the early Christian debate on marriage', *Recherches Augustiniennes* 21, 139-62.

Collins, Adela Yarbro 1985. *Feminist Perspectives on Biblical Scholarship* (Chico, California).

Consolino, Franca Ela 1984. 'Il significato del *Inventio Crucis* nel *de obitu Theodosii*', *Annali della facoltà di lettere e filosofia* 5, Firenze, 161-80.

────── 1986a. *Elogio di Serena* (Venice).

────── 1986b. 'Modelli di comportamento e modi di sanctificazione per l'aristocrazia femminile d'occidente', in Giardina, A., ed., *Società romana e impero tardoantico I. Istituzioni, ceti, economie* (Rome), 273-306, 684-99.

Cox, Patricia 1983. *Biography in Late Antiquity* (Berkeley and Los Angeles).

Crossan, Dominic 1975. *The Dark Interval. Towards a Theology of Story* (Niles, Illinois).

────── 1976. 'Parable, allegory and paradox', in Patte 1976, 247-81.

Dagron, Gilbert 1978. *Vie et miracles de Sainte Thècle*. Subsidia Hagiographica 62 (Brussels).

Davies, Stevan L. 1980. *The Revolt of the Widows. The Social World of the Apocryphal Acts* (London and Amsterdam).

Davis, Natalie Z. 1976. 'Women's history in transition: the European case', *Feminist Studies* 3, 83-103.

de Ste. Croix, G.E.M. 1975. 'Early Christian attitudes to property and slavery', *Studies in Church History* 12, 1-38.

Dodds, E.R. 1965. *Pagan and Christian in an Age of Anxiety* (Cambridge).

Eadie, John W. and Ober, Josiah, eds. 1985. *The Craft of the Ancient Historian* (Lanham, Maryland).

Fiorenza, E. Schussler 1983. *In Memory of Her: a feminist theological reconstruction of Christian origins* (New York).

────── 1985. 'Remembering the past in creating the future: historical-critical scholarship and feminist Biblical interpretation', in Collins 1985, 43-64.

Flanagan, J.W. and Robinson, A.W., eds., 1975. *No Famine in the Land* (Missoula).

Foucault, M. 1983. *Le Souci de soi* (Paris).

────── 1986. 'The battle for chastity', in Ariès and Béjin 1986, 14-25.

Gabba, E., ed., 1983. *Tria Corda. Studi in onore di Arnaldo Momigliano* (Como).

Garsoian, M., Mathews, T., Thomson, R., eds., 1983. *East of Byzantium: Syria and Armenia in the formative period* (Washington, D.C.).

Giannarelli, E. 1980. *La tipologia femminile nella biografia e nell'autobiografia cristiana del IV secolo* (Rome).

Girard, R. 1977. *Violence and the Sacred* (Eng. trans., Baltimore and London).

———— 1978. *Des choses cachées depuis l'origine du monde* (Paris).

Graef, Hilda 1985. *Mary. A History of Doctrine and Devotion* (London, combined repr. of 1963 and 1965 ed.).

Hägg, T. 1983. *The Novel in Antiquity* (Oxford).

Harnack, A. 1908. *The Mission and Expansion of Christianity in the first three centuries*, 2 vols. (Eng. trans., London and New York).

Harvey, Susan Ashbrook 1983. 'Women in early Syrian Christianity', in Cameron and Kuhrt 1983, 288-98.

Hayes, H.R. 1964. *The Dangerous Sex: the myth of feminine evil* (New York).

Herrin, Judith 1983a. 'In search of Byzantine women: three avenues of approach', in Cameron and Kuhrt 1983, 167-90.

———— 1983b. 'Women and faith in icons in early Christianity', in Samuel and Stedman Jones, 56-83.

Holum, K. 1983. *Theodosian Empresses* (Berkeley and Los Angeles).

Judge, E.A. 1960. *The Social Pattern of Christian Groups in the First Century*, (London).

———— 1982. *Rank and Status in the World of the Caesars and St. Paul*, Broadhead Memorial Lecture 1981, Canterbury, N.Z.

Kappeler, Susanne 1986. *The Pornography of Representation* (Cambridge).

Kelly, J.N.D. 1975. *Jerome. His Life, Writings and Controversies* (London).

Kennedy, G.A. 1983. *Greek Rhetoric under Christian Emperors* (Princeton, N.J.).

Kermode, F. 1979. *The Genesis of Secrecy* (Cambridge).

Koch, H. 1937. *Virgo Eva, Virgo Maria. Neue Untersuchungen über die Lehre von der Jüngfrauschaft und der Ehe Mariens in der ältesten Kirche* (Berlin).

Kresic, S., ed. 1981. *Contemporary Literary Hermeneutics and the Interpretation of Literary Texts* (Ottawa).

Lefkowitz, Mary R. 1986. *Women in Greek Myth* (London).

Lichtenstein, Jacqueline 1987. 'Making up representation: the risks of femininity', *Representations*, 20, 77-87.

MacDonald, Denys R. 1983. *The Legend and the Apostle* (Philadelphia).

Meeks, W. 1983. *The First Urban Christians* (New Haven).

———— 1986. *The Moral World of the First Christians* (Philadelphia).

Momigliano, A. 1985. 'The Life of St. Macrina by Gregory of Nyssa', in Eadie and Ober 1985, 443-58.

Mortley, R. 1986. *From Word to Silence, I-II, Theophaneia* 31-2 (Bonn).

Padel, Ruth 1983. 'Women: model for possession by Greek daemons', in Cameron and Kuhrt 1983, 3-19.

Pagels, Elaine 1979. *The Gnostic Gospels* (New York).

———— 1985. 'The politics of Paradise: Augustine's exegesis of Genesis 1-3 versus that of John Chrysostom', *Harvard Theol. Rev.* 78, 67-100.

———— 1988. *Adam, Eve and the Serpent* (London).

Palmer, Richard 1981. 'Allegorical, philological and philosophising hermeneutics: three modes in a complex heritage', in Kresic 1981, 15-38.

Patlagean, Evelyne 1976. 'L'Histoire de la femme déguisée en moine et l'évolution de la sainteté féminine à Byzance', *Studi Medievali* 17, 597-623.

———— 1977. *Pauvreté sociale et pauvreté économique à Byzance, IVe au VIIe siècle* (Paris).

Patte, Daniel, ed. 1976. *Semiology and Parables* (Pittsburgh).

Pope, Barbara Corrado 1985. 'Immaculate and powerful: the Marian revival in the nineteenth century', in Atkinson et al. 1985, 173-200.

Ricoeur, Paul 1965. *History and Truth* (Eng. trans., Evanston, Ill.).

———— 1977. *The Rule of Metaphor* (Eng. trans., Toronto).

—— 1980. *Essays on Biblical Interpretation*, ed. L.S. Mudge (Philadelphia).

Rossi, Mary Ann 1984. 'The passion of Perpetua, everywoman of Late Antiquity', in Smith and Lounibos 1984, 53-86.

Rousselle, Aline 1983a. *Porneia* (Paris).

—— 1983b. 'Parole et inspiration: le travail de la voix dans le monde romain', *History and Philosophy of the Life Sciences* Section 2, Pubblicazioni della Stazione Zoologica di Napoli 5, 129-57.

Ruether, Rosemary R. 1969. *Gregory of Nazianzus, Rhetor and Philosopher* (Oxford).

—— 1974. 'Misogynism and virginal feminism in the Fathers of the Church', in Ruether, R., ed., *Religion and Sexism* (New York), 150-83.

—— 1979. 'Word, spirit and power', in Ruether and McLaughlin 1979, 30-70.

—— 1979. 'Mothers of the Church', ibid., 72-98.

—— 1979. (ed. with McLaughlin, E.), *Women of Spirit. Female Leadership in the Jewish and Christian Traditions* (New York).

Samuel, R. and Stedman Jones, G., eds. 1983. *Culture, Ideology and Politics* (London).

Schoedel, W.R. and Wilken, R., eds. 1979. *Early Christian Literature and the Classical Intellectual Tradition. In honorem Robert Grant* (Paris).

Shaw, Brent. 1987. 'The Age of Roman girls at marriage: a reconsideration', *JRS* 77, 30-46.

Smith, Robert C. and Lounibos, John, eds. 1984. *Pagan and Christian Anxiety. A Response to E.R. Dodds* (Lanham, Maryland).

Söder, R. 1932. *Die apokryphen apostelgeschichten und die romanhäfte Literatur der Antike* (Stuttgart), repr. 1969.

Swidler, L. 1971. 'Jesus was a feminist', *The Catholic World* 212, 171-183.

—— 1979. *Biblical Affirmations of Women* (Philadelphia).

Theissen, Gerd 1978. *The Sociology of Early Palestinian Christianity* (Eng. trans., Philadelphia).

—— 1982. *The Social Setting of Pauline Christianity* (Eng. trans., Philadelphia).

Tsirpanlis, C. 1985. 'Saint Gregory the Theologian on marriage and the family', *Patristic and Byzantine Review* 1, 33-8.

Veyne, Paul 1978. 'La famille et l'amour sous la Haut-Empire romain', *Annales E.S.C.* 33, 35-63.

—— 1983. *L'Elégie érotique romaine* (Paris).

—— 1987. 'The Roman Empire', in Ariès and Duby 1987, 5-234.

Via Jr., Dan O. 1967. *The Parables* (Philadelphia).

Votaw, C.W. 1970. *The Gospels and Contemporary Biography in the Greco-Roman World* (Philadelphia).

Warner, Marina 1976. *Alone of All Her Sex. The Myth and Cult of the Virgin Mary* (London).

—— 1981. *Joan of Arc* (New York).

Wicker, K. 1975. 'First-century marriage ethics: a comparative study of the household codes and Plutarch's conjugal precepts', in Flanagan and Robinson 1975, 141-53.

—— 1978. 'Mulierum Virtutes (Moralia 242e-263c)', in Betz 1978, 106-34.

Wuellner, W. 1979. 'Greek rhetoric and Pauline argumentation', in Schoedel and Wilken 1979, 177-88.
Yarbrough, Anne 1976. 'Christianisation in the fourth century: the example of Roman women', *Church History* 45, 149-65.

Postlude: what next with history?

In their differing ways, all the essays in this volume have been concerned with the same issues – first, the nature of the written materials which the historian must use and the techniques which he might employ in using them, and second, the status of his own written production. In company with literary critics, ethnographers and philosophers, some historians at any rate have lost their old faith in the certainty of historical method and its capacity to produce objective reporting. At the same time, attempts to get round this dilemma by appealing to statistical or sociological methods now seem less persuasive as the theoretical foundations of scientific method are themselves coming into question. In the field of ancient history, moreover, any statistical evidence that does exist is liable to be extremely defective in coverage, and often depends on the very literary sources that have already been found suspect.

On the other hand, extreme positions of scepticism, such as the view that history is *only* a mode of rhetoric, or that historical explanation is never possible even in principle, are unlikely to hold the field: historians will still go on trying to find out what 'really happened', at least in their own view, and to understand for themselves why it did. It may be logically difficult, or even strictly impossible, to prove that this or that 'really happened' in the past, but it is part of the definition of a historian to be concerned not with fictional narratives in the present, but with events in the past.

At least some elements in most historical narratives can in principle be falsified; it follows then that a historian's relation to some such concept as 'truth' must of necessity be different from that of, say, a novelist or a literary critic. The abandonment of this relation not only brings history into a Derridan denial of its own value, but also removes all distinction between it and other narative forms.

Since for these reasons it seems unlikely that many historians will actually embrace such an extreme position as their espousal of fashionable theory may strictly imply, it is bound to seem easier to some simply to ignore the theory, or to deal with it by relegating it to some convenient corner where it can be quietly forgotten. But as this book shows, it is actually a delusion to imagine that there can be such a separation. Whether they are aware of it or not, historians who continue to claim objectivity, or to present the unadorned and simple 'facts', are doing so in a world which has changed about them. If, as several of the papers included here emphasise, it is after all part of a historian's job to convince his audience, he will not succeed if he writes without considering their response, and it is this response which, rightly or wrongly, and whether we like it or not, is now substantially changing. Writing of literary criticism, Edward Said has defined the change in terms of 'a loss of objectivity, in the sense of objecthood'.[1] He goes on to argue that emphasis has moved from the object to the practice of criticism, 'from a kind of objectivized historicism' to 'a kind of international critical apparatus important for its activity'. But this emphasis does not simply apply to literary criticism; interestingly enough, in the same essay Said moves from literature to history, for the general concern, he argues, is with 'the text's situation in the world', which includes the world of the past. His own book, *Orientalism* (New York, 1978), is a brilliant study of the influence exerted on historical attitudes by textuality, in this case by a certain range of texts about the orient. The texts of writers and historians have in turn restricted the possibilities for further description; only by exploring the nature both of those texts, and of their influence on subsequent attitudes can anything approaching a more 'objective' picture emerge. Moreover, part of history is the history of texts. Texts do not only have power to shape our own conception of history (or indeed of the present) – they have also shaped history itself, and the tracing of their history will enable us to understand better the cultural development of the past. The history of culture was of course the concern of Foucault, who is an important subject in Said's essay. But it is a sign of the extent to which these ideas are entering the consciousness of historians in general that cultural history is beginning to be seen at least by some not as some specialised field, like the 'history of ideas', but as the central, if not the only proper subject of the historian.

Ancient historians have one particular advantage over modernists, that because of the very nature of their subject matter and especially of the available materials for its study, they have for the most part to be generalists, and thus are much less likely to be pigeonholed as specialists in one type of history or another (cultural history *as opposed to* political or economic); typically, they will have to use whatever sources they can find – epigraphic, literary, documentary or anything else that might come to hand. As their choice of sources is therefore more eclectic, they should therefore be more flexible themselves in how they use them. On the other hand, at least in the Anglo-Saxon tradition, a high premium has traditionally been placed on 'source-criticism', with the assumption, explicit or implicit, that the

[1] Edward Said, *The World, the Text and the Critic* (London, 1984), 142.

result of good source-critical method will be both objective and reliable. Indeed, the model was provided in the fifth century BC by Thucydides, when he rejected the history of the distant past as unreliable on the grounds of the nature of the available source material, and laid down a programme for himself and many generations of successors which involved the close scrutiny of sources as close to the events as possible, followed by the application of the reasoned judgement of the historian.[2] Although these claims by Thucydides have been seen to have coexisted with a strong sense of drama and emotion infusing his whole narrative of the war between Athens and Sparta it is only relatively recently that his history has attracted the kind of attention from the point of view of an interest in rhetoric and textuality which would not seem obvious;[3] indeed, he often continues to stand for the 'scientific' or 'objective', historical method which now seems increasingly problematic. Herodotus, on the other hand, condemned in antiquity as a 'liar' and implicitly criticised by Thucydides as credulous and lacking in historical rigour, is now available for a far more sympathetic reading than the one he has tended to receive in recent times.

With this background, however, a lingering positivism remains a feature of much ancient history written within the Anglo-Saxon tradition. It was not the purpose of this collection necessarily to undermine it or to argue against a training which most of us have had and which we cannot do without. Rather, it was to show that we are not immune from the changes which have been taking place within other disciplines, or in the intellectual world generally; that while movements like deconstruction and semiotics do unfortunately tend to slip into their own private special languages, at worst deliberately obscurantist, it is not enough to write them off for this reason. 'Once an intellectual,' to quote Edward Said again, 'the modern critic has become a cleric in the worst sense of the word.'[4] But the greatest treason would be for history to leave criticism to the clerics.

---

[2] See especially Thucydides, 1.20f., and on the contrast between Thucydides and Herodotus and their respective influence in antiquity, Arnaldo Momigliano, 'Historiography on written tradition and historiography on oral tradition', in *Studies in Historiography* (London, 1966), 211-20; 'The place of Herodotus in the history of historiography', ibid., 127-42.

[3] See e.g. Virginia Hunter, *Thucydides the Artful Reporter* (Toronto, 1973).

[4] *The World, the Text and the Critic*, 292.